Enhancing

PROFESSIONAL

PRACTICE

A FRAMEWORK FOR TEACHING

2nd Edition

ASCD

Alexandria, Virginia USA

CHARLOTTE DANIELSON ▶

1703 N. Beauregard St. • Alexandria, VA 22311-1714 USA
Phone: 800-933-2723 or 703-578-9600 • Fax: 703-575-5400
Web site: www.ascd.org • E-mail: member@ascd.org
Author guidelines: www.ascd.org/write

Gene R. Carter, *Executive Director;* Nancy Modrak, *Director of Publishing;* Julie Houtz, *Director of Book Editing & Production;* Darcie Russell, *Project Manager;* Georgia Park, *Senior Graphic Designer;* Cynthia Stock, *Typesetter;* Vivian Coss, *Production Specialist*

All Web links in this book are correct as of the publication date but may have become inactive or otherwise modified since that time. If you notice a deactivated or changed link, please e-mail books@ascd.org with the words "Link Update" in the subject line. In your message, please specify the Web link, the book title, and the page number on which the link appears.

ASCD Member Book, No. FY07-5 (February 2007, P). ASCD Member Books mail to Premium (P), Comprehensive (C), and Regular (R) members on this schedule: Jan., PC; Feb., P; Apr., PCR; May, P; July, PC; Aug., P; Sept., PCR; Nov., PC; Dec., P.

PAPERBACK ISBN: 978-1-4166-0517-1   ASCD product #106034
Also available as an e-book through ebrary, netLibrary, and many online booksellers (see Books in Print for the ISBNs).

Quantity discounts for the paperback edition only: 10–49 copies, 10%; 50+ copies, 15%;
for 1,000 or more copies, call 800-933-2723, ext. 5634, or 703-575-5634. For desk copies: member@ascd.org.

Library of Congress Cataloging-in-Publication Data
Danielson, Charlotte.
    Enhancing professional practice : a framework for teaching / Charlotte Danielson. —
2nd ed.
       p. cm.
    Includes bibliographical references and index.
    ISBN-13: 978-1-4166-0517-1 (pbk. : alk. paper) 1. Teaching. 2. Classroom environment. 3. Educational planning. I. Title.

    LB1025.3.D35 2007
    371.1'02—dc22

                                                                    2006030286

18 17 16   13 14 15 16 17

Enhancing PROFESSIONAL PRACTICE
A FRAMEWORK FOR TEACHING
2nd Edition

I came into this school year expecting, as well as fearing, a lot. A lot of everything. I guess because it's a new start so I can have a completely new experience.

I suppose I expect the most from myself as a student, a friend, and a part of the community. I expect to do as well as I can in every class every day. I expect myself not to become discouraged if I don't do as well as I wanted to do on a test or anything else.

I expect my fellow students to be as supportive of the rest of the class as I am to them. I want to always feel comfortable speaking in class.

I expect my teachers to always listen to every student as an equal and to always be fair.

These are the words of a 9th grade student describing her expectations at the beginning of a new year in a new school. We must never forget the students' voices as we, the professional educators, plan for their academic success. This book is dedicated to all students who entrust their daily lives to their teachers.

Preface to the Second Edition

Since the framework for teaching was first published in 1996, it has been adopted by thousands of educators in the United States and around the world. The success of the framework is a reflection, in my view, of both the recognition of the vital importance of high-quality teaching and an awareness of its complexity. That combination of factors has led both practitioners and policymakers to embrace a definition of teaching that is simultaneously clear and succinct (it can be written on a single page) and respectful of the intricacies of the work.

The work of teaching has not changed significantly since then; the work was enormously complex then, and it remains so today. However, in the years since 1996, educational research has proceeded, yielding greater insights into teachers' work. And the educational landscape has changed significantly; schools are under greater pressure than ever to achieve results with all their students; and everyone, from policymakers to practitioners, recognizes the pivotal importance of good teaching.

In my work with educators since 1996, I have been overwhelmed by their commitment, their passion, and their expertise. Although the nature of teaching has not changed much since 1996, the second edition of *Enhancing Professional Practice: A Framework for Teaching* includes a few additions and revisions:

• The importance of state curriculum frameworks and standards has been recognized throughout the framework.

• In the first edition, Component 3d was restricted to what its name suggested: Providing Feedback to Students. In the second edition, it has been expanded to incorporate other elements of using assessment in instruction. In the new 3d, providing feedback to students is merely one element of a broader concept. This expansion has resulted in a slight revision to Component 1f, Assessing Student Learning. It is now clearly situated within Domain 1 (Planning and Preparation) and has been renamed Designing Student Assessments.

• In the first edition of the framework for teaching, Component 4d was called Contributing to the School and District. It is clear, however, that teachers' engagement with their schools and districts is not in addition to their regular work; rather, it is integral to that work. Hence, Component 4d in the second edition of the framework for teaching has a new name: Participat-

ing in a Professional Community. The elements are the same; only the name is different.

• The expanded second edition of this book includes frameworks for a host of education specialists, including school nurses, counselors, and psychologists. These specialists work closely with teachers and administrators, and all work together for the benefit of the students, as the expanded frameworks in Chapter 5 describe.

• Common themes such as equity and high expectations are manifested in much of the work of teaching. In the second edition, the incorporation of those themes in the rubrics is more explicit than was the case in the first edition.

Therefore, although the essential nature of teaching described in the second edition of the framework is the same as that in the first edition, the second edition contains some additions and enhancements that will ensure its applicability to educators today and for many years to come.

PREFACE TO THE FIRST EDITION

In 1987, Educational Testing Service (ETS) began a large scale project to provide a framework for state and local agencies to use for making teacher licensing decisions. The resulting program is called The Praxis Series: Professional Assessments for Beginning Teachers®. Many states use Praxis I: Pre-Professional Skills Assessments and Praxis II: Subject Assessments to grant an initial teaching license. Praxis III: Classroom Performance Assessments is for use in assessing actual teaching skills and classroom performance.

I worked with ETS to help prepare and validate the criteria for Praxis III. The criteria were based on formal analyses of important tasks required of beginning teachers; reviews of research; analyses of state regulations for teacher licensing; and extensive field work that included pilot testing the criteria and assessment process (Dwyer and Villegas, 1993; Dwyer, 1994; Rosenfeld, Freeberg, & Bukatko, 1992; Rosenfeld, Reynolds, & Bukatko, 1992; Rosenfeld, Wilder, & Bukatko, 1992).

My particular responsibility in the development of Praxis III was to design the training program for assessors. Because the Praxis system is used to license beginning teachers, assessors for Praxis III must be able to make professionally and legally defensible judgments. Indeed, throughout the pilot and field testing of both the instrument and the training program, the rates of interrater agreement were high.

As valuable as Praxis III is for states in the licensing of qualified teachers, I came to see its usefulness as extending far beyond that limited role. In training hundreds of assessors to use the Praxis III framework for assessing the teaching of novices, I witnessed the quality of the participants' conversation. It became clear that in their daily lives, educators have (or make) little opportunity to discuss good teaching. As participants watched videotapes and read scenarios of teaching during the assessor training, they had to determine how what they observed represented the application of the various criteria in different contexts. For example, they noticed that a kindergarten teacher's actions to help students extend their thinking were quite different from those employed by a chemistry teacher. And yet, both teachers might be extending their students' thinking, so both sets of action constituted examples of a particular criterion in different contexts.

As educators (particularly teachers) watched and discussed the videotapes with one another, they also engaged in side conversations or reflection about their own teaching. That is, they saw a teacher's action that they could adopt or adapt to their own setting. They heard a teacher phrase a question such that it provoked deep thinking by students—and they might determine to try something similar. Hence, as teachers went through the training program, they interacted with the activities on several different levels. On the surface, of course, they were preparing to become certified assessors, which meant that they had to pass a proficiency test. On a deeper level, they were finding that the conversations themselves were helpful and that their own practice would be changed as a result.

Because of its impact on their own teaching, many Praxis III assessors reported that the experience of training was some of the most powerful professional development they had ever participated in. It gave them a structured opportunity to discuss teaching with colleagues in a concrete and research-based setting. Such opportunities are indeed rare in our schools. A par-

ticipant's statement expresses the thinking of many: "By participating in the Praxis III training, I have focused more on my own teaching. I have become more thoughtful in my teaching and more concerned that my instructional activities fulfill my goals." I, too, was changed by the experience. I developed a profound appreciation for the power of structured conversation to enrich the professional lives of teachers.

To restrict such conversations to those who serve as Praxis III assessors in states that choose to use that framework for licensing beginning teachers appeared to be too narrow an application. What about teachers in every state? What about those who already have their license? What about those who supervise student teachers or mentor beginning teachers? Wouldn't all those relationships and experiences be enriched by a comprehensive framework for teaching?

This line of thinking resulted in *Enhancing Professional Practice: A Framework for Teaching*. The framework is based on the Praxis III criteria, augmented to apply to experienced as well as to novice teachers and used for purposes beyond the licensing of beginning teachers. It is a framework that will, I hope, enrich the professional lives of those who choose to use it.

Other work also influenced the development of the framework: documents from the standards committees of the National Board for Professional Teaching Standards (NBPTS); work at the University of Wisconsin (Newmann, Secada, & Wehlage, 1995); Michael Scriven's (1994) conceptions of teacher duties; and recent research on the pedagogical implications of constructivist learning. The framework has been subjected to a further intensive review by ETS colleagues Carol Dwyer, Ruth Hummel, and Alice Sims Gunzenhauser. The research foundation for the framework is provided in the Appendix.

1

The Framework for Teaching: An Overview

The framework for teaching described in this book identifies those aspects of a teacher's responsibilities that have been documented through empirical studies and theoretical research as promoting improved student learning. Although they are not the only possible description of practice, these responsibilities seek to define what teachers should know and be able to do in the exercise of their profession.

In this framework, the complex activity of teaching is divided into 22 components clustered into the following 4 domains of teaching responsibility:

- Domain 1: Planning and Preparation
- Domain 2: The Classroom Environment
- Domain 3: Instruction
- Domain 4: Professional Responsibilities

Each component defines a distinct aspect of a domain; two to five elements describe a specific feature of a component. For example, Domain 2, The Classroom Environment, contains five components. Component 2a is Creating an Environment of Respect and Rapport, which consists of two elements: "Teacher interaction with students" and "Student interactions with other students." This component applies in some manner to all settings, as do all the other components. But although teachers at all levels and in all subjects establish rapport with and convey respect for their students, they do so in different ways. Figure 1.1 summarizes the components and their elements; Chapter 4 describes them in detail.

The components of professional practice constitute a comprehensive framework reflecting the many different aspects of teaching. Although the components are distinct, they are, of course, related to one another. A teacher's planning and preparation affect instruction, and all these are affected by the reflection on practice that accompanies a unit or lesson. In addition, many features of teaching, such as the appropriate use of technology or a concern for equity, do not each constitute a single component but rather apply to them all. Chapter 3 identifies the common themes that apply to many of the components.

WHY HAVE A FRAMEWORK?

A framework for professional practice is not unique to education. Indeed, other professions—medicine, accounting, and architecture, among many others—have well-established definitions of expertise and procedures to certify novice and advanced practitioners. Such procedures are the public's guarantee that the members of a profession hold themselves and their colleagues to high standards of practice. Similarly, a framework for teaching is useful not only to practicing educators but also to the larger community, because it conveys that educators, like other professionals, are members of a professional community.

A framework for professional practice can be used for a wide range of purposes, from meeting novices' needs to enhancing veterans' skills. Because teaching is complex, it is helpful to have a road map through the territory, structured around a shared understanding of teaching. Novice teachers, of necessity, are concerned with day-to-day survival; experienced teachers want to improve their effectiveness and help their colleagues do so as well; accomplished teachers may want to move toward advanced certification and serve as a resource to less-experienced colleagues.

A Reflection of the Complexity of Teaching

The complexity of teaching is well recognized, and this complexity extends over several aspects of the work. Teaching is physically demanding; teachers are active, moving from one part of the classroom, and of the school, to another. Student teachers, as every cooperating teacher knows, are physically exhausted at the end of a day. Teaching is also emotionally demanding, and the more caring a teacher is, the more demanding it is. Many teachers struggle to not care too much about the plights of some of their students, particularly if they are able to exert only minimal influence on the contributing factors. But even when teachers exercise self-discipline, they are frequently emotionally drained at the end of a day.

More recent research has confirmed that teaching is also cognitively demanding; a teacher makes hundreds of nontrivial decisions daily, from designing lessons, to responding to students' questions, to meeting with parents. In other words, teaching is a *thinking* person's job; it is not simply a matter of following a script or carrying out other people's instructional designs.

FIGURE 1.1

Domains, Components, and Elements of the Framework for Teaching

Domain 1: Planning and Preparation

Component 1a: Demonstrating Knowledge of Content and Pedagogy
- Knowledge of content and the structure of the discipline
- Knowledge of prerequisite relationships
- Knowledge of content-related pedagogy

Component 1b: Demonstrating Knowledge of Students
- Knowledge of child and adolescent development
- Knowledge of the learning process
- Knowledge of students' skills, knowledge, and language proficiency
- Knowledge of students' interests and cultural heritage
- Knowledge of students' special needs

Component 1c: Setting Instructional Outcomes
- Value, sequence, and alignment
- Clarity
- Balance
- Suitability for diverse learners

Component 1d: Demonstrating Knowledge of Resources
- Resources for classroom use
- Resources to extend content knowledge and pedagogy
- Resources for students

Component 1e: Designing Coherent Instruction
- Learning activities
- Instructional materials and resources
- Instructional groups
- Lesson and unit structure

Component 1f: Designing Student Assessments
- Congruence with instructional outcomes
- Criteria and standards
- Design of formative assessments
- Use for planning

Domain 2: The Classroom Environment

Component 2a: Creating an Environment of Respect and Rapport
- Teacher interaction with students
- Student interactions with other students

Component 2b: Establishing a Culture for Learning
- Importance of the content
- Expectations for learning and achievement
- Student pride in work

Component 2c: Managing Classroom Procedures
- Management of instructional groups
- Management of transitions
- Management of materials and supplies
- Performance of noninstructional duties
- Supervision of volunteers and paraprofessionals

Component 2d: Managing Student Behavior
- Expectations
- Monitoring of student behavior
- Response to student misbehavior

Component 2e: Organizing Physical Space
- Safety and accessibility
- Arrangement of furniture and use of physical resources

(figure continues)

FIGURE 1.1

Domains, Components, and Elements of the Framework for Teaching (continued)

Domain 3: Instruction

Component 3a: Communicating with Students
- Expectations for learning
- Directions and procedures
- Explanations of content
- Use of oral and written language

Component 3b: Using Questioning and Discussion Techniques
- Quality of questions
- Discussion techniques
- Student participation

Component 3c: Engaging Students in Learning
- Activities and assignments
- Grouping of students
- Instructional materials and resources
- Structure and pacing

Component 3d: Using Assessment in Instruction
- Assessment criteria
- Monitoring of student learning
- Feedback to students
- Student self-assessment and monitoring of progress

Component 3e: Demonstrating Flexibility and Responsiveness
- Lesson adjustment
- Response to students
- Persistence

Domain 4: Professional Responsibilities

Component 4a: Reflecting on Teaching
- Accuracy
- Use in future teaching

Component 4b: Maintaining Accurate Records
- Student completion of assignments
- Student progress in learning
- Noninstructional records

Component 4c: Communicating with Families
- Information about the instructional program
- Information about individual students
- Engagement of families in the instructional program

Component 4d: Participating in a Professional Community
- Relationships with colleagues
- Involvement in a culture of professional inquiry
- Service to the school
- Participation in school and district projects

Component 4e: Growing and Developing Professionally
- Enhancement of content knowledge and pedagogical skill
- Receptivity to feedback from colleagues
- Service to the profession

Component 4f: Showing Professionalism
- Integrity and ethical conduct
- Service to students
- Advocacy
- Decision making
- Compliance with school and district regulations

On a more general level, it is useful to think of teaching as similar to not one but several other professions, combining the skills of business management, human relations, and theater arts.

Business managers set goals for groups of subordinates and try to lead them toward accomplishing the goals. Such managers must allocate time and other scarce resources as they balance task-related and socioemotional considerations. They distribute rewards and sanctions to those in their charge. Similarly, teachers must motivate students to engage in learning, set goals and subgoals, manage time and other resources, and be accountable for the results.

Human relations work involves understanding the dynamics of a large group of individuals, each with a complex set of needs and desires. A teacher must also consider the range of individual personalities and take advantage of any opportunities for motivating students. A teacher must be able to connect with diverse students and establish relationships of caring and concern. In addition, in interactions with parents and colleagues, teachers must demonstrate sensitivity to multiple aspects of those relationships—personal, professional, and cultural.

Theater arts include many types of professionals, such as director, stage manager, actor, set designer, and even playwright. Teaching includes an equivalent of all the components of the theater arts. But although a director can, for example, delegate responsibility for props and sets, a teacher must manage all materials. Moreover, teachers may have to follow a "script" they do not particularly like, and the "audience" is frequently not attending voluntarily.

Other metaphors come to mind. Teachers have been likened to orchestra conductors, gardeners, engineers, and artists. Indeed, depending on which aspect of the job one is considering, any of these references may be appropriate. Many metaphors include students, such as Theodore Sizer's "student as worker; teacher as coach." These metaphors remind us of the intellectual and emotional demands of teaching and the many, sometimes competing, aspects of the job.

But even more demanding than its complexity is the level of stress that teaching generates. Planning for the productive activity of 30 or more individuals (some of them present reluctantly) and successfully executing those plans, all within the context of multiple (and sometimes conflicting) demands from the school, district, community, and state, leave many teachers—particularly novices—buffeted, confused, or discouraged. As noted, the physical demands of the job are daunting, requiring enormous stamina. Most teachers leave school exhausted at the end of the day, knowing that their students will return the next day rested and ready for more. "Will I be ready?" teachers ask themselves. "Can I be ready? What will we *do* all day? How will I engage my students in learning important content?"

An environment of high-stakes accountability only exacerbates teachers' levels of stress. Schools are being asked to, in Michael Fullan's phrase, "raise the bar and narrow the gap" (2005). Teachers are under enormous external pressure, as never before, to prepare their students for productive lives in the knowledge economy and success in externally mandated assessments.

A Common Language for Professional Conversation

Every profession establishes a language of practice, one that captures the important concepts and understandings shared by members of the profession. Similarly, a framework for teaching offers educators a means of communicating about excellence. This is not a new finding; because of Madeline Hunter's work, most educators know what is meant by "anticipatory set," "input and modeling," and "teaching for transfer." Now, as our understanding of teaching expands and deepens, we need a vocabulary that is correspondingly rich, one that reflects the realities of a classroom where students are engaged in learning important content. Such a framework is valuable for veterans as well as novices as they all strive to enhance their skills in this complex work.

During conversations about practice, particularly when such conversations are organized around a common framework, teachers are able to learn from one another and to thereby enrich their own teaching. It is this joint learning that makes the conversations so rich—and so valued. Therefore, although attendance at courses and workshops is an important vehicle for professional learning, so is focused conversation with colleagues.

It is through serious, professional conversations about the framework's components that the components are validated for any particular setting. As educators study the components and consider them within their own contexts, they can determine which components and elements are applicable and which are not. This process is critical both to enriching the professional lives of educators and to ensuring that the components used in a given setting actually do apply there. Only educators in that setting can make those determinations.

By providing an agreed-upon framework for excellence, a framework for teaching serves to structure conversations among educators about exemplary practice. A uniform frame-work allows those conversations to guide novices as well as to enhance the performance of veterans.

A Structure for Self-Assessment and Reflection on Practice

It is not only through conversation, however, that teachers can use a framework for teaching to strengthen their practice. Clear descriptions of practice enable teachers to consider their own teaching in light of the statements. Indeed, the statements, particularly when accompanied by descriptions of levels of performance, *invite* teachers to do so. It is virtually impossible for teachers to read clear statements of what teachers do, and how those actions appear when they are done well, and not engage in a thought process of "finding themselves" in the descriptors. It is natural, then, to read the statement at the next-higher level and to think to oneself, "Oh, I can do *that*."

THE TRADITION OF FRAMEWORKS FOR TEACHING

Even before the initial publication of the framework for teaching in 1996, there was a long and highly respectable tradition of attempting to definitively describe good practice. Although the purposes of such frameworks have ranged from accountability to enhancing the profession, their value has been consistently recognized.

Contributions of a Research Base

The origin of identified components of professional practice lies in a combination of Madeline Hunter's work and research in process-product and cognitive science. Hunter was one of the first educators to argue persuasively that teaching is not only an art but also a science; some instructional practices are demonstrably more effective than others. This idea was also the message of process-product research, which sought to establish relationships among certain teaching practices and enhanced student achievement, as measured by standardized tests (Wittrock, 1986). The optimistic title of a book by Gage is instructive: *The Scientific Basis of the Art of Teaching* (1977). Identifying effective practices (and, in the case of Hunter, promulgating them) became the research focus in teaching during the 1970s and 1980s. Wittrock (1986) contributed to the collective knowledge base of educators by publishing the series *Handbook of Research on Teaching*.

State Standards

Exactly how to best use the results of research on teaching became the next challenge for educators. On a statewide basis, Georgia took the lead and used the research to create a performance assessment system as the basis for awarding a permanent license to teach in the state. Other states (particularly in the Southeast) followed suit, with systems that were modeled on Georgia's and yet had their own distinctive features. By 1990, state performance assessment systems were in place in North Carolina, Florida, and Connecticut, with others proposed (but never implemented) in Kansas and Louisiana. Over the years since then, policymakers in many states (and in numerous countries) have promulgated teaching standards to guide both teacher preparation and the evaluation of teaching. In response to, and in some cases independently of, the policy

requirements, practitioners have discovered the value of clear standards of practice in structuring professional conversations.

The earliest systems of teaching standards tended to identify specific teaching behaviors (such as writing learning objectives on the board) supposedly derived from the research on effective teaching, and to rate teachers on their demonstration of these practices. The later systems adopted a more complex view of teaching and considered the quality of a teacher's judgment. For example, a Connecticut competency states that teachers should be able to "formulate meaningful questions about the subject matter." These developments reflect an increasing recognition of the complexity of teaching and the role of professional autonomy.

National Frameworks

Nationally prominent organizations have proposed sets of standards primarily for student teachers. For example, the Interstate New Teacher Assessment and Support Consortium (INTASC) developed standards for new teachers and has created a portfolio system designed to permit assessment of those standards. This combination has served as the foundation of standard-setting efforts in many states. A correlation of the framework offered here and the INTASC standards is shown in Figure 1.2. Similarly, the National Association of State Directors of Teacher Education and Certification (NASDTEC) and the National Council for Accreditation of Teacher Education (NCATE) have both proposed standards for beginning teacher competencies. And Educational Testing Service, in designing the Praxis series of assessments for states to adopt for licensing, developed Praxis III: Classroom Performance Assessments, in which trained and

FIGURE 1.2

Correlation of the INTASC Standards with the Framework for Teaching Components

INTASC Standard	Description of Teacher Performance	Framework Component	Description of Teacher Performance
Principle 1	Understands the central concepts, tools of inquiry, and structure of the disciplines taught; creates learning experiences to make them meaningful to students.	1a 1e 3c	Demonstrates knowledge of content and pedagogy. Designs coherent instruction. Engages students in learning.
Principle 2	Understands how children learn and develop; provides learning opportunities that support their development.	1b 1c 1f 3b 3c	Demonstrates knowledge of students. Sets instructional outcomes. Designs student assessments. Uses questioning and discussion techniques. Engages students in learning.
Principle 3	Understands how students differ in their approaches to learning; creates instructional opportunities adapted to diverse learners.	1b 1e 2a 2b 3b to 3e	Demonstrates knowledge of students. Designs coherent instruction. Creates an environment of respect and rapport. Establishes a culture for learning. Instruction Domain.
Principle 4	Understands and uses a variety of instructional strategies.	1d 1e 3b to 3e	Demonstrates knowledge of resources. Designs coherent instruction. Instruction Domain.
Principle 5	Creates a learning environment that encourages positive social interaction, active engagement in learning, and self-motivation.	1e 2a 2b 2c 2d 2e 3c	Designs coherent instruction. Creates an environment of respect and rapport. Establishes a culture for learning. Manages classroom procedures. Manages student behavior. Organizes physical space. Engages students in learning.

FIGURE 1.2

Correlation of the INTASC Standards with the Framework for Teaching Components *(continued)*

INTASC Standard	Description of Teacher Performance	Framework Component	Description of Teacher Performance
Principle 6	Uses knowledge of communication techniques to foster active inquiry, collaboration, and supportive interaction.	2a 3a 3b 3c	Creates an environment of respect and rapport. Communicates with students. Uses questioning and discussion techniques. Engages students in learning.
Principle 7	Plans instruction based on knowledge of subject matter, students, the community, and curriculum goals.	1a to 1e 3c 3e	Planning and Preparation Domain. Engages students in learning. Demonstrates flexibility and responsiveness.
Principle 8	Understands and uses formal and informal assessment strategies.	1b 1f 3d 3e 4a 4b 4c	Demonstrates knowledge of students. Designs student assessments. Uses assessment in instruction. Demonstrates flexibility and responsiveness. Reflects on teaching. Maintains accurate records. Communicates with families.
Principle 9	Reflects on teaching.	4a 4d 4e	Reflects on teaching. Participates in a professional community. Grows and develops professionally.
Principle 10	Fosters relationships with colleagues, parents, and agencies in the larger community.	1d 4c 4d 4f	Demonstrates knowledge of resources. Communicates with families. Participates in a professional community. Shows professionalism.

certified assessors observe classroom teaching and evaluate performance against established criteria (Reynolds, 1992).

The National Board for Professional Teaching Standards (NBPTS) has made an enormous contribution to teaching standards. It was created in 1987 following the publication of *A Nation Prepared* (Carnegie Forum on Education and the Economy's Task Force on Teaching as a Profession, 1986). Through rigorous assessments, NBPTS offers teachers the equivalent of advanced board certification in medicine. Just as a medical doctor earns an initial license to practice medicine and then passes a test for board certification in, for example, pediatrics, the theory of the national board is that teachers should be able to earn advanced certification in any of multiple disciplines or levels—for example, early childhood or high school mathematics. NBPTS offers more than 30 separate certificates to teachers; increasing numbers of teachers have taken advantage of this opportunity, finding the experience to be both challenging and professionally rewarding.

By-products of the Movement Toward Frameworks

The use of frameworks that define and describe excellence in teaching has produced powerful side effects. Even when the original purpose was to demonstrate accountability, practitioners themselves have enjoyed enormous benefits.

It has long been recognized that articulating clear standards for student learning, illustrated by examples of exemplary student work, enhances the quality of that work and students' sense of purpose. Teachers have discovered that when they are clear to students about the criteria used to evaluate a science project, for example, students are far more focused, and the resulting projects are of higher quality than when such criteria are not provided. Furthermore, students who might have believed that high grades were beyond their reach now see clearly how to achieve them.

The same phenomenon is at work with a framework for teaching. When teachers are beginning their careers, the challenge of becoming a skilled practitioner is daunting. Teaching is so complex and its various components so intertwined that many novices feel overwhelmed. A framework for teaching offers a structure for teachers to assess their practice and to organize improvement efforts. In addition, to implement teacher mentoring and licensing systems or to certify teachers under NBPTS, many educators must be trained as mentors or assessors. During such training, practitioners think seriously about teaching, learn to recognize the various components in different contexts, and as a result, reflect deeply on their own practice. This reflection, conducted in a professional and supportive environment and in the service of another purpose (becoming a mentor or a certified assessor), is an enriching experience. Practitioners report that the experience is their first opportunity in many years to discuss *teaching* seriously—in its complex entirety—with respected colleagues.

➤ *The components of professional practice are part of a long tradition of applying standards to both student learning and the complex role of teaching. The benefits—for individuals, universities, or schools and districts—are enormous.*

USES FOR A FRAMEWORK

A framework for professional practice has many distinct, though related, uses. These are described briefly here and in greater detail in Chapter 6.

The Preparation of New Teachers

Many teacher educators, both in the United States and in other countries, have found the framework for teaching to be of value as they structure their programs to prepare students for the demanding and important work of teaching. The framework contributes to the organization of the program itself, the courses offered, and the supervision of student teachers.

Teacher educators have found that when they recognize the existence of a clearly articulated framework for teaching that describes the work for which they are preparing their students, they must be able to offer assurance that their graduates are, in fact, proficient in the knowledge and skills described in that framework. Such recognition leads naturally to an "audit" of their own practice, to ensure that their programs include what students will need to be successful as teachers. Furthermore, during the clinical phase of teacher preparation, teachers-in-training benefit from a clear framework for teaching, both in their observations of experienced teachers and as an organizing structure for the feedback they receive from their supervisors.

The Recruitment and Hiring of Teachers

Many school districts have discovered that recruitment and hiring are facilitated if those activities are informed by a coherent definition of good teaching, one that is aligned with their approaches to mentoring, professional development, and teacher evaluation. As a result, they have created interview questions based on the components and elements of the framework for teaching, ensuring consistency in the interview process and in the skills of teachers who join the faculty. Furthermore, through their questions, educators convey to teaching candidates what the district values and how it defines good teaching; as a result, when the new teachers are later working in the schools, they are not surprised by the district's conceptualization of good teaching.

A Road Map for Novices

Most professions designate a period of apprenticeship for a novice practitioner. Doctors work as interns and residents before assuming complete responsibility for patients. Attorneys practice as clerks for experienced lawyers or judges and then join a firm or an agency where they practice with attorneys experienced in the different specialty areas. Social workers employed in public agencies work under supervision before they earn a license to practice on their own.

But teachers, from the moment they are awarded their first license and work as the teacher of record, are considered full members of the profession. The responsibilities of a first-year teacher are just as complex (in some situations, more so) as those of a 20-year veteran. In very few locations do teachers have an experience equivalent to the internship of a doctor or a social worker; they are plunged immediately into the full responsibilities of a teacher. A newly licensed architect, for example, would never be asked to design a major building the first week on the job, all alone. But this is exactly what teachers are asked to do, and it reflects a structural challenge in the profession. Any structural solutions that might be effective, such as professional development schools that include a full-year internship, are expensive to implement.

Given the complexity of teaching, a map of the territory is invaluable to novices, providing them with a pathway to excellence. If the map is used well and shared by mentors, it can help make the experience of becoming an accomplished professional a rewarding one. Furthermore, well-designed mentoring programs significantly reduce the rate of attrition of new teachers.

Guidance for Experienced Professionals

A framework for professional practice offers the teaching profession the same definition long afforded other professions. A framework answers the questions "What does an effective teacher know?" and "What does an accomplished teacher do in the performance of her duties?" A framework is useful for all teachers, from those just entering the profession, to veterans who may have lost enthusiasm for their work, to master teachers who are trying to convey their wisdom to others. Thus far, educators have lacked an agreed-upon structure that reflects new understandings of teaching and learning and offers a context for describing and discussing excellence. They rarely devote precious time to professional dialogue and sharing of techniques. A framework for teaching provides the structure for such discussions and an opportunity for genuine professionalism.

A Structure for Focusing Improvement Efforts

When novice teachers meet with their mentors or when experienced teachers consult with their coaches or supervisors, they need a framework to determine which aspects of teaching require their attention. They must decide which parts, of all the complex elements of instruction reflected in any lesson, to concentrate on. A framework for teaching provides such a structure.

Without a framework, the structure is reduced to whatever the mentor, coach, or supervisor has in her head, and it thus reflects the personal beliefs that individual holds about teaching, regardless of whether these have ever been made explicit. Many teachers have had the experience of conducting what they thought was a brilliant lesson only to have a principal react negatively because, for example, students were talking to one another. The teacher and the principal did not share a common understanding of what represented effective teaching.

With a framework for teaching in hand, however, participants can conduct conversations about where to focus improvement efforts within the context of shared definitions and understandings. When a teacher is struggling in the classroom, when a lesson is ineffective, or when students are not engaged, a comprehensive framework is useful in identifying the source of the difficulty and therefore in guiding improvement efforts. These conversations focus on means, not ends, and they are conducted in an environment of professional respect.

Communication with the Larger Community

An important step to enhancing the stature of educators in the family of professions is defining clearly what constitutes excellence in teaching. As long as practitioners present teaching as a mysterious art form without well-defined duties and competencies, the larger community will regard it with mistrust. For example, many in the general public do not understand the need for teachers to attend courses and workshops: "They went to college, didn't they?" The clarity that a framework for teaching provides, including Component 4e, Growing and Developing Professionally, can situate such activities squarely within the responsibilities of teaching.

A framework for professional practice has important uses in the service of teaching and learning. These uses demonstrate the framework's power to elevate professional conversations that characterize the interaction of exemplary teachers everywhere.

ASSUMPTIONS AND FEATURES OF
THE FRAMEWORK FOR TEACHING

The framework for teaching represents all aspects of a teacher's responsibilities that are reflected in daily work. It derives from the most recent theoretical and empirical research about teaching and aims to apply to all situations. This chapter describes general features of the framework and the assumptions upon which it is based.

UNDERLYING ASSUMPTIONS

All descriptions of teaching rest on certain assumptions, whether they are stated explicitly or not. Some of these assumptions, such as how children learn, rest (or claim to rest) on academic research; others express statements of value, such as defining what is important for students to learn. But whatever their origin, underlying assumptions should be stated clearly and succinctly so that when users are evaluating different sets of teaching standards they can determine which best match their needs.

Important Learning for Students

First, and possibly most important, definitions of teaching are grounded in a view of what constitutes important learning for students. Educators, researchers, and policymakers concur that the traditional view of learning, focused on knowledge and procedures of low cognitive challenge and the regurgitation of superficial understanding, does not meet the demands of the present and future. Competitive industries in the 21st century will be those whose workers can solve complex problems and design more efficient techniques to accomplish work. Furthermore, a democratic society depends on an educated citizenry both to make informed choices at the ballot box and to discharge the complex responsibilities of serving as a juror. To be sure, much basic knowledge is important for students to understand. But deep, conceptual understanding—knowledge that lasts longer than the time it takes for a student to pass a test—is also needed. And the skill of evaluating arguments, or analyzing information and drawing conclusions, is critical.

It is the premise of the framework for teaching that it is important for students—all students—to acquire deep and flexible understanding of complex content, to be able to formulate and test hypotheses, to analyze information, and to be able to relate one part of their learning to another. To bring about this type of outcome for students, teachers themselves must have deep and flexible understanding of their content and the skills to enable students to move beyond memorization to analysis and interpretation. Thus, high-level learning by students requires high-level instruction by their teachers.

The Nature of Learning and How to Promote It

Understanding how students acquire high-level understanding and advanced cognitive skills and how to develop the intellectual capabilities needed for acquiring and processing information is at the heart of the advanced instructional skills that teachers require. In the professional community, teachers continue their search for how to develop such skills.

Educators and policymakers have focused their attention (again) on "constructivism" and a constructivist approach to learning (and therefore teaching). This orientation has become de rigueur in education circles and is reflected in many of the curriculum standards promulgated by both professional organizations and many states. We must recognize, however, that this movement is not new. Constructivism stems from a long and respected tradition in cognitive psychology, especially the writings of Dewey, Vygotsky, and Piaget. Although not universally accepted throughout all of the 20th century, constructivism is now acknowledged by cognitive psychologists as providing the most powerful framework for understanding how children (and adults) learn.

So what is the constructivist approach, and how does it help educators teach for conceptual understanding? First, it is essential to state, in very clear terms, what constructivism is *not*. A constructivist orientation does not hold that educators relinquish control of what students learn to the students themselves. It is not an "anything goes" philosophy. Teachers who embrace a constructivist orientation understand that they are the adults and that they, together with their colleagues and in line with state standards, determine what it is that students will learn. At issue is *how* the students learn it. Is the content "transmitted" to students somehow, or do they "construct" their understanding?

Constructivism recognizes that, for all human beings—adults as well as children—it is the *learner* who does the learning. That is, people's understanding of any concept depends entirely on their experience in deriving that concept for themselves.

Teachers can, of course, guide the process, but students must develop understanding through what they do. The constructivist approach makes explicit that different individuals, depending on their experiences, knowledge, *and their cognitive structures at the time,* will understand a given presentation differently. People remember an experience based on what their pre-existing knowledge and cognitive structures allow them to absorb—regardless of a teacher's intentions or the quality of an explanation.

An example of constructivist teaching may be provided by considering a teacher's goal in having students understand the concept of pi, a mathematical concept equal to approximately 3.14. The teacher could make a presentation about pi, saying that it is a constant equal to about 3.14 and giving examples of how it is used. This approach has the virtue of being brief. However, most students will not remember anything about pi, perhaps not even its value, nor could they be said to *understand* it.

To teach the concept of pi in a constructivist manner, the teacher needs to engage students in developing their own understanding. For example, the teacher might present students with many round objects and ask them to measure their diameters and circumferences and to analyze the resulting data. Regardless of how students display their information (for example, by making a graph or presenting a table), they will discern patterns in the data. The students will recognize, possibly with teacher guidance, that the graph they have made is a straight line or that the circumference divided by the diameter is always the same. The slope of the line and the quotient are both a little greater than 3 and represent what mathematicians call *pi*. Only when students have engaged in such an investigation can

they be said to truly *understand* pi and appreciate its value in mathematics.

The goals of a constructivist approach are no different than those of a more traditional approach—in this case, to understand pi. Pi figures into the formulas for calculating area and volume of geometric figures in the most traditional presentations of mathematics. But a teacher using a constructivist approach recognizes that if students are to understand the concept, they must do much of the intellectual work themselves; they must see the patterns and derive the relationships. Such an approach also suggests that students can acquire an understanding of pi in many ways; many instructional sequences could achieve the goal. Within a single class, some students may use the graphing method, while others might calculate the quotients. Others may devise yet another method of investigation. But all will notice patterns in the data and will derive the relationship between the two sets of numbers.

As another example, consider a middle school class learning about the Civil War. In a traditional class, a teacher may ask students to write a report on a battle, such as the Second Battle of Bull Run. And typically, the reports will include barely disguised encyclopedia or Internet accounts of the encounter; students will have learned little from the exercise.

Instead of a report, however, suppose the teacher asks students to imagine that they are soldiers (either Union or Confederate) in the battle and to write a letter home. The directions could be fairly specific: describe the terrain, the weather that day, what (if anything) the soldiers had to eat, the events of the battle, what happened to one's buddies, and so on. Students will need not only to learn information about the battle from as many sources as possible but also to *do something* with the information. They will have to coordinate versions from different perspectives, draw their own conclusions, and personalize the information.

Nothing in this approach is particularly new or controversial; teachers have used such techniques for years. But constructivist teaching does take time, because students require more time to explore a concept than simply to be told about it. Therefore, educators must be selective; they must determine which topics and concepts in the curriculum are critical for students to understand, which ones warrant the time needed to develop understanding. But although the time required for instruction in an inquiry manner is longer than in a formal lecture, student learning tends to be more permanent. Once students have derived pi, for example, they are likely to remember it. So although fewer topics may be covered, more is actually learned.

It is important to keep in mind that construction of knowledge is not the same as physical involvement with manipulative materials. So-called hands-on learning may or may not be constructivist. Students can follow directions as mindlessly when using physical objects as they can when completing a worksheet. In a constructivist approach, students are cognitively engaged in what they are doing; the activities, in other words, must be "minds-on." Although in many situations physical involvement with real objects aids this process, physical involvement provides no guarantee that students will be mentally engaged.

Of course, not all valuable learning is constructivist. Other types of learning, such as rote memorization, have an important role, too—as, for example, in learning foreign language vocabulary words. The instructional challenge for a teacher is in knowing when to use which approach. To take another example from mathematics, suppose the goal is for students to understand the concept of addition, which is grounded in developmental structures of number conservation and additive composition. They must construct the understanding that each time 5 and 3 are added together in any order and using any representation, the answer is always 8. But once the concept is thoroughly understood, memorizing the addition facts can proceed by rote. Patterns can help the learning process; but in the end, students must know the facts.

The constructivist approach has important implications for teaching and for the role of the teacher in student learning. When considering an environment where students are constructing their own understanding, educators may conclude that a teacher has nothing to do. On the contrary, a teacher's role in a constructivist class is no less critical than the teacher's role in a traditional class. It is different. Teaching no longer focuses solely on making presentations (although those are still sometimes appropriate) or assigning questions and exercises. Instead, teaching focuses on designing activities and assignments—many of them framed as problem solving—that engage students in constructing important knowledge.

The framework for teaching is grounded in the constructivist approach. It assumes that the primary goal of education is for students to understand important concepts and to develop important cognitive skills, and that it is each teacher's responsibility, using the resources at hand, to accomplish those goals. Naturally, this is a highly complex view of teaching, one that recognizes the many decisions that must be made daily to realize such a vision. But the framework also takes the position that to meet the needs of our citizens of the future, nothing less will do.

The Purposeful Nature of Teaching

Another important assumption underlying the framework for teaching is that instructional decisions are purposeful. Activities and assignments are not chosen merely because they are fun. They are selected or designed because they serve the instructional goals of the teacher, as guided by the students' interests and strengths.

This focus on purpose sets this framework apart from many other teaching frameworks. Generally, teachers are asked to demonstrate that their students are on task or that students treat one another with respect. But teachers are rarely asked to explain the reasons for students to be on-task or to behave respectfully. The questions that should be asked are questions such as these: "What instructional purpose is being served?" "Is this instructional purpose worthwhile?" Even instructional practices that are widely regarded as good, such as integrated, thematic units, may not have a significant purpose.

In the framework for teaching, purpose is central. Component 1c (Setting Instructional Outcomes) extends a long reach over all of teaching. The instructional outcomes must themselves be valuable, aligned to curriculum standards, and suitable to the students. In addition, the instructional methods, the proposed assessment techniques, and the teacher's reflection on the lesson must address those same outcomes. The outcomes, in other words, provide the organizing structure for all the decisions the teacher makes. Do the activities and materials serve to achieve the instructional purpose that the teacher has established? Will the assessment techniques actually assess student achievement of the outcomes, and will they respect both the content and the processes inherent in those outcomes? Can the formative assessments the teacher has planned serve next steps by both the teacher and the students?

The Nature of Professionalism

Teaching has struggled for some time with its role in the world of the professions. Generally speaking, it is neither as prestigious nor as well paid as other occupations, such as medicine, accounting, architecture, and law, which are openly recognized as professions. Many historical reasons account for this situation; teaching is characterized by high degrees of government oversight, bureaucratic organization, and low status. Teaching has been treated—and, to some degree, has treated itself—as a job, with almost an assembly-line mentality, in which teachers follow a "script" that has been designed by someone else, presumably more expert.

However, when one considers the work of teaching and compares that work to the defining characteristics of a profession, it is clear that teaching is, indeed, a profession. For example, all professions have a body of knowledge that is shared by the community of professionals; so does teaching. Teachers apply their professional knowledge in making hundreds of decisions daily, often under conditions of uncertainty and frequently under the pressure of time. Furthermore, teaching, like other professions, occurs at the intersection of theoretical and practical considerations. That is, both the theory and the practice of teaching inform each other. And lastly, teachers, like members of other professions, conduct themselves in accordance with high ethical standards of professional practice.

The work of teachers, as described in the framework for teaching, operates on the assumption that teaching is indeed professional work, with both the privileges and obligations conferred by that status. The framework recognizes the complexity and the importance of teaching; decisions that teachers make in designing and executing instructional plans are far from trivial. These decisions depend on a sophisticated understanding of the content to be learned, the students in one's care, and the nature of learning itself. They require familiarity with the context and sophisticated judgments about the likely consequences of different courses of action. The implications of this professionalism are evident in each of the components of the framework for teaching.

FEATURES OF THE FRAMEWORK

The framework for teaching embodies a number of features that ensure both its validity and its applicability to a wide range of instructional settings.

Comprehensive

The framework aims to describe *all* of teaching, in all its complexity. It is comprehensive, referring not only to what occurs in the classroom but also to what happens behind the scenes and beyond the classroom walls. The comprehensive nature of the framework for teaching sets it apart from other, earlier attempts to describe teaching.

These broader responsibilities include many activities, such as the following:

- Planning for instruction and reflecting on next steps.
- Interacting with colleagues in the faculty lounge, on school and district committees, and in pursuit of instructional improvement.
- Communicating with parents and the larger community.

The comprehensive nature of teaching, as described in the framework, has important implications for how teachers reflect on their practice and how they demonstrate their skill. Because much of the important work of teaching happens outside the classroom, a comprehensive examination of practice cannot be restricted to observations of classroom teaching. What happens in the classroom is, of course, central to good teaching. But it does not fully define it.

Domain 2 (The Classroom Environment) and Domain 3 (Instruction) are demonstrated principally through a teacher's interaction with students. But many other components, including all of Domain 4 (Professional Responsibilities), are manifested in the interactions a teacher has with families; colleagues, both within the school and district and in larger groups, such as professional organizations and university classes; and the community of business and civic leaders. Domain 1 (Planning and Preparation) is revealed through a teacher's plans for instruction. Although the success of those plans is only fully demonstrated in the classroom and primarily through what happens in Domain 3 (Instruction), the success of the instructional design *as a design* is revealed through unit and lesson plans.

Teachers can also demonstrate many components through materials they create and interpret. For example, a class or homework assignment that shows samples of student work sheds light on Component 3c (Engaging Students in Learning); class newsletters and logs of contact with families can document Component 4c (Communicating with Families); and logs of committee meetings and school events can document Component 4d (Participating in a Professional Community).

Some components are not directly observable and must be inferred. For example, Component 2d concerns the management of student behavior. One element is "Expectations," meaning that all students understand the standards of conduct and have participated, if possible, in establishing those standards. If a mentor or coach visits a class in December, the standards will probably have been established, so they may not be discussed during a lesson. The observer, however, may be able to infer—perhaps from displayed material or by the interaction of students with their peers and teacher—whether such standards have been successfully established. What is *observed* is behavior—both students' and the teacher's. But what is *inferred* relates to the standards of conduct established in the class.

Grounded in Research

To the greatest extent possible, the framework for teaching is grounded in a body of research that seeks to identify principles of effective practice and classroom organization. Such principles maximize student learning and promote student engagement. Some of this research is empirical; that is, it is grounded in experience, with formal research data to support it. Some is theoretical; that is, it is derived from theoretical research on cognition.

The educational environment presents formidable challenges for empirical research, and these challenges have been well documented. Research design depends on clear outcomes, measures of those outcomes, and control of other variables that might influence the outcomes. Unfortunately, educational research does not routinely meet any of these conditions.

The goals of education are frequently clear neither to the policy community nor to educators. However, even when the goals are clear and include such items as high-level cognitive skills, measures of achievement (consisting primarily of scores on standardized tests) are poorly suited to documenting whether students have attained those goals. Thus, success by individual students, and by schools and school districts, is translated to mean achieving a high score on a multiple-choice, machine-scorable test. Standardized tests are fairly reliable in assessing bits of information, low-level knowledge, and routine procedures. But they are unsatisfactory for assessing conceptual understanding. For example, a thorough understanding of buoyancy, and how it is related to sinking and floating, is different from the ability to select its correct definition from a list of choices. And other broadly accepted goals of public schools—such as developing social maturity—don't lend themselves to assessment by any type of test at all.

An additional difficulty with educational research concerns control over extraneous variables. Clean research design requires that any technique tried with a group of students be compared with an alternate approach. Insofar as possible, both the students and the teachers involved in the research must be comparable. But common sense, as well as convincing research, has made it clear that outside influences contribute enormously, and in ways not completely understood, to student learning. Controlling for those influences is notoriously difficult. In particular, it is not sufficient to simply determine which students, or students in which classes, score highest on a test, because some of them might have been able to pass the test with no instruction at all.

Education researchers have made advances in the design of "value-added" research, which determines students' knowledge and skill at the outset of an instructional sequence and calculates their predicted level of achievement at the end. Then, by comparing students' actual with their predicted achievement, the effectiveness of the instruction can be ascertained. But even with these advances, making sound conclusions from educational research studies involves large numbers of students and must assume that there are no systematic biases in the assignment of different students to different experimental groups. Furthermore, such techniques require valid assessments in the different fields that teachers teach; for a secondary teacher of biology or Spanish, for example, such tests are not available.

But given these limitations and caveats, the framework for teaching derives as much as possible from sound educational research. (The research supporting each of the components is described in the Appendix.) In those cases in which empirical research has not yet been conducted, the framework derives from recommendations of experts in curriculum, instruction, and assessment and draws extensively on the most current theoretical research literature and writings of leading authorities.

Public

One of the main principles of the framework for teaching is that it is publicly known. The framework has no "gotcha" mentality behind it—an attribute that is particularly important if it is used for supervision.

Implications for promulgating the framework are profound. First and most important, such action puts the opportunity for meaningful discussion about the components in the hands of those who must use them—namely, teachers. Decisions on the applicability of each element to a given situation must be made by those who are most familiar with that situation—again, teachers. Many schools and districts engage in a systematic "book study" of the framework for teaching, in which teachers examine each component in depth and determine what modifications, if any, would have to be made to the wording to make the framework applicable to their own setting.

Second, when a framework is public, discussion becomes an important vehicle for professional development. Dialogue that centers on the framework and how the different components are revealed in different contexts becomes a powerful catalyst for meaningful discussion about the enhancement of teaching.

Third, if the framework is used for mentoring or supervision, it ensures that teachers know what an observer is "looking for." Without an agreed-upon definition of good teaching, an observer relies on her own, perhaps idiosyncratic, view of good practice, a view that may never have been explicitly communicated to the teacher. In addition, the framework can help a teacher select improvement goals. Through self-assessment, reflection, and analysis, a teacher can identify the components on which to concentrate, with a mentor or supervisor available as a coach. If the framework were kept secret, this opportunity would not be available.

Generic

It is well known—certainly by teachers—that every teaching situation is unique. Each day, in each classroom, a particular combination of factors defines the events that occur. The personalities of both teacher and students interacting with one another and with the content create a unique environment. Many educators believe that, because of this uniqueness, there can be no generic framework that defines teaching. They point to the systematic differences in technique between teaching mathematics and foreign language; they cite the different approaches to learning exhibited by 1st graders and high school sophomores. And they point out that the makeup of a class—for example, whether the students are from urban or rural areas or whether student cultural traditions match those of the educators—heavily influences the decisions a teacher makes about organizing the curriculum and engaging students in learning.

Yet beneath the unique features of each situation are powerful commonalties. It is these commonalties that the framework addresses. For example, in every classroom, an effective teacher creates an environment of respect and rapport (Component 2a). How that is done and what is specifically observed are very different in a kindergarten class and a high school biology class, in an urban setting and a rural setting. But the underlying construct is the same: students feel respected by the teacher and their peers; they believe that the teacher *cares* about them and their learning. Similarly, the specific techniques used to engage students in writing a persuasive essay are fundamentally different from those used to engage students in a conceptual understanding of place value. But in both cases, students are deeply engaged in the task at hand and take pride in their work. The framework for teaching captures this engagement and pride. And because a teacher's actions are a function of the contexts in which they occur, it follows that good teaching does not consist of a listing of specific behaviors; it cannot, because the behaviors themselves depend on the context. It also follows that there is only one framework for teaching; there is not a framework specific to high school English or middle school social studies. Although those different contexts imply very different decisions by teachers about what they do every day, the framework for teaching captures those aspects of teaching that are common across contexts.

When mentors, coaches, or supervisors observe colleagues' classrooms, they must beware of imposing their own preferences on what they see. The question is not "Has this teacher established a physical environment in the same way I would do it?" but rather "Given this teacher's situation—the age of the students and the nature of the school and the class—has this teacher successfully established a physical environment conducive to learning? What suggestions can I make, *given this context and given this teacher's general approach*?" Thus, although the components apply in some form to all contexts, their manifestations vary greatly in ways that make them appropriate to diverse settings.

Although the framework for teaching is comprehensive and generic, it is a framework for *teaching;* it is not a framework for the work done by school nurses, guidance counselors, or even media resource teachers. Individuals who hold these specialist positions are regarded for organizational purposes as teachers, and they typically do some teaching. But their primary responsibilities lie outside the walls of a single classroom. And even if they do some teaching, their jobs include other responsibilities as well, such as, in the case of a school librarian, maintaining the collection and serving as a resource for other teachers. Hence, specialists need their own frameworks, documents that reflect their work. Chapter 5 contains frameworks that practitioners could adapt for their work.

Coherent in Structure

The framework for teaching divides the complex work of teachers into four domains: (1) Planning and Preparation, (2) The Classroom Environment, (3) Instruction, and (4) Professional

Responsibilities. Each of these domains is further elaborated by either 5 or 6 components, for a total of 22 components. Each component describes an important aspect of teaching, and, taken together, the components in a domain fully capture everything important about that domain. In addition, each component is further divided into 2 to 5 essential elements, for a total of 76 elements. Again, each of the elements describes an important aspect of that component, and, taken together, they capture all the important aspects of the component. This hierarchical structure is designed for ease of navigation; that is, when considering practice, one can first determine the broad domain, and then the component, and, if necessary, the element. The structure is coherent in that the different aspects of practice "hang together" to describe increasingly broad areas of practice; they are not just a random collection of unrelated skills.

Furthermore, the different domains and components represent areas of roughly equal "size" or "heft." One domain is not noticeably larger than the others, nor does one component within a domain reflect a much larger part of a teacher's responsibility within that domain than do the other components. The domains and the components within the domains are, in other words, of roughly equal grain size.

The structure of the framework for teaching carries some implications. First, the framework is organized around the "tasks" of teaching, which means that the components and elements of the framework are nonredundant. Each concept is included only once. Even in those cases in which the same words are used (for example, *activities* in the elements for Components 1e and 3c), distinctly different aspects of the concept are being described. The *activities* referred to in Component 1e are the learning activities as designed in the instruc-

tional plan; the *activities* in Component 3c are the activities as implemented in the classroom.

Another aspect of the framework's structure deals with anticipating its possible applications. That is, the framework has been structured with an eye on its "downstream" uses. Because the framework is organized around the tasks of teaching, it is useful for supervisors of student teachers, or mentors or coaches, or teachers themselves, as a means to analyze practice. This is a critical feature when a purpose of a description of teaching is to structure efforts at improvement. And if the framework is to be used for supervision and evaluation, it is essential that it describe actual practice. That is, it is possible, from the manner in which the statements are written, to imagine ways in which a teacher might demonstrate skill in that area.

Furthermore, because the framework for teaching describes the tasks of teaching, the verbs used concern performance, rather than the beliefs or dispositions of teachers. Thus, it states that teachers "demonstrate flexibility and responsiveness" rather than that teachers "are committed to student learning." It is probably the case that a teacher's flexibility reflects a commitment to student learning, but the critical feature here is the performance, because that is what can be observed and analyzed.

Independent of Any Particular Teaching Methodology

Some previous attempts to develop frameworks for teaching have been grounded in a specific approach to teaching and presume that the approach will be effective in any setting. In fact, the history of educational practice is littered with attempts to find new and better ways to enhance student learning, such as cooperative learning, learning styles, TESA, brain hemisphericity, multiple intelligences, and so on. Although such formulations make a contribution, prescribing them seems to violate the very notion of professionalism. Even when an idea is well grounded and a requirement to use it is well motivated, reflecting the promulgation of a "scientific basis for the art of teaching" (Gage, 1977), the requirement seems to assume that the same approach will be effective for all types of learning with all types of students.

Partly to respond to the overly prescriptive models presented in the early 1980s, many educators and researchers delved into the field of learning and teaching styles. Based on their research, they argued that just as students bring different strengths to aid their learning, so, too, teachers have different strengths, which are expressed as their "style"; none is better than any other. Where one teacher may be nurturing, another may be firm; where one teacher lectures, another may use small-group instruction.

The framework for teaching is grounded in the belief that both positions are inadequate. Indeed, selecting instructional approaches rests absolutely with a teacher; this decision is a critical element of professionalism. Not all choices, however, are effective; not all are equally appropriate. Decisions about instructional strategies and learning activities involve matching the desired outcomes of a lesson or a unit (that is, what the students are to learn) with the approaches selected. Not only should the instructional goals be worthwhile, but the methods and materials chosen should be appropriate for those goals and help students attain them.

What is required, then, is that teachers have a repertoire of strategies from which they can select a suitable one for a given purpose. No single approach will be effective in every situation, for each set of instructional purposes, or with all individuals or groups of students. These choices and decisions represent the heart of professionalism. And for many educators, adding to the repertoire is their primary purpose in attending workshops and inservice sessions and taking university courses. Teachers know that they are never finished acquiring strategies to suit different goals. They can always gain new insights and new approaches to meet their (and their students') instructional purposes.

A diagram that is helpful in analyzing different approaches and organizational patterns is provided in Figure 2.1, which identifies four ways of grouping students for instruction. In the first pattern, students are together in a large group and involved in a single activity that a teacher or another student leads. This activity can be a lecture, a discussion, or a student presentation. In the second pattern, a teacher works with a small group of students, while other students work alone or independently in small groups. This pattern is the basic "reading group" organization. In the third pattern, students work in small groups, and the teacher circulates to assist as needed. Science teachers frequently use this organization when students are completing a laboratory assignment. Teachers in all disciplines use it to structure small-group work. In the last pattern, students work alone, with the teacher circulating, providing feedback, or conducting conferences with individual students. Many types of tasks fall into this grouping, from worksheets, to writing assignments, to problem sets.

The figure also indicates different levels of student initiative. The levels range from low (for example, the level of initiative required to answer questions from a teacher or a

FIGURE 2.1

Approaches to Classroom Organization and Instruction

Grouping Pattern	Level of Student Initiative		
	Low	Moderate	High
Teacher or student leads large-group presentation.	(A)		(B)
Teacher works with small groups; other students work alone or in small groups.		(C)	
Students work in small groups; teacher circulates.	(D)		
Students work alone; teacher monitors.	(E)		(F)

textbook), to moderate (for example, the level required to write an essay on one of several topics that a teacher has proposed), to high (for example, the level required to devise an experiment to test a theory a student has generated).

The letters in parentheses indicate various combinations of grouping patterns and levels of student initiative. Therefore, a teacher lecture or a student presentation is an example of (A); a student-led discussion on a topic the class selects is an example of (B). A teacher meeting with a group of students to discuss a book that they have selected from a range of choices the teacher has offered is an example of (C); a science lab in which students are following an established procedure illustrates (D). Students completing a worksheet assignment by the teacher fits (E); students writing an essay on a topic of their own choosing is an example of (F).

No arrangement is superior to the others; all can promote high-quality learning. At any time in a classroom, students will be working individually or in a group, and they will be engaged in a task at some level of initiative. They may be working in several different group patterns and at different levels of initiative in succession.

Which method a teacher selects depends on both the content to be learned and the students' age and preferred approach. The teacher is the person most knowledgeable about those factors. Another professional, however, might have selected a different approach to accomplish the same purposes with the same students; this approach might have been as effective, or perhaps more so. But the discussion is about the *appropriateness* of different choices; there are no right and wrong choices.

The framework for teaching does not endorse any particular teaching style for all teachers; it does, however, enable educators to engage in conversations about the appropriateness of choices made at many points in a lesson or unit. No one approach is a "one size fits all." But some approaches will be better suited to certain purposes than others. Making good and defensible choices is the hallmark of a professional educator.

— *The framework for teaching is based on important assumptions about what is important for students to learn, the nature of learning and how to promote it, the purposeful nature of teaching, and the nature of professionalism. The framework for teaching also has a number of important features: it is comprehensive, grounded in research, public, generic, coherent in structure, and independent of any particular teaching methodology.*

THE FOUR DOMAINS OF
TEACHING RESPONSIBILITY

Although teachers sometimes feel pulled in many different directions—at one moment serving as a counselor, at another moment as a business manager—a unifying thread runs through the entire framework for teaching and provides an organizing structure. That thread consists of engaging students in learning important content. All the components of the framework serve this primary purpose. And in pursuit of important learning, a teacher creates, with the students, a community of learners, where all students feel respected and honored.

Each of the four domains of the framework refers to a distinct aspect of teaching. To some degree, the components within each domain form a coherent body of knowledge and skill that can be the subject of focus independent of the other domains. This chapter describes each domain, identifies common themes that run through the components, and explains the concepts underlying the four levels of performance that are displayed by teachers with different levels of skill.

DOMAIN 1 : PLANNING AND PREPARATION

The components in Domain 1 describe how a teacher organizes the content that the students are to learn—how the teacher *designs* instruction (see Figure 3.1). The domain covers all aspects of instructional planning, beginning with a deep

---

FIGURE 3.1

Components of Domain 1: Planning and Preparation

Component 1a: Demonstrating Knowledge of Content and Pedagogy

Component 1b: Demonstrating Knowledge of Students

Component 1c: Setting Instructional Outcomes

Component 1d: Demonstrating Knowledge of Resources

Component 1e: Designing Coherent Instruction

Component 1f: Designing Student Assessments

---

understanding of content and pedagogy and an understanding and appreciation of the students and what they bring to the educational encounter. But understanding the content is not sufficient; every adult has encountered the university professor who, while truly expert in a subject, was unable to engage students in learning it. The content must be transformed through instructional design into sequences of activities and exercises that make it accessible to students. All elements of the instructional design—learning activities, materials, and strategies—must be appropriate to both the content and the students, and aligned with larger instructional goals. In their content and process, assessment techniques must also reflect the instructional outcomes and should serve to document student progress during and at the end of a teaching episode. Furthermore, in designing assessment strategies, teachers must consider their use for formative purposes and how assessments can provide diagnostic opportunities for students to demonstrate their level of understanding during the instructional sequence, while there is still time to make adjustments.

It is difficult to overstate the importance of planning. In fact, one could go further and argue that a teacher's role is not so much to *teach* as it is to *arrange for learning*. That is, a teacher's essential responsibility is to ensure that students learn, to design (or select or adapt) learning activities such that students learn important content. Thus, planning is a matter of design. Teachers who excel in Domain 1 design instruction that reflects an understanding of the disciplines they teach—the important concepts and principles within that content, and how the different elements relate to one another and to those in other disciplines. They understand their students—their backgrounds, interests, and skills. Their design is coherent in its approach to topics, includes sound assessment methods, and is appropriate to the range of students in the class.

Skills in Domain 1 are demonstrated primarily through the plans that teachers prepare to guide their teaching, by how they describe the decisions they make, and ultimately through the success of their plans as implemented in the classroom. But planning is about design. In other words, the instructional design, *as a design,* works. For example, a unit plan is a successful design if it is coherent and concepts are developed through a sequence of varied learning activities that progress from simple to complex. It's possible to envision, from reading the plans, how a teacher intends to engage students in the content. Furthermore, a teacher's intentions for a unit or a lesson are reflected not only in the written plans but also in the actual activities and assignments (worksheets, activity directions, and so on) the teacher gives to students for completion either during class or for homework. The level of cognitive challenge of such assignments is an important indication of the type of intellectual engagement the teacher intends for the students. The plans and the student assignments may be included in a teacher's professional portfolio; the plan's effects must be observed through action in the classroom.

DOMAIN 2: THE CLASSROOM ENVIRONMENT

The aspects of an environment conducive to learning are captured in Domain 2 (see Figure 3.2). These aspects of teaching are not associated with the learning of any particular content; instead, they set the stage for all learning. The components of Domain 2 establish a comfortable and respectful classroom environment that cultivates a culture for learning and creates a safe place for risk taking. The atmosphere is businesslike, with non-

---

FIGURE 3.2

Components of Domain 2: The Classroom Environment

Component 2a: Creating an Environment of Respect and Rapport

Component 2b: Establishing a Culture for Learning

Component 2c: Managing Classroom Procedures

Component 2d: Managing Student Behavior

Component 2e: Organizing Physical Space

---

instructional routines and procedures handled efficiently; student behavior is cooperative and nondisruptive; and the physical environment is supportive of the stated instructional purposes.

When students remember their teachers years later, it is often for the teacher's skill in Domain 2. Students recall the warmth and caring their favorite teachers demonstrated, their high expectations for achievement, and their commitment to students. Students feel safe with these teachers and know that they can count on the teachers to be fair and, when necessary, compassionate. Students also notice the subtle messages they receive from teachers as to their capabilities; they don't want their teachers to be "easy." Instead, they want their teachers to push them while conveying confidence that they know the students are up to the challenge. Students are also sensitive to teachers' own attitudes toward their subjects and their teaching; they are motivated by teachers who care about what they are doing, who love their subjects, and who put their heart into their teaching.

Teachers who excel in Domain 2 create an atmosphere of excitement about the importance of learning and the significance of the content. They care deeply about their subject and invite students to share the journey of learning about it. These teachers consider their students as real people, with interests, concerns, and intellectual potential. In return, the students regard their teachers as concerned and caring adults and are willing to make a commitment to the hard work of learning. They take pride in a job well done. Such teachers never forget their proper role as adults, so they don't try to be pals. They also know that their natural authority with students is grounded in their knowledge and expertise rather than in their role alone. These teachers are indisputably in charge, but their students regard them as a special sort of friend, a protector, a challenger, someone who will permit no harm. As such, these teachers are remembered for years with appreciation.

Skills in Domain 2 are demonstrated through classroom interaction and captured on paper through interviews with or surveys of students. These skills are observed in action, either in person or on videotape.

DOMAIN 3: INSTRUCTION

Domain 3 contains the components that are at the essential heart of teaching—the actual engagement of students in content (see Figure 3.3). It is impossible to overstate the importance of Domain 3, which reflects the primary mission of schools: to enhance student learning. The components in Domain 3 are unified through the vision of students developing

---

FIGURE 3.3

Components of Domain 3: Instruction

Component 3a: Communicating with Students

Component 3b: Using Questioning and Discussion Techniques

Component 3c: Engaging Students in Learning

Component 3d: Using Assessment in Instruction

Component 3e: Demonstrating Flexibility and Responsiveness

---

complex understanding and participating in a community of learners. Domain 3 components represent distinct aspects of instructional skill.

Domain 3 represents the implementation of the plans designed in Domain 1. As a result of success in executing the components of Domain 1, teachers prepare plans appropriate to their students, grounded in deep understanding of the content, aligned with state standards, and designed to engage students in important work. As a result of success in Domain 3, teachers demonstrate, through their instructional skills, that they can successfully implement those plans. Their students are engaged in meaningful work, which carries significance beyond the next test and which can provide skills and knowledge necessary for answering important questions or contributing to important projects. Such teachers don't have to motivate their students, because the ways in which teachers organize and present the content, the roles they encourage students to assume, and the student initiative they expect serve to motivate students to excel. The work is real and significant, and it is important to students as well as to teachers.

Teachers who excel in the components of Domain 3 have finely honed instructional skills. Their work in the classroom is fluid and flexible; they can shift easily from one approach to another when the situation demands it. They seamlessly incorporate ideas and concepts from other parts of the curriculum into their explanations, relating, for example, what the students have just learned about World War I to patterns about conflicts they have previously learned in their studies about other wars. Their questions probe student thinking and serve to extend understanding. They are attentive to different students in the class and the degree to which the students are thoughtfully engaged; when they observe inattention, they move to correct it. And above all, they carefully monitor student understanding as they go (through well-designed questions or activities) and make minor midcourse corrections as needed.

Skills in Domain 3 are demonstrated through classroom interaction, observed either in person or on videotape. In addition, samples of student work can reveal the degree of cognitive challenge expected from students and the extent of their engagement in learning.

DOMAIN 4: PROFESSIONAL RESPONSIBILITIES

The components in Domain 4 are associated with being a true professional educator; they encompass the roles assumed outside of and in addition to those in the classroom with students (see Figure 3.4). Students rarely observe these activities; parents and the larger community observe them only intermittently. But the activities are critical to preserving and enhancing the profession. Educators exercise some of them (such as maintaining records and communicating with families) immediately upon entering the profession, because they are integral to their work with students. Others (such as participating in a professional community) they develop primarily after their first few years of teaching, after they have mastered, to some degree, the details of classroom management and instruction.

One of the contributions of the framework for teaching is its inclusion of the components of Domain 4; previous enumerations of the work of teaching did not identify this important area. But the work of professional educators manifestly extends beyond their work in the classroom; in fact, it is through the skills of Domain 4 that highly professional teachers distinguish

---

FIGURE 3.4

Components of Domain 4: Professional Responsibilities

Component 4a: Reflecting on Teaching

Component 4b: Maintaining Accurate Records

Component 4c: Communicating with Families

Component 4d: Participating in a Professional Community

Component 4e: Growing and Developing Professionally

Component 4f: Showing Professionalism

---

themselves from their less proficient colleagues. And when teachers present evidence of their work in this area—through logs, summaries of their work on school and district committees, or descriptions of workshops for parents—they are frequently surprised (and impressed) by the extent of their professional engagement.

Domain 4 consists of a wide range of professional responsibilities, from self-reflection and professional growth, to participation in a professional community, to contributions made to the profession as a whole. The components also include interactions with the families of students, contacts with the larger community, the maintenance of records and other paperwork, and advocacy for students. Domain 4 captures the essence of professionalism by teachers; teachers are, as a result of their skills in Domain 4, full members of the teaching profession and committed to its enhancement.

Teachers who excel in Domain 4 are highly regarded by colleagues and parents. They can be depended on to serve students' interests and those of the larger community, and they are active in their professional organizations, in the school, and in the district. They are known as educators who go beyond the technical requirements of their jobs and contribute to the general well-being of the institutions of which they are a part.

Skills in Domain 4 are demonstrated through teacher interactions with colleagues, families, other professionals, and the larger community. Some of these interactions may be documented in logs and placed in a portfolio. It is the interactions themselves, however, that must be observed to indicate a teacher's skill and commitment.

THE INTERRELATEDNESS OF THE DOMAINS AND COMPONENTS

The four domains of the framework for teaching, and the components they contain, are described separately from one another. This is not to suggest, however, that teachers *do* each of them independently or in isolation. That is clearly not the case. Teaching is a holistic endeavor; all the different aspects of teaching are entangled in multiple ways. This interaction of the components of teaching may be illustrated by selecting any component for further examination. For example, selecting Component 3b, Using Questioning and Discussion Techniques, we could ask, "If a teacher is truly skilled at questioning and discussion, which other components of the framework would that teacher, of necessity, demonstrate at a high level?" Certainly, the teacher would have to thoroughly know the content (1a) in order to formulate important questions or to recognize

whether a student's question was worthy of further discussion. The teacher would have to know her students (1b) to formulate questions suitable to a particular group of students or for an individual. The teacher would have to have established clear instructional outcomes (1c) to ensure that the discussion, even if students take significant initiative, is moving in a direction consistent with the teacher's purpose. As for the components in Domain 2, there must be an environment of respect and rapport (2a) so students feel comfortable speaking in class, knowing that they will not be ridiculed. The teacher will have established routines (2c) about class discussions (do students raise their hands when they want to speak, or not?). And the teacher may have encouraged students to move their desks or chairs so they can see one another during the discussion (2e.) These interconnections among the different components of teaching may be illustrated by examining any component in depth.

This then leads to the question of the purpose of identifying the domains and components separately. If teaching is holistic, what is to be learned by listing them and describing them one at a time? A theater-in-the-round provides a useful analogy. If the teaching is considered the play, in a theater-in-the-round, the audience is sitting all around the action. And because the audience is sitting all around, the spotlights must come from every direction. The domains and components of the framework can be considered as the lights. To better understand the teaching, one may choose to "focus" on the quality of the interactions, or the routines and procedures, or the degree of student participation in discussion. That is, the components of the framework for teaching become a diagnostic tool to understand how a teacher's performance can be strengthened, while acknowledging that every aspect of teaching is connected to many others.

The framework for teaching divides the complex work of teaching into four major domains: Planning and Preparation, The Classroom Environment, Instruction, and Professional Responsibilities; each is further divided into five or six smaller components.

COMMON THEMES

Some educators, when they first study the framework for teaching, are concerned that it seems to exclude some important aspects of practice; they might ask, for example, "Where are concerns for individual differences, or cultural awareness? What about technology, or high expectations?" Those concepts are, indeed, essential to good teaching; abundant research supports their inclusion in any comprehensive description of good practice. However, these items do not reflect the *work* of teaching; they are not what teachers *do*. Instead, they are reflected in the *manner in which teachers do what they do*. For example, a successful teacher's instructional outcomes and feedback to students, as well as the teacher's interaction with families of students, all reflect high expectations and attention to the needs of individual students. The same considerations apply to the other common themes; they permeate all the different components and elements of the framework for teaching and serve to define performance at a high level. These themes are described in the following sections.

Equity

Implicit in the entire framework, particularly those domains relating to interaction with students (Domains 2 and 3), is a commitment to equity. In an environment of respect and rapport, *all* students feel valued. When students are engaged in a discussion of a concept, *all* students are invited and encouraged to participate. When feedback is provided to students on their learning, it is provided to *all* students.

This equity imperative is particularly meaningful in the context of an educational tradition of elitism. Schools in the United States have traditionally served many students well. Students have been offered academic courses of high quality and have graduated to pursue opportunities in higher education. But our public schools have not served all students equally well. Those who have been underserved are primarily students of color or students living in poverty, especially in urban areas; and females, particularly in science and mathematics. And even when the inequities have not been institutionalized, as they were in segregated schools before 1954, they have been nearly as insidious.

A commitment to excellence is not complete without a commitment to equity. Such a commitment provides (1) equal opportunities for stimulating academic achievement, with the open doors to higher education and careers that result from success in that arena, and (2) additional levels of support for those traditionally underserved, to enable them to overcome individual and community-wide doubts about their capability to succeed with distinction. In a school committed to equity, one would never hear a science teacher or a physical education teacher in the faculty lounge say, "She did pretty well, *for a girl.*" Nor would teachers, even implicitly, accept lower performance from some students because of their perceived ability or their background. This practice constitutes a particularly insidious form of bigotry.

Cultural Competence

Students may arrive at school with traditions that are different from or in conflict with those of many U.S. classrooms. Children in some cultures, for instance, are taught not to look adults in the eye because it is a sign of disrespect; yet many U.S. teachers interpret a child's looking away as insolence. Similarly, the way questions are used in many classes is unfamiliar to some students. For example, when teachers use questions that they know the answer to as a way of checking whether students have done the assigned reading, these students are baffled: "Why would a teacher ask a question to which he already knows the answer? Clearly, this is not a real question; but if it is not a question, what is it?" Such thoughts interfere with a student's ability to participate fully, and the teacher may well conclude that the student is a slow learner. Other such examples abound in the research literature (Villegas, 1991).

Teachers who are sensitive to the cultures of their students pay particular attention to Component 1b (Demonstrating Knowledge of Students). In learning about students' backgrounds, these teachers ensure that they are aware of relevant information about cultural traditions, religious practices, and patterns of interaction that may affect a student's classroom participation. In addition, the teachers ensure that the materials they use (Components 1e and 3c) and the examples they

employ (Components 3a and 3c) do not refer to items or traditions unfamiliar to students, or that they explain such materials and examples fully. And they take particular care that in their communication with families (Component 4c), they demonstrate cultural respect.

Cultural competence extends far beyond an awareness of the traditions, dress, and foods of a particular culture. Although "Mexican Day," for example, can provide an opportunity for students to demonstrate their skill in dance, to wear traditional dress, and to share traditional foods, real cultural competence goes much further. By the time they enter school, children will have absorbed from their communities a sense of the world and their place in it. Schools have an obligation to help students recognize that in a democracy, no one, and no cultural group, is marginalized (Irvine, 1990).

High Expectations

For years, research has confirmed the importance of high expectations in promoting high levels of student achievement, particularly for those students traditionally underserved by schools. Accomplished professionals believe that all students are capable of extremely high standards of learning, and they organize their teaching accordingly. They are also aware of the dynamics of expectations and the connections between expectations and reality. When teachers believe that some students are particularly capable or slow in learning, such expectations tend to become self-fulfilling prophecies.

High expectations are reflected in many components of the framework for teaching. For example, teachers set their instructional outcomes (Component 1c) at a high and challenging level. The rigorous culture for learning (Component 2b) explicitly includes, as one element, high expectations. The questions posed during a lesson (Component 3b) are at a high cognitive level. The feedback students receive (Component 3d) during class or as comments on their papers reflects the teacher's confidence that they are capable of high-level work. And the teacher's communication with families about their children's work (Component 4c) sends the same message of high-level learning.

High expectations are necessarily grounded in clear and open standards for achievement. The characteristics of a good persuasive essay, for example, are rigorous, known to all students, and apply to all. And, echoing the commitment to equity, teachers are committed to helping all students reach the standard. Based on their unique characteristics, some students may require additional time or support to reach a standard. They may have a learning disability, or they may learn very slowly. In these cases, high expectations will be based on the students' own unique history and will reflect significant achievement for *them*. But regardless of the absolute level of mastery, every student is challenged by high expectations for learning.

Embedded in the concept of high expectations for students is a culture of hard work and perseverance. Skilled teachers do not accept sloppy work from students or work that does not represent sincere effort; such practices convey the message that just submitting an assignment is good enough, regardless of its quality. The culture of hard work is a direct consequence of the teacher's presentation of the task at hand as important and representing important learning. But significant learning requires concentration and intellectual "elbow grease." When

teachers permit students to "blow it off," they communicate that such a level of achievement is the best they can expect from those individuals.

Developmental Appropriateness

How students engage with academic content is shaped in part by their level of intellectual development. Teachers observe important patterns of development despite students' many individual differences. These patterns are especially important in certain academic areas—science and mathematics at all levels, and literature and the social sciences at the high school level. For example, until students can conserve number, which is usually achieved by the time they are 6 or 7, they cannot fully understand addition facts. (They might be able to memorize the correct answers, but until their concept of number is stable, they cannot truly *understand* the concept.) Similarly, until students understand the concept of separating and controlling variables, usually by age 11, they cannot design a scientific experiment independently. And until students can achieve formal thought (at about age 14), they will have trouble understanding the role of chance in history or engaging in serious literary criticism.

Developmental considerations are central to a constructivist view of learning, as described in Chapter 2. How students understand a concept is influenced by their cognitive structures at the time they are introduced to it. The research literature is filled with examples of student misconceptions of certain ideas, sometimes with amusing consequences. For example, even many university graduates believe that the reason it is warmer in the summer than in the winter is that the earth is closer to the sun in the summer. This belief conforms to their naive understanding of heat transmission, but it is false; the earth is actually closer to the sun in the winter. In spite of having been taught in their science classes that the explanation for the seasons lies in the *tilt* of the earth rather than in its proximity to the sun, many people—even into adulthood—persist in holding this erroneous belief.

Attention to developmental appropriateness relates to many components of the framework for teaching, particularly (though not exclusively) those in Domain 1 (Planning and Preparation). Teachers who are sensitive to developmental patterns choose their instructional outcomes (Component 1c), activities and materials (Components 1e and 3c), and assessment strategies (Component 1f) carefully. But attention to child development also influences the other domains. Teachers demonstrate respect in developmentally appropriate ways (Component 2a). They ask developmentally appropriate questions (Component 3b) and provide feedback (Component 3d) in ways that stretch but do not intellectually overwhelm students.

Attention to Individual Students, Including Those with Special Needs

Every classroom is composed of individual learners; therefore, the challenge of teaching includes not only organizing the group but also attending to the particular characteristics of individuals. This is not a trivial matter; organizing for the productive learning of a large number of students, each with unique characteristics, is a daunting prospect. It is made all the more challenging by external insistence on ensuring that all students attain certain standards of performance.

But, fundamentally, learning is done by individuals, not by groups. So although it is essential for a teacher to know that some students in the class learn quickly, or that another group of individuals does not understand a particular concept, the knowledge of group needs is only a compilation of the knowledge of individual characteristics. Therefore, in planning learning experiences for students, skilled teachers design activities that are challenging on a number of different levels simultaneously and thus are appropriate for more students than would be possible with more narrowly focused activities.

Sensitivity to individual students must be extended to include appropriate accommodations for students with special needs. Some of these needs are intellectual; others are physical or emotional. And with greater inclusion of students with disabilities in regular classrooms, all teachers require at least some understanding of special needs.

Attention to individual students has implications throughout the framework for teaching. Naturally, the teacher's knowledge of students (Component 1b) includes knowledge of individuals. Attentive teachers' instructional plans and assessment strategies (Components 1e and 1f) are suitable to the needs of every student in the class. Interactions with students are appropriate to individuals (Component 2a), and feedback (Component 3d) is suitable for where each student is in his or her learning. Records are maintained to permit ongoing monitoring of progress (Component 4b.) And, of course, in communicating with families (Component 4c), attentive teachers are responsive to the situations of each student.

Furthermore, teachers who have students with physical limitations must also attend to the implications of how physical space is organized (Component 2e). Students with visual or hearing impairments must be situated in a classroom so they can see and hear to the maximum extent possible. Students with emotional needs impose particular responsibilities on teachers as they respond to student behavior (Component 2d), as well as to other aspects of student interaction in Domain 2 (The Classroom Environment).

Appropriate Use of Technology

Calculators, computers, CD-ROMs, video players, overhead projectors, cameras, and other tools of technology are, to varying degrees, available in U.S. schools and classrooms, and to a large extent students have access to electronic technology at home. Using these tools to enhance learning is an important responsibility of today's teachers. Such tools can be used in classrooms with students (Components 3a and 3c), to help with records management (Component 4b), or to communicate with families (Component 4c). Moreover, teachers can use the Internet in their planning (Domain 1) and in pursuing opportunities for professional learning (Component 4e). The use of e-mail has greatly enhanced the reach of many teachers, in their participation in a professional community (Component 4d) and in their ongoing communication with families (Component 4c). And most school districts and many schools maintain Web sites that describe the school's program; in some cases, teachers use this resource to post homework assignments, and they use e-mail to communicate with students after the school day.

Educators need to remember that technological tools are just that—tools. They should never be considered ends in themselves, and they should not be misused. For example, if

students learn to perform operations by using a calculator exclusively, they may not know how to do the problem without it. That is, if students don't understand the *concept* of multiplication or how multiplying by 10 affects a product, then using a calculator to get the right answers leaves them vulnerable. They may discover that their computational skill is dependent on access to a calculator. Similarly, it is essential for students to know their multiplication facts so they can recall them quickly and easily. But once students have acquired the necessary concepts, the calculator can save them a great deal of time.

Teachers and schools must also be aware that the private resources available to students in the area of technology are extremely uneven. Many families now have computers at home, complete with games and all the latest enhancements. Many others do not. Thus children's familiarity with technology is diverse and is reflected in how they can use technological tools in their academic work. Part of a school's responsibility is to provide access to technology for all students.

For many teachers, the use of electronic technology represents a foray into unfamiliar territory; they did not grow up with such tools, and some resist acquiring the necessary skill. Being new to these tools is frightening; one is forever concerned about making an error, or breaking the equipment, or losing important documents. These hesitations are overcome through experience, by increasing familiarity with the machines and what they will do. Of course, learning about technology is, for teachers, a task that is never finished. Just when one has mastered a new tool, another becomes available. Staying abreast of developments in technology is an important component of professional development for many teachers.

Student Assumption of Responsibility

It is important to remember that small children direct their own learning—and do so with great energy and commitment. Babies *want* to learn to walk, although for many of them, at least at first, it is a slower way to get around than crawling. Children are naturally curious about their environment and actively seek to understand it. It would be a rare 5-year-old who displayed intellectual laziness; however, by the time students are 12, many of them have become lethargic about their schoolwork.

An important aspect of the framework, and one that is manifest in many of the components, is student assumption of responsibility—for the work students undertake, for the physical arrangement of the class, and for their participation in a purposeful learning community. This is not to suggest that the teacher is not in charge, but part of being in charge is to enlist student energy in ensuring the success of the class.

A class in which a teacher is clearly setting the agenda, however, can still become a community of learners. For example, as students learn more about the Civil War, they will—and should be encouraged to—formulate questions that the teacher may not have considered. Depending on the teacher's instructional purposes, such questions may be suitable for investigation. And once students have gained some insight, even on questions the teacher has posed, they are in a position to share those insights with other students, entering into a dialogue about the subject with their peers and resource people, which the teacher monitors and facilitates but does not always direct.

The framework for teaching is clear about a teacher's role in creating an environment for productive learning. Setting the broad agenda is part of a teacher's responsibility. The environment, however, can consist of a learning community. In such a community, the lines between teachers and learners become somewhat blurred; individuals move back and forth across that line in the course of their work, without relinquishing responsibility. Teachers are not afraid to acknowledge when they do not know a particular fact, and they recognize and specifically use student contributions to the production of knowledge.

It is a hallmark of a community of learners that every individual is highly engaged and is invested in the endeavor. It is the hallmark of an accomplished professional that the classroom has made the shift from a learning environment completely managed by the teacher to one in which students themselves assume some responsibility. It is manifested in many aspects of the teacher's practice. For example, the teacher's instructional outcomes (Component 1c) may reflect suggestions from students, and students may have suggested the evaluative criteria to be used to assess student work (Component 1f). In the classroom, students themselves will ensure standards of civility (Component 2a); they will take initiative in implementing, or even improving, the routines and procedures (Component 2c); they will ensure compliance with the standards of conduct (Component 2d); and they may make suggestions for how the room arrangement could better support their learning (Component 2e). Similarly, in Domain 3, students will formulate questions and ensure that all students participate in class discussions (Component 3b), and they will actively use formative assessment results in their learning (Component 3d).

Inexperienced teachers tend to be fearful of allowing students to share responsibility for the class. Indeed, it can be a frightening prospect; some teachers have had the experience of students behaving irresponsibly when given too much latitude. Or they may have found that some students, when given a choice in the matter, will choose to not work at all. Creating an environment in which students take responsibility not only for their own learning but also for that of their classmates might, in some situations, represent a considerable departure from past practice. However, with experience, many teachers find that students respond to such efforts with enthusiasm and reward their teachers with a renewed commitment to learning.

Seven common themes pervade the framework for teaching: (1) equity, (2) cultural competence and sensitivity, (3) high expectations, (4) developmental appropriateness, (5) attention to individual students, including those with special needs, (6) appropriate use of technology, and (7) student assumption of responsibility.

LEVELS OF PERFORMANCE

As teachers remain in the profession, gaining experience and developing expertise, their performance becomes more polished. As has been noted, teaching is highly complex work; teachers juggle multiple demands simultaneously. When they are new to the profession, it is not unusual for teachers to be overwhelmed by the various aspects of the task and for even their best-laid plans to go awry.

Increasingly, it has been possible to study the development of expertise in many professions—chess players, air traffic controllers, athletes, and emergency room doctors. Since the mid-1980s, researchers have observed common patterns in the development of expertise in these diverse fields. The common

principles apply to pedagogy as well. Drawing on these other fields, it is now possible to describe, with some certainty, what it is that improves with experience and how expertise in teaching is acquired. It should be noted that *expertise* is not the same thing as *experience;* that is, not all experienced teachers are experts. However, experience is necessary for the acquisition of expertise. But although it is necessary, it is not sufficient; the development of expertise requires conscious effort by teachers.

So what does expertise in teaching consist of? How is it manifested? How can it be acquired by novices? Expertise in teaching appears to consist of at least two distinct, though related, characteristics (Berliner, 2001, 2004). First, experts develop *automaticity* in their work. That is, routines are established and patterns are set so they no longer require constant attention. Experienced teachers set their routines early in the school year, but even then, they know what to expect in a certain situation and how to respond. Because much of their practice has become automatic and they no longer have to think consciously about the details, expert teachers are able to devote more of their conscious attention to other matters than is possible for novices. Therefore, when it appears that experts can do more than one thing at a time, it is because they, in fact, can; this is a result of automaticity. As a consequence of automaticity, an expert teacher's classroom appears to be running itself, and the teacher's actions demonstrate flexibility and fluidity.

Second, when expert teachers look around their classrooms, they *see* more than do novices. This has been demonstrated by showing novice and expert teachers short video clips of classrooms. When asked to report on what they see, the novices tend to describe actions literally: a student entered the room; the student in the blue shirt asked a question. Experts, on the other hand, interpret what the see: the student who entered appeared to be returning from a special class; the student's question revealed a lack of understanding. Related to their more insightful observations, expert teachers (like experts in all fields) are also adept at noticing exceptions to the general rule. They know what typical patterns are and can quickly notice discrepancies.

The higher levels of performance in the framework for teaching represent both greater experience and increased expertise. As teachers' performance moves to higher levels, they are more effective in their work and incorporate many of the features of expert performance. And if experience in other professions can guide educators, teachers should expect to need at least five years to exhibit proficient performance in all areas, and longer to develop the skills described at the highest level.

In the framework for teaching, levels of performance are provided for the 4 domains and for each of the elements that make up the 22 components of the domains. The levels of performance are Unsatisfactory, Basic, Proficient, and Distinguished. The levels range from describing teachers who are still striving to master the rudiments of teaching (Unsatisfactory) to highly accomplished professionals who are able to share their expertise (Distinguished). It is important to recognize that the levels are levels of performance of *teaching,* not of *teachers.* This distinction is significant and reflects the fact that performance is highly variable; whereas at a general level there are patterns and consistencies, any individual lesson may be highly successful or it may fall apart.

The levels of performance are especially useful when the components are used to support mentoring, coaching, or professional growth. The levels can inform a professional discussion and suggest areas for further learning. Although the levels are also useful for supervision and teacher evaluation, it is important that they be used to structure professional conversations and not in a "gotcha" manner.

Unsatisfactory

The teacher performing at the Unsatisfactory level does not yet appear to understand the concepts underlying the component. Working on the fundamental practices associated with the elements will enable the teacher to grow and develop in this area. In some areas of practice, performance at the Unsatisfactory level represents teaching that is below the licensing standard of "do no harm." For example, students are treated with sarcasm or put-downs (Component 2a), the environment is chaotic (Component 2c), or learning is shut down (Component 3c.) Therefore, if a supervisor encounters performance at the Unsatisfactory level, it is very likely time to intervene. For a mentor, a component at the Unsatisfactory level represents a first priority for coaching.

Basic

The teacher performing at the Basic level appears to understand the concepts underlying the component and attempts to implement its elements. But implementation is sporadic, intermittent, or otherwise not entirely successful. Additional reading, discussion, visiting classrooms of other teachers, and experience (particularly supported by a mentor) will enable the teacher to become proficient in this area.

Performance at the Basic level is characteristic of student teachers or teachers new to the profession—those for whom virtually everything they do, almost by definition, is being done for the first time. So it is not surprising that not everything goes according to plan. Even when experienced teachers try a new activity, its implementation may be rough or inconsistent (for example, it may take longer than planned or not as long, or the directions for the activity may not be clear). In fact, when trying a new activity or when teaching in a new assignment, experienced teachers may perform at the Basic level for the same reason a new teacher might—they are doing something for the first time.

For supervision or evaluation purposes, this level is generally considered minimally competent for teachers early in their careers; improvement is likely to occur with experience, and no actual harm is being done to students. But enhancement of skill is important, and a mentoring or coaching program will ensure that such improvement occurs in a supportive environment.

Proficient

The teacher performing at the Proficient level clearly understands the concepts underlying the component and implements it well. Most experienced, capable teachers will regard themselves and be regarded by others as performing at this level.

Teachers at the Proficient level are experienced, professional educators. They thoroughly know their content, they know their students, they know the curriculum and have a broad repertoire of strategies and activities to use with students, and they can move easily to Plan B if that turns out to

be necessary. And they have eyes in the backs of their heads! Many of the routines of teaching have become automatic, and proficient teachers have developed a sophisticated understanding of classroom dynamics and are alert to events that don't conform to the expected pattern.

Teachers performing at the Proficient level have mastered the work of teaching while working to improve their practice. They can also serve as resources to one another as they participate in a professional community.

Distinguished

Teachers performing at the Distinguished level are master teachers and make a contribution to the field, both in and outside their school. Their classrooms operate at a qualitatively different level from those of other teachers. Such classrooms consist of a community of learners, with students highly motivated and engaged and assuming considerable responsibility for their own learning. All the common themes are manifested, as appropriate, in the classroom of a teacher performing at a Distinguished level.

A classroom functioning at the Distinguished level seems to be running itself; it almost appears that the teacher is not doing anything. It is seamless; the students know what to do and get right to work. When novice teachers observe a class at this level, they typically don't recognize what they are seeing; they can observe the results of what the teacher has created but aren't always aware of how the teacher did it.

Distinguished-level performance is very high performance, and, indeed, some teachers (particularly with some groups of students) may never attain it consistently. As some educators have phrased it, "Distinguished-level performance is a good place to visit, but don't expect to live there." The student component is important, because with some groups of students it is a daunting challenge to create a community of learners. It may take all year to make much progress at all. But the Distinguished level remains a goal for all teachers, regardless of how challenging it may be in any particular set of circumstances.

As a summary of the levels of performance, a swimming metaphor is helpful. The teacher at the Unsatisfactory level could be compared to a nonswimmer who has been thrown in deep water and is drowning. The swimmer who can manage the dog paddle, but nothing else, is similar to the teacher per-

forming at the Basic level; the swimmer can get across the lake but may be swamped if any waves come up. A swimmer with command of a number of different strokes, and the knowledge of when to use which, is similar to a teacher performing at the Proficient level. And a competitive swimmer who is perfecting her strokes, or a swimming teacher, would be the equivalent of the teacher performing at the Distinguished level.

Figure 3.5 summarizes the levels of performance for the four domains.

➤ *The framework for teaching includes four levels of performance—Unsatisfactory, Basic, Proficient, and Distinguished—that serve to more fully describe the components and elements of each domain. They are useful primarily for structuring professional conversation.*

FIGURE 3.5

Domain Levels of Performance

	Unsatisfactory	**Basic**	**Proficient**	**Distinguished**
Domain 1 Planning and Preparation	Teacher's plans reflect little understanding of the content, the students, and available resources. Instructional outcomes are either lacking or inappropriate; assessment methodologies are inadequate.	Teacher's plans reflect moderate understanding of the content, the students, and available resources. Some instructional outcomes are suitable to the students as a group, and the approaches to assessment are partially aligned to the goals.	Teacher's plans reflect solid understanding of the content, the students, and available resources. Instructional outcomes represent important learning suitable to most students. Most elements of the instructional design, including the assessments, are aligned to the goals.	Teacher's plans, based on extensive content knowledge and understanding of students, are designed to engage students in significant learning. All aspects of the teacher's plans—instructional outcomes, learning activities, materials, resources, and assessments—are in complete alignment and are adapted as needed for individual students.

(figure continues)

FIGURE 3.5

Domain Levels of Performance *(continued)*

	Unsatisfactory	Basic	Proficient	Distinguished
Domain 2 The Classroom Environment	Classroom environment is characterized by chaos and conflict, with low expectations for learning, no clear standards of student conduct, poor use of physical space, and negative interactions between individuals.	Classroom environment functions somewhat effectively, with modest expectations for student learning and conduct, and classroom routines and use of space that partially support student learning. Students and the teacher rarely treat one another with disrespect.	Classroom environment functions smoothly, with little or no loss of instructional time. Expectations for student learning are high, and interactions among individuals are respectful. Standards for student conduct are clear, and the physical environment supports learning.	Students themselves make a substantive contribution to the smooth functioning of the classroom, with highly positive personal interactions, high expectations and student pride in work, seamless routines, clear standards of conduct, and a physical environment conducive to high-level learning.
Domain 3 Instruction	Instruction is characterized by poor communication, low-level questions, little student engagement or participation in discussion, little or no use of assessment in learning, and rigid adherence to an instructional plan despite evidence that it should be revised or modified.	Only some students are engaged in learning because of only partially clear communication, uneven use of discussion strategies, and only some suitable instructional activities and materials. The teacher displays some use of assessment in instruction and is moderately flexible in adjusting the instructional plan and in response to students' interests and their success in learning.	All students are engaged in learning as a result of clear communication and successful use of questioning and discussion techniques. Activities and assignments are of high quality, and teacher and students make productive use of assessment. The teacher demonstrates flexibility in contributing to the success of the lesson and of each student.	All students are highly engaged in learning and make material contributions to the success of the class through their participation in discussions, active involvement in learning activities, and use of assessment information in their learning. The teacher persists in the search for approaches to meet the needs of every student.
Domain 4 Professional Responsibilities	The teacher demonstrates low ethical standards and levels of professionalism, with poor record-keeping systems and skills in reflection, little or no communication with families or colleagues, and avoidance of school and district responsibilities and participation in activities for professional growth.	The teacher demonstrates moderate ethical standards and levels of professionalism, with rudimentary record-keeping systems and skills in reflection, modest communication with families or colleagues, and compliance with expectations regarding participation in school and district projects and activities for professional growth.	The teacher demonstrates high ethical standards and a genuine sense of professionalism by engaging in accurate reflection on instruction, maintaining accurate records, communicating frequently with families, actively participating in school and district events, and engaging in activities for professional development.	The teacher's ethical standards and sense of professionalism are highly developed, showing perceptive use of reflection, effective systems for record keeping and communication with families, leadership roles in both school and district projects, and extensive professional development activities. Where appropriate, students contribute to the systems for record keeping and family communication.

4

THE FRAMEWORK FOR
PROFESSIONAL PRACTICE

This chapter describes the 22 components of professional practice within the framework of the 4 domains. Each description has three parts: Rationale and Explanation, Demonstration, and a figure showing the elements of the component and how the four levels of performance (Unsatisfactory, Basic, Proficient, and Distinguished) apply to each element.

DOMAIN 1: PLANNING AND PREPARATION

Domain 1 describes the critical, behind-the-scenes work of organizing for classroom instruction. Even in schools or districts with an established curriculum, teachers put considerable effort into transforming that curriculum so it is accessible to their students. That effort includes having a deep knowledge of the content itself and designing instruction that is appropriate to the diverse learners in one's charge.

COMPONENT 1A: DEMONSTRATING KNOWLEDGE OF CONTENT AND PEDAGOGY

Rationale and Explanation

"A person cannot teach what he or she does not know." This statement captures the essence of why content knowledge is important in teaching. Regardless of teachers' instructional techniques, they must have sufficient command of a subject to guide student learning. This requirement is independent of teachers' approaches to teaching; regardless of whether teachers have structured their lessons as a presentation or as guided by student inquiry, they must understand the content to be learned, the structure of the discipline of which that content is a part, and the methods of inquiry specific to that discipline. Teachers must be aware of the connections among different divisions of the discipline (for example, between scientific concepts and inquiry) and among the different disciplines themselves (for example, between the history and the literature of a particular period).

The term *content* includes, of course, far more than factual information. It encompasses all aspects of a subject: concepts, principles, relationships, methods of inquiry, and outstanding issues. Teachers who understand their subjects know which questions sit on the fringes of what is known and which are likely to interest students, yield greater understanding, or represent conceptual dead ends. Furthermore, the *content* of a discipline includes, in addition to its facts and concepts, skills in analyzing the facts and concepts, comparing them to one another, or identifying connections with other aspects of the discipline or with other disciplines.

Students look to teachers as their source of information about a subject. Although teachers may sometimes withhold information to encourage student inquiry, what they do convey should be accurate. For example, teachers of world languages should be able to speak those languages with an appropriate accent. Teachers of physical education should be able to demonstrate or explain the skills they are teaching. Content must also be presented so that it respects the nuances of a discipline. When engaging students in a discussion, teachers should demonstrate that they understand the complexities and patterns of the content to be learned and must be able to challenge students to recognize the relationships between what they know and important questions yet to be explored.

Knowledgeable teachers know which concepts are central to a discipline and which are peripheral. For example, the concepts of pattern are crucial to understanding mathematics; those of revolution and counterrevolution are central to understanding history. Furthermore, frequently it is not sufficient to understand the central concepts in a discipline; one must also understand how those concepts interact with one another. For example, in mathematics, how are area and perimeter related to one another? Can several shapes have the same perimeter but different areas? How many such shapes are there? And which shape yields the greatest area? How do you know? Or, in science, how are buoyancy and floating related to each other? Can a buoyant object sink? Can you demonstrate that?

In addition, some disciplines—mathematics, for example—contain important prerequisite relationships. For example, students must understand place value before they can understand addition and subtraction with regrouping. Other disciplines have similar internal constraints; students need to learn some concepts or skills before they can tackle others. Knowledgeable teachers know where these important relationships are in the subjects they teach.

Although necessary for good teaching, subject knowledge is not enough. Many adults can recall the teacher who was an expert in chemistry but could not share that knowledge or engage students in the subject. Teachers use pedagogical techniques particular to the different disciplines to help convey information and teach skills. General pedagogical skill is insufficient to ensure student learning; every discipline has its own approaches to instruction. Techniques used in writing, for example, are different from those used in science.

A teacher's knowledge of content and pedagogy is also reflected in an awareness of common student misconceptions or likely sources of error—and how these should be handled. Elementary students, for example, sometimes have difficulty with regrouping, partly because of a weak understanding of the underlying concept of place value. A knowledgeable teacher recognizes that many students make mistakes in regrouping, and the teacher knows how to anticipate or correct the situation. Or students may hold a naive and incorrect understanding of a concept in science, such as how light is transmitted. Teachers who are knowledgeable about subject-based pedagogy anticipate such misconceptions and work to dispel them.

Knowledge of content and pedagogy is not stagnant but evolves over time. Even when teachers specialize at the university level in the disciplines they later teach, their knowledge, unless renewed, can become dated and stale. Teachers must keep apprised of developments in the field and in the accepted best methods of engaging students with it. And if teachers'

responsibilities for instruction change, they have an even greater need to become thoroughly acquainted with their new field or subfield. For example, a teacher who has been teaching high school chemistry for many years may switch to biology. That change will require content and pedagogical preparation in addition to that required if the teacher continued to teach only chemistry.

Knowledge of content and pedagogy are appropriately different for teachers at different levels of schooling. Content specialists who teach only one subject (typically at the secondary level) may be held to a higher standard than generalists (mostly at the elementary level) who teach many. Moreover, the balance between content and pedagogical knowledge varies from one discipline to another. In some disciplines, such as reading, the content does not change, but the pedagogy is critical. In others, such as science, both the content and the pedagogy change over time. That is, in reading, the instructional goal is for students to be able to derive meaning from written text. Although this goal has remained stable over many years, the approaches used (such as phonics and whole language) have been the subject of much controversy. Alternatively, science teachers must alter not only their instructional strategies over time but also the topics taught as new knowledge evolves.

When entering the profession, teachers wrestle with "survival" issues and the challenges of daily preparation. Even when teaching in a field in which they are relatively expert, the task of transforming that content into meaningful learning experiences for students is daunting. As teachers become more experienced and enhance their expertise, they become increasingly flexible in how they weave aspects of the content together, and they can make connections with other disciplines.

Demonstration

Teachers provide evidence of their knowledge of content and pedagogy through their performance in the classroom. For example, evidence is found in their clear explanation of concepts, their knowledgeable responses to students' questions, and their skill in engaging students in learning, and by developing instructional plans and participating in professional growth activities.

Teachers can also demonstrate knowledge of the subjects they teach through instructional artifacts, comments on student work, and their classroom interactions with students. Content errors reflect a shaky understanding of the subject, and evasive responses to students may suggest only a thin knowledge of content. Although some responses are deliberately unrevealing, because the teacher wants to engage students in their own investigations, the teacher, in conversation, should be able to demonstrate a solid understanding of the subject. (See Figure 4.1.)

COMPONENT 1B: DEMONSTRATING KNOWLEDGE OF STUDENTS

Rationale and Explanation

Teachers do not teach their subjects in a vacuum; they teach them to students. To maximize learning, teachers must know not only their subject and its accompanying pedagogy, but also their students.

Each age group has certain developmental characteristics—intellectual, social, and emotional. For example, students in the early primary years are consolidating their understanding of the concept of number and the relationships between sounds and symbols; those in their late-elementary and middle school years are assembling an array of facts and concepts in different disciplines and learning skills related to friendship and peer relationships. The skill of separating and controlling variables in a scientific investigation or the concept of proportional reasoning is not available to most students until they are about 12. Teachers' knowledge of their students should include the students' stage of developmental understanding.

Another aspect of knowing one's students is understanding the general principles underlying learning, particularly those involved in developing conceptual understanding. What students can learn and understand is based on their prior knowledge and experiences; they build their understanding on what they already know. For example, their current understanding of fractions influences what else they can learn and understand about the topic. Their current skill in writing dictates their next steps in developing basic competency. Experienced teachers know that it is not sufficient to *present* information to students; they must *represent* it in such a manner that it relates to students' prior knowledge and engages them in developing their own understanding. The teacher's role in this complex undertaking is to structure the learning environment—the activities and tasks, the materials, and the student groupings—so that it reflects the essential constructivist nature of human learning. A teacher's blind adherence to a grade-level curriculum is unlikely to be effective if students lack the understanding or skill needed to master the content. Furthermore, as students grow older, they become more capable of monitoring and assuming responsibility for their own learning and behavior.

It is important for teachers to realize that some students may hold erroneous beliefs. Recent research has verified the

FIGURE 4.1

DOMAIN 1: PLANNING AND PREPARATION
Component 1a: Demonstrating Knowledge of Content and Pedagogy
Elements: Knowledge of content and the structure of the discipline • Knowledge of prerequisite relationships • Knowledge of content-related pedagogy

ELEMENT	LEVEL OF PERFORMANCE			
	UNSATISFACTORY	BASIC	PROFICIENT	DISTINGUISHED
Knowledge of content and the structure of the discipline	In planning and practice, teacher makes content errors or does not correct errors made by students.	Teacher is familiar with the important concepts in the discipline but may display lack of awareness of how these concepts relate to one another.	Teacher displays solid knowledge of the important concepts in the discipline and how these relate to one another.	Teacher displays extensive knowledge of the important concepts in the discipline and how these relate both to one another and to other disciplines.
Knowledge of prerequisite relationships	Teacher's plans and practice display little understanding of prerequisite relationships important to student learning of the content.	Teacher's plans and practice indicate some awareness of prerequisite relationships, although such knowledge may be inaccurate or incomplete.	Teacher's plans and practice reflect accurate understanding of prerequisite relationships among topics and concepts.	Teacher's plans and practices reflect understanding of prerequisite relationships among topics and concepts and a link to necessary cognitive structures by students to ensure understanding.
Knowledge of content-related pedagogy	Teacher displays little or no understanding of the range of pedagogical approaches suitable to student learning of the content.	Teacher's plans and practice reflect a limited range of pedagogical approaches or some approaches that are not suitable to the discipline or to the students.	Teacher's plans and practice reflect familiarity with a wide range of effective pedagogical approaches in the discipline.	Teacher's plans and practice reflect familiarity with a wide range of effective pedagogical approaches in the discipline, anticipating student misconceptions.

power and stability of students' misconceptions, particularly in mathematics and science. Teachers' knowledge of students includes knowing what these misunderstandings and misconceptions are; only then can they determine the appropriate next steps in learning for each student and for groups of students.

Furthermore, many schools include large numbers of students for whom English is not their native language. Awareness of the challenges these students confront is essential for the design of learning experiences.

Students vary enormously in their interests and talents. For example, many teachers know that a particular student is artistic, another is a whiz at numbers, and a third has highly creative ideas. A student may be highly knowledgeable in a certain area—for example, the nuances of basketball. The educational literature is filled with examples of teachers who have succeeded in engaging students in, for example, writing, when the students could use what they know, and are passionate about, to complete assignments. Skilled teachers help students build on these strengths and interests while developing all areas of competence.

Students' academic knowledge is not the only area that affects their learning. Students bring out-of-school knowledge of everyday events and activities, as well as misunderstandings and parents' opinions, to school with them. This knowledge influences school-based learning. For instance, students' understanding that a closed car becomes hot on a sunny but cold winter day, and that water sitting in a hose becomes hot in the summer, can assist a teacher in introducing students to the concept of passive solar energy. Students may participate in sports, scouting, music, or drama activities. Such out-of-school experiences provide rich material for teachers in designing learning experiences and developing analogies and metaphors for new content. But to make use of students' experiences, teachers must first be aware of them.

Students also come to school with social and cultural characteristics that influence how they interpret events, participate in learning activities, and absorb new information. For example, in some cultures, challenging an adult's authority is considered disrespectful. Children from these environments find it difficult to question a teacher's—or a textbook's—interpretation of, say, a historical event. Moreover, students from some ethnic or cultural backgrounds may have experienced a lack of respect or trust in the mainstream culture. These experiences influence how students view the world and their place in it. They may have concluded that the enterprise called "school" has winners and losers, and that because they have little chance—in their view—of being among the winners, they have stopped trying. Knowing that some students experience this type of alienation is important for teachers and can guide them in their interactions with students as they attempt to overcome the effects of such experiences.

Many classes contain students with special needs. Part of knowing students is knowing which ones require additional assistance in learning parts of the curriculum or which ones must demonstrate knowledge in unique ways. Teachers' knowledge of students should include information about such special cases, which can then be used in instructional planning. Furthermore, some students have serious medical conditions their teachers need to be aware of.

Experienced teachers know that it is not always easy to come to know one's students; many students display only a limited side of themselves in the classroom. When teachers are serious about wanting to know the interests and strengths of their students, they frequently must actively solicit the information through such techniques as interest inventories, speaking with other teachers, and paying attention to which students are active in extracurricular activities. Some teachers make extraordinary efforts to see their students display the full range of their interests and skills; they attend athletic events or school performances, make home visits, or attend events in the community.

A teacher's knowledge of students varies, of necessity, depending on the teaching assignment. A high school music or physical education teacher who interacts with 400 students a week confronts a different challenge than that of the kindergarten teacher with a class of 19 children. It is only reasonable that the extent of their knowledge of students is correspondingly different. However, even the teacher with 400 students interacts with each one as an individual and can engage in ongoing efforts to understand the various factors that shape their world.

Demonstration

Teachers demonstrate their knowledge of students in the classroom orally and in writing. They can describe their students and what those students bring with them to the classroom. Their knowledge of students is evident in the instructional plans they create and in their interaction with students in the classroom. But because a teacher's knowledge of students is typically far greater than that which is demonstrated in any single unit or lesson plan, it's desirable for teachers to have the opportunity to describe this understanding. (See Figure 4.2.)

FIGURE 4.2

DOMAIN 1: PLANNING AND PREPARATION
Component 1b: Demonstrating Knowledge of Students

Elements: Knowledge of child and adolescent development • Knowledge of the learning process • Knowledge of students' skills, knowledge, and language proficiency • Knowledge of students' interests and cultural heritage • Knowledge of students' special needs

ELEMENT	LEVEL OF PERFORMANCE			
	UNSATISFACTORY	BASIC	PROFICIENT	DISTINGUISHED
Knowledge of child and adolescent development	Teacher displays little or no knowledge of the developmental characteristics of the age group.	Teacher displays partial knowledge of the developmental characteristics of the age group.	Teacher displays accurate understanding of the typical developmental characteristics of the age group, as well as exceptions to the general patterns.	In addition to accurate knowledge of the typical developmental characteristics of the age group and exceptions to the general patterns, teacher displays knowledge of the extent to which individual students follow the general patterns.

(figure continues)

FIGURE 4.2

DOMAIN 1: PLANNING AND PREPARATION
Component 1b: Demonstrating Knowledge of Students (continued)

Elements: Knowledge of child and adolescent development • Knowledge of the learning process • Knowledge of students' skills, knowledge, and language proficiency • Knowledge of students' interests and cultural heritage • Knowledge of students' special needs

ELEMENT	LEVEL OF PERFORMANCE			
	UNSATISFACTORY	BASIC	PROFICIENT	DISTINGUISHED
Knowledge of the learning process	Teacher sees no value in understanding how students learn and does not seek such information.	Teacher recognizes the value of knowing how students learn, but this knowledge is limited or outdated.	Teacher's knowledge of how students learn is accurate and current. Teacher applies this knowledge to the class as a whole and to groups of students.	Teacher displays extensive and subtle understanding of how students learn and applies this knowledge to individual students.
Knowledge of students' skills, knowledge, and language proficiency	Teacher displays little or no knowledge of students' skills, knowledge, and language proficiency and does not indicate that such knowledge is valuable.	Teacher recognizes the value of understanding students' skills, knowledge, and language proficiency but displays this knowledge only for the class as a whole.	Teacher recognizes the value of understanding students' skills, knowledge, and language proficiency and displays this knowledge for groups of students.	Teacher displays understanding of individual students' skills, knowledge, and language proficiency and has a strategy for maintaining such information.
Knowledge of students' interests and cultural heritage	Teacher displays little or no knowledge of students' interests or cultural heritage and does not indicate that such knowledge is valuable.	Teacher recognizes the value of understanding students' interests and cultural heritage but displays this knowledge only for the class as a whole.	Teacher recognizes the value of understanding students' interests and cultural heritage and displays this knowledge for groups of students.	Teacher recognizes the value of understanding students' interests and cultural heritage and displays this knowledge for individual students.
Knowledge of students' special needs	Teacher displays little or no understanding of students' special learning or medical needs or why such knowledge is important.	Teacher displays awareness of the importance of knowing students' special learning or medical needs, but such knowledge may be incomplete or inaccurate.	Teacher is aware of students' special learning and medical needs.	Teacher possesses information about each student's learning and medical needs, collecting such information from a variety of sources.

COMPONENT 1C: SETTING INSTRUCTIONAL OUTCOMES

Rationale and Explanation

Teaching is a purposeful activity—it is goal directed and designed to achieve certain well-defined purposes. Even when operating within the confines of an established curriculum (and virtually all teachers are), teachers must determine the appropriate learning for a given class on a given day. It is through the articulation of instructional outcomes that the teacher describes these purposes; they should be clear and relate to what it is that the students are intended to learn as a consequence of instruction.

In general, it is a teacher's responsibility to establish instructional outcomes. In classrooms organized as a community of learners, however, teachers engage students in determining these outcomes, frequently in ways intended to extend their learning beyond the established curriculum. For example, after exploring the events leading up to the Civil War, students might wonder whether similar factors were at work in the run-up to the Revolutionary War and undertake an investigation. And as students assume greater responsibility for their own learning, they may increasingly select their own learning tasks in pursuit of established outcomes.

When teachers establish instructional outcomes, they must take into account a number of factors: a district's curriculum (generally grounded in state or discipline-based curriculum frameworks), the requirements of external mandates (for example, state testing or voluntary programs such as Advanced Placement examinations), and community expectations. But even if the established curriculum requires only recall of facts, teachers with a deep knowledge of the subject can extend that mandate to include higher-level learning. Instructional outcomes for a given instructional episode should "fit" within the sequence of learning about that topic or concept. That is, the learning should not reflect an isolated, random event.

Instructional outcomes must be worthwhile and represent learning central to a discipline as well as high-level learning for the students. Not all knowledge and skill in a discipline are worth learning; trivial facts, although they may be true, are of little lasting value. This is not to discount the value of some facts that students should have at their disposal; an important characteristic of educated people, after all, is that they know a lot. And the important ideas in a discipline are grounded in multiple instances of the idea. For example, general characteristics of revolutions can be understood only by examining a number of revolutions throughout history. Furthermore, it is not sufficient to say that we can always look up, for example, the answer to 5×6; students should simply know their multiplication facts. In selecting instructional outcomes, then, teachers should consider the importance of the outcomes they select for students both now and for what future learning the outcomes make possible. Instructional outcomes should represent important learning, high expectations for students, and intellectual rigor.

Above all, instructional outcomes must be clear and stated in terms of student learning rather than student activity: "What will students *learn* as a result of the instructional engagement?" not "What will students *do*?" For example, "Students will know the distinction between different trees on the school's property" is a statement of an outcome, whereas "Students will take a walking tour of the school grounds" states an activity.

To determine whether a statement is an outcome or an activity, it is helpful to consider what would count as evidence.

Instructional outcomes can be assessed in terms of student learning and performance. They must be stated in clear language that permits viable methods of evaluation and the establishment of performance standards. Verbs that define instructional outcomes should be unambiguous and suggest assessment techniques. For example, the goal "The student will write for a variety of purposes and audiences" is too general to suggest assessment methodologies or standards of performance. It is satisfactory as a broad program goal or outcome; however, for instructional planning and assessment, the instructional outcome should be narrowed, tightened, and made more specific. If possible, it should be illustrated with a sample of student work.

There are many types of instructional outcomes, and they may reflect diverse long-range purposes of schooling. The outcomes may deal with knowledge and understanding (factual, conceptual, and procedural), high-level thinking and analysis, or communication and social skills. Indeed, they may include dispositions, such as perseverance or open-mindedness. They may even include what could only be called "values"; for example, most teachers want to teach their students not only *how to* read; they want them *to like to* read. Furthermore, content and process outcomes are usually present simultaneously; far from conflicting with one another, they complement and build on one another. Thus, just because instructional outcomes are stated clearly does not mean they need to be restricted to knowledge and skill, or low-level in their cognitive challenge.

Together, instructional outcomes should reflect a balance among different types of learning. Some may represent factual knowledge or conceptual understanding. Others may include reasoning skills, social skills, or communication skills. Still others may include dispositions, such as a willingness to listen to all points of view or taking pride in one's work. A single lesson may incorporate only a few types of outcomes; a longer unit generally includes a balance.

The outcomes must be appropriate to the diverse students in a teacher's charge, providing for the students' age and developmental levels, prior skills and knowledge, and interests and backgrounds. Not all outcomes are equally suitable for all students, nor are the same outcomes always appropriate for all students in a class. Skilled teachers adjust their instructional outcomes to accommodate the diversity of their students.

Furthermore, although most instructional outcomes are stated in terms of the main content to be learned (such as English literature), many skilled teachers are alert to opportunities to coordinate the content with other disciplines (such as history). At an even more advanced level, teachers occasionally collaborate to create truly integrated learning experiences for their students. Thus, a study of the 19th century could include instructional outcomes from both history and literature; the history provides a context for the literature, while the literature offers another perspective on the history. At the elementary level, of course, because they are responsible for all the major subjects, teachers can design such integrated units themselves or together with their grade-level colleagues. Opportunities for coordination and integration may even be available in what seem to be the least likely situations. For example, teachers of mathematics and science find that when students write about their understanding of a concept, the activity helps them improve their skill in expository writing and deepens their level of understanding.

Demonstration

Teachers demonstrate their skills in setting instructional outcomes either orally or in writing. They should be able to describe how the outcomes relate to district curriculum guidelines, state frameworks, content standards, and curriculum outcomes in a discipline. They should also be able to explain how the outcomes are appropriate for their students and how they fit within a sequence of learning and reflect the balance among different types of learning. When appropriate, teachers will also be able to describe the potential for coordination and integration of curriculum topics and skills. The suitability of instructional outcomes for a diverse group of students is best observed during a classroom visit. (See Figure 4.3.)

COMPONENT 1D: DEMONSTRATING KNOWLEDGE OF RESOURCES

Rationale and Explanation

Resources fall into a number of different categories and come from a variety of sources. Skilled teachers are knowledgeable about them all and constantly add to the reservoir of possible aids to their work, persistently searching for new resources that can assist them in their teaching and their students in learning.

The first and most obvious form of resources consists of the myriad things used in any classroom. They may be simple or complex, and they may be purchased or made by the teacher or students. They include texts and supplemental materials; physical objects, such as math manipulatives or models or science laboratory equipment; and print materials, such as

maps, primary source materials, or trade books. Resources also include those that are available outside the classroom, such as museums, concert performances, and materials from local businesses. Teachers can also draw from a wide variety of human resources, from experts within the classroom community (students and parents) to those from the larger business and civic world. When teachers are aware of this wide range of resources, they can plan instruction to incorporate the resources into their teaching.

Another type of resource, related also to the substance of what students are learning, consists of those materials that students can investigate on their own. This would include supplemental reading material, items in the school or town library or historical society, or informative Web sites. Teachers may not be familiar with every item available for student use, but they should at least be aware of their existence and how to get access to them.

Teachers use additional resources to extend their own knowledge of content. They might take a course at a local university or pursue knowledge on their own. The Internet has made much information readily available to teachers, including information that previously was not so easy to find. Thus, when teaching in a new assignment or when striving to stay current with the quickly changing knowledge base of the subjects they teach, experienced teachers seek out assistance, either in the school or district (through courses or through the expertise of colleagues) or on their own through books or on the Internet.

In addition, teachers can learn about new developments in pedagogy, but they must know the resources are available before they can use them. Many teachers belong to professional

FIGURE 4.3

DOMAIN I: PLANNING AND PREPARATION
Component 1c: Setting Instructional Outcomes
Elements: Value, sequence, and alignment • Clarity • Balance • Suitability for diverse learners

ELEMENT	LEVEL OF PERFORMANCE			
	UNSATISFACTORY	BASIC	PROFICIENT	DISTINGUISHED
Value, sequence, and alignment	Outcomes represent low expectations for students and lack of rigor. They do not reflect important learning in the discipline or a connection to a sequence of learning.	Outcomes represent moderately high expectations and rigor. Some reflect important learning in the discipline and at least some connection to a sequence of learning.	Most outcomes represent high expectations and rigor and important learning in the discipline. They are connected to a sequence of learning.	All outcomes represent high expectations and rigor and important learning in the discipline. They are connected to a sequence of learning both in the discipline and in related disciplines.
Clarity	Outcomes are either not clear or are stated as activities, not as student learning. Outcomes do not permit viable methods of assessment.	Outcomes are only moderately clear or consist of a combination of outcomes and activities. Some outcomes do not permit viable methods of assessment.	All the instructional outcomes are clear, written in the form of student learning. Most suggest viable methods of assessment.	All the outcomes are clear, written in the form of student learning, and permit viable methods of assessment.
Balance	Outcomes reflect only one type of learning and only one discipline or strand.	Outcomes reflect several types of learning, but teacher has made no attempt at coordination or integration.	Outcomes reflect several different types of learning and opportunities for coordination.	Where appropriate, outcomes reflect several different types of learning and opportunities for both coordination and integration.
Suitability for diverse learners	Outcomes are not suitable for the class or are not based on any assessment of student needs.	Most of the outcomes are suitable for most of the students in the class based on global assessments of student learning.	Most of the outcomes are suitable for all students in the class and are based on evidence of student proficiency. However, the needs of some individual students may not be accommodated.	Outcomes are based on a comprehensive assessment of student learning and take into account the varying needs of individual students or groups.

associations, most of which publish journals or newsletters and sponsor workshops and conferences. Taking advantage of these resources helps teachers stay current with new developments in pedagogy in the subjects they teach. Some teachers also join study groups, in their schools or online, to share approaches and lesson plans. Many teachers have discovered the power of various Web sites where they can observe video clips of exemplary teachers using a skill or strategy they want to acquire. Participating in such communities of inquiry can help teachers remain fresh in their teaching and current with evolving techniques.

Knowledge of resources to assist students is part of every teacher's responsibility. Students' full potential can be realized only if their teachers are aware of what is available. Resources include items and services available both through and beyond the school. They can take the form of special services, such as an instructional aide to help a student with a hearing impairment or resource room assistance for elementary students with learning disabilities. They may also take the form of courses geared for different levels of challenge at the secondary level. Moreover, some schools establish peer-tutoring programs in which older students offer assistance to younger ones. Some outside resources help academic learning, such as tutoring services and homework hotlines. Others meet nonacademic needs—for example, Big Brother and Big Sister programs and mentoring programs. Most communities have agencies to help students with acute physical needs (for example, by providing winter coats and shoes) and students who are victims of physical or sexual abuse or who themselves abuse alcohol or drugs.

When teachers begin their professional careers, they typically find the task of preparing lessons for large numbers of students, most of whom they do not yet know well, truly challenging. It is natural that they would stick fairly close to the "official" materials provided by the school or the district and learn to use those effectively. But as teachers gain skill and experience, they realize that they can enrich their students' experience by locating supplemental materials that can help them achieve their instructional purposes better than if they restricted themselves to only the materials provided. This flexibility, reinforced by an awareness of what is available, is a mark of an expert.

In addition, as they gain experience, teachers are increasingly in a position to seek out and take advantage of resources to assist them in their content and pedagogical knowledge. As they become more comfortable in the school environment, they will become increasingly aware of areas they want to strengthen in their teaching and will be able to seek out courses, workshops, study groups, and networks, both in person and online.

Demonstration

Teachers demonstrate their knowledge of resources through their ability to articulate how they have planned a unit or a lesson to incorporate the best of what the school, district, and community have to offer. Their knowledge is also evident in how they can describe a potential lesson or unit, or how they plan to address a student's instructional or noninstructional needs. (See Figure 4.4.)

COMPONENT 1E: DESIGNING COHERENT INSTRUCTION

Rationale and Explanation

A teacher translates instructional outcomes into learning experiences for students through the design of instruction; it is

FIGURE 4.4

DOMAIN 1: PLANNING AND PREPARATION
Component 1d: Demonstrating Knowledge of Resources
Elements: Resources for classroom use • Resources to extend content knowledge and pedagogy • Resources for students

ELEMENT	LEVEL OF PERFORMANCE			
	UNSATISFACTORY	BASIC	PROFICIENT	DISTINGUISHED
Resources for classroom use	Teacher is unaware of resources for classroom use available through the school or district.	Teacher displays awareness of resources available for classroom use through the school or district but no knowledge of resources available more broadly.	Teacher displays awareness of resources available for classroom use through the school or district and some familiarity with resources external to the school and on the Internet.	Teacher's knowledge of resources for classroom use is extensive, including those available through the school or district, in the community, through professional organizations and universities, and on the Internet.
Resources to extend content knowledge and pedagogy	Teacher is unaware of resources to enhance content and pedagogical knowledge available through the school or district.	Teacher displays awareness of resources to enhance content and pedagogical knowledge available through the school or district but no knowledge of resources available more broadly.	Teacher displays awareness of resources to enhance content and pedagogical knowledge available through the school or district and some familiarity with resources external to the school and on the Internet.	Teacher's knowledge of resources to enhance content and pedagogical knowledge is extensive, including those available through the school or district, in the community, through professional organizations and universities, and on the Internet.
Resources for students	Teacher is unaware of resources for students available through the school or district.	Teacher displays awareness of resources for students available through the school or district but no knowledge of resources available more broadly.	Teacher displays awareness of resources for students available through the school or district and some familiarity with resources external to the school and on the Internet.	Teacher's knowledge of resources for students is extensive, including those available through the school or district, in the community, and on the Internet.

here that teachers' knowledge of the content, knowledge of their students, clarity of instructional outcomes, and knowledge of resources come together to result in a plan of action. Even in classrooms where students assume considerable responsibility for their learning, the teacher is in charge of organizing the environment, managing the learning process, and establishing the framework for investigations.

A critical feature of an instructional design is *coherence;* that is, the different elements of the plan—the instructional outcomes, the activities, the materials, the methods, and the grouping of students—all hang together. They are aligned both with one another and with any external requirements, such as state tests and community expectations. Another aspect of coherence relates to sequencing. The sequence of activities should be logical and should progress from easier to harder, from simple to more complex, from attention to one domain of learning to integration across several. It should be clear from looking at either a lesson or a unit plan how the concepts are developed and how students are to engage with increasingly complex aspects of the topic. In other words, the sequence of activities, even within a single lesson, has a clearly recognizable *structure.*

Furthermore, designing instruction is a different skill from implementing a plan in the classroom, and both skills are critical to the enhancement of learning. Good planning is essential to student learning. Although experienced teachers can, perhaps, manage to "fly by the seat of their pants," even they cannot do so for long. On the other hand, even the best-prepared lessons may need modification in the face of real students; so there is, inevitably, a balance between careful planning and flexibility in execution.

Because instructional outcomes are varied, the teacher's choice of instructional strategies is also likely to vary from one context to another. For example, the methods used in helping students understand a routine procedure, such as how to clean laboratory glassware, are likely to be different from those used in enabling students to engage in independent projects. Some lessons consist of presentations, whereas others are more like workshops, with the teacher's role correspondingly different.

Of all the elements of an instructional plan, the most critical is the design of instructional activities. The important question to be answered is this: "What could the students *do* in order to learn X?" There are many choices, of course. They could listen to a presentation or they could work—either alone or in groups—to solve a problem or to engage in a project. They could participate in a class discussion or reflect in a journal on new information. The list is endless, and skilled teachers draw on an extensive repertoire in making their decisions. Given the importance of students' active intellectual engagement in learning, skilled teachers, in their design of activities, favor those that challenge students to be cognitively active, that offer students the opportunity to select an activity from among several options, and that permit students the opportunity to develop their own understanding.

An advanced skill in the design of instructional activities is to create opportunities, in the same task, for students of varying skill and knowledge to find appropriate challenge. For example, in a mathematics class, a teacher might pose a problem in which, at the simplest level, students determine the solution. Students for whom that task is too simple can explore a more advanced question of whether the problem has more than one solution. If not, can they demonstrate why only one solution is possible? Or, alternatively, is there more than one method by which to arrive at the correct solution? Of the possible approaches, is one clearly more efficient, or elegant, than the others? Why is this so? Similar extensions of even routine learning tasks are possible in most disciplines and represent an important strategy in differentiating instructional plans for different students.

Activities and assignments that promote learning tend to share certain characteristics: (1) they emphasize thinking and problem-based learning; (2) they permit student choice and initiative; and (3) they encourage depth rather than breadth.

Emphasize thinking and problem-based learning.
Many successful constructivist activities and assignments require that students solve a problem or answer an important question. For example, when 4th graders determine which set of objects conducts electricity, or when high school students determine if the number of delegates to the Constitutional Convention was related to each state's population, they are engaging in problem solving. That each question actually has a correct answer does not make it trivial. The students must determine an approach, interpret their findings, and possibly formulate additional questions. From their point of view, they are answering a question and engaging in problem-based learning, and their work requires high-level thinking (Newmann, Secada, & Whelage, 1995).

Permit student choice and initiative.
Many well-designed activities encourage or even require students to make choices and take initiative. For example, when students are asked to write an essay in the style of Hemingway, they can write whatever they choose, but their choice is constrained by the directions for the task. The highest level of student engagement occurs when students exercise initiative in formulating their own questions and designing their own investigations.

Encourage depth rather than breadth.
Activities and assignments designed to enhance student engagement are not superficial. They challenge students to search for underlying causes, explain their thinking, and justify a position. Work designed for depth represents an appropriate cognitive challenge for students, not permitting easy answers or flippant responses. Typically such activities engage students in generating knowledge, finding patterns, and testing hypotheses.

In addition to having certain characteristics, the sequence of activities should have some variety. For example, small-group work and reporting out may be an effective approach, but as a steady diet, such a procedure would become tedious. Furthermore, some approaches may be more appropriate to some students than to others; by offering a variety, teachers ensure that all students have access to methods suitable to them.

Another element in instructional design is the choice of materials and resources. Teachers should select these carefully and make sure they clearly support the instructional outcomes. Concrete materials may illustrate a concept better than a verbal description alone, and a drawing on the board may be better than either. Perhaps students can learn more about a topic by going online than by reading the textbook alone. Naturally the materials and resources should be suited to the students, offering an appropriate level of challenge.

The establishment of instructional groups is a well-recognized aspect of planning; the groups must be suitable to both the instructional outcomes and the students. There are many choices to be made here. Which students work well together, and which poorly? Is it desirable that the groups be mixed in ability and background, or for a certain activity will homogeneous groups accomplish the goals of the lesson or unit better? Which activities are best conducted with the class as one single group, which should students engage in independently, and which are best achieved with students in small groups? And what is the teacher's role with respect to the groups? Should the teacher lead the work with one group while the others work independently, or should the teacher circulate to monitor and provide assistance? These are all questions whose answers can have a significant impact on the success of a lesson. And, of course, where appropriate, students themselves should take some initiative in choosing their own work group.

A coherent instructional unit has a well-defined structure. Individual activities support the whole, with each activity playing an important role. Time allocations are reasonable, with opportunities for students to engage in reflection and closure. Topics from one part of the unit are connected with others; students explore a subject from many different angles and understand the relationship of the parts to the whole.

Demonstration

Long-range planning for coherent instruction is demonstrated by a unit plan encompassing several weeks. That time span enables teachers to demonstrate their skill in organizing and sequencing learning activities that engage students, in using a variety of materials and groups appropriately, and in allocating reasonable time. In addition, when teachers design instruction for individual lessons, all the characteristics of long-range planning—purposeful activities, appropriate materials

and student groups, and a coherent structure—are displayed, albeit on a smaller scale. (See Figure 4.5.)

COMPONENT 1F: DESIGNING STUDENT ASSESSMENTS

Rationale and Explanation

The professional community of educators has gradually recognized the central role of assessment in learning. As a result, teachers have found that they have another powerful instructional tool at their disposal. It is well worth the challenge of mastering the techniques of using it to maximum benefit.

Assessment in teaching has two related, though distinct, uses. The first is to determine that students have, in fact, achieved the instructional outcomes established through the planning process. That is, it is assessment *of* learning. But in addition, teachers can design assessment *for* learning—that is, assessment that provides both them and their students with valuable information to guide future learning. Teachers should consider each of these purposes when they design their approaches to assessment. Although assessment *of* learning is frequently undertaken by groups of teachers working together; assessment *for* learning is more typically undertaken by teachers on their own, in response to their individual groups of students.

In creating assessments of learning, teachers must ensure that each instructional outcome can be assessed in some way. Moreover, the assessment methodologies must be appropriate to the different types of outcomes. For example, a science unit may contain seven instructional outcomes: one related to factual knowledge, one to conceptual understanding, two to data analysis, two to communication of findings, and one to

FIGURE 4.5

DOMAIN 1: PLANNING AND PREPARATION
Component 1e: Designing Coherent Instruction
Elements: Learning activities • Instructional materials and resources • Instructional groups • Lesson and unit structure

ELEMENT	LEVEL OF PERFORMANCE			
	UNSATISFACTORY	BASIC	PROFICIENT	DISTINGUISHED
Learning activities	Learning activities are not suitable to students or to instructional outcomes and are not designed to engage students in active intellectual activity.	Only some of the learning activities are suitable to students or to the instructional outcomes. Some represent a moderate cognitive challenge, but with no differentiation for different students.	All of the learning activities are suitable to students or to the instructional outcomes, and most represent significant cognitive challenge, with some differentiation for different groups of students.	Learning activities are highly suitable to diverse learners and support the instructional outcomes. They are all designed to engage students in high-level cognitive activity and are differentiated, as appropriate, for individual learners.
Instructional materials and resources	Materials and resources are not suitable for students and do not support the instructional outcomes or engage students in meaningful learning.	Some of the materials and resources are suitable to students, support the instructional outcomes, and engage students in meaningful learning.	All of the materials and resources are suitable to students, support the instructional outcomes, and are designed to engage students in meaningful learning.	All of the materials and resources are suitable to students, support the instructional outcomes, and are designed to engage students in meaningful learning. There is evidence of appropriate use of technology and of student participation in selecting or adapting materials.
Instructional groups	Instructional groups do not support the instructional outcomes and offer no variety.	Instructional groups partially support the instructional outcomes, with an effort at providing some variety.	Instructional groups are varied as appropriate to the students and the different instructional outcomes.	Instructional groups are varied as appropriate to the students and the different instructional outcomes. There is evidence of student choice in selecting the different patterns of instructional groups.

FIGURE 4.5

DOMAIN 1: PLANNING AND PREPARATION
Component 1e: Designing Coherent Instruction (continued)
Elements: Learning activities • Instructional materials and resources • Instructional groups • Lesson and unit structure

ELEMENT	LEVEL OF PERFORMANCE			
	UNSATISFACTORY	BASIC	PROFICIENT	DISTINGUISHED
Lesson and unit structure	The lesson or unit has no clearly defined structure, or the structure is chaotic. Activities do not follow an organized progression, and time allocations are unrealistic.	The lesson or unit has a recognizable structure, although the structure is not uniformly maintained throughout. Progression of activities is uneven, with most time allocations reasonable.	The lesson or unit has a clearly defined structure around which activities are organized. Progression of activities is even, with reasonable time allocations.	The lesson's or unit's structure is clear and allows for different pathways according to diverse student needs. The progression of activities is highly coherent.

collaboration skills. Clearly, no single approach is suitable for all these outcomes. A simple factual test may be appropriate for the factual knowledge but other approaches are necessary to assess conceptual understanding, data analysis, communication of findings, and collaboration skills. And if possible, assessment methodologies should reflect authentic, real-world applications of knowledge and understanding. Although not always possible, such authenticity motivates students and provides teachers with excellent insight into student learning.

A well-designed approach is clear about how student work will be evaluated. Again, this requirement is relatively easy with a test in which questions have a single right answer, student responses can be counted, and percentages calculated. But even when assessing students' factual knowledge, asking students to explain a concept in their own words provides much richer information than asking them to simply select a definition from a list of options. Furthermore, for more complex instructional outcomes and for responses that don't yield a single correct answer, part of designing an assessment is to determine a scoring system or a rubric for evaluating student work. For example, an instructional outcome might state, "Students will write a descriptive essay." For the goal to be meaningful, a teacher needs to specify the length and organization of the essay, the importance of mechanics, and use of language. The criteria, in other words, define the important characteristics of a successful response.

Such a rubric not only identifies the criteria of an acceptable response but also establishes standards of performance. In other words, it answers the question "How good is good enough?" Not only are these standards of performance clear, but they are known to students. Secrecy has no role in assessment—such an environment feels like "gotcha" to students. Of course, the exact items that will appear on an assessment should not be given to students in advance. But there is no reason they can't be informed about the *type* of items that will be presented and the content to be covered. Then, by studying that content and by reviewing exemplary responses to sample items, students can better prepare for the assessment.

Furthermore, many teachers have discovered that when students participate in the design of assessments, they are able to be purposeful about their learning. If students don't know the characteristics of an effective essay, for example, the very activity of developing a rubric to evaluate student essays will help them understand those characteristics clearly. And when students have the opportunity to compare successive iterations of their own work against the rubric (for example, comparing writing samples from the beginning and end of the school year), they have tangible evidence of their progress in learning. For many students, this kind of comparison is highly motivational.

But the full power of assessment is realized only when teachers also include assessment *for* learning in their instructional planning. Such a use of assessment is typically termed *formative* to indicate that its purpose is not to certify mastery of content by students but to provide information to both students and teachers as to what has not yet been learned and to guide next steps. But for formative assessment to be truly effective, it must be designed to yield maximum information (Guskey, 2005; Wiliam, 2004).

Expert teachers design their formative assessments to provide diagnostic information. In some disciplines, particularly science and mathematics, careful analysis of students' wrong answers enables teachers to see where students went astray and may reveal student misconceptions about the content or a procedure. Student writing also offers teachers much information as to their level of understanding. When students describe, for example, the relationship between floating and buoyancy, teachers can readily determine those students for whom the distinction is still cloudy.

For assessment to yield useful information, teachers must give careful attention to student responses. Gathering assessment information can sometimes be an informal process—done, for example, during a class discussion. But when it is gathered more systematically, such as through an assignment or a quiz, it is essential for teachers to examine and analyze the student work, to determine what has not yet been learned. In addition, of course, this analysis also provides important information to teachers regarding the instructional approaches used. After examining student work, they may conclude, "That approach didn't work!"

Demonstration

Teachers demonstrate their skill in designing student assessment through the plans they create. With respect to assessment *of* learning, a unit plan should include the method to be used to assess student understanding, including, if appropriate, a scoring guide or rubric for evaluating student responses. When teachers also include assessment *for* learning in their plan, then the details of such assessments should be part of the plan. In addition, teachers should be able to explain how they intend to use assessment of learning in their instruction, and how they plan to include students in assessment activities. (See Figure 4.6.)

FIGURE 4.6

DOMAIN 1: PLANNING AND PREPARATION
Component 1f: Designing Student Assessments
Elements: Congruence with instructional outcomes • Criteria and standards • Design of formative assessments • Use for planning

ELEMENT	LEVEL OF PERFORMANCE			
	UNSATISFACTORY	BASIC	PROFICIENT	DISTINGUISHED
Congruence with instructional outcomes	Assessment procedures are not congruent with instructional outcomes.	Some of the instructional outcomes are assessed through the proposed approach, but many are not.	All the instructional outcomes are assessed through the approach to assessment; assessment methodologies may have been adapted for groups of students.	Proposed approach to assessment is fully aligned with the instructional outcomes in both content and process. Assessment methodologies have been adapted for individual students, as needed.
Criteria and standards	Proposed approach contains no criteria or standards.	Assessment criteria and standards have been developed, but they are not clear.	Assessment criteria and standards are clear.	Assessment criteria and standards are clear; there is evidence that the students contributed to their development.
Design of formative assessments	Teacher has no plan to incorporate formative assessment in the lesson or unit.	Approach to the use of formative assessment is rudimentary, including only some of the instructional outcomes.	Teacher has a well-developed strategy to using formative assessment and has designed particular approaches to be used.	Approach to using formative assessment is well designed and includes student as well as teacher use of the assessment information.
Use for planning	Teacher has no plans to use assessment results in designing future instruction.	Teacher plans to use assessment results to plan for future instruction for the class as a whole.	Teacher plans to use assessment results to plan for future instruction for groups of students.	Teacher plans to use assessment results to plan future instruction for individual students.

DOMAIN 2: THE CLASSROOM ENVIRONMENT

The classroom environment is a critical aspect of a teacher's skill in promoting learning. Students can't concentrate on the academic content if they don't feel comfortable in the classroom. If the atmosphere is negative, if students fear ridicule, if the environment is chaotic, no one—neither students nor teacher—can focus on learning. So although Domain 2 does not deal with instructional skills, its components make the teacher's exercise of instructional skills possible.

COMPONENT 2A: CREATING AN ENVIRONMENT OF RESPECT AND RAPPORT

Rationale and Explanation

Teaching depends, fundamentally, on the quality of relationships among individuals. When teachers strive to engage students in a discussion or an activity, their interactions with them speak volumes about the extent to which they value students as people.

When adults recall their favorite or least favorite teachers years later, they tend to remember those who treated them with respect or those who demeaned them. These memories often overwhelm other memories of school, such as the teachers who really knew their subjects or who gave wonderful explanations. Depending on how old they are when they tell the story, adults may recall a single day, or even a single episode, from 30 or 40 years earlier. The memories are powerful and can have tremendous influence on individuals' sense of

themselves that becomes integral to their identities. These powerful memories relate to how one was treated; therefore, all relationships between teacher and students, and among students, should be grounded in mutual respect and trust.

An essential skill of teaching is that of managing relationships with students and ensuring that those among students are positive and supportive. Although children may be smaller than adults, they are no less human; they have feelings and aspirations, hopes and fears—and those deserve careful attention. In interviews, students consistently report that one of the characteristics they most value in their teachers is that of respecting them and their lives outside school. The out-of-school part has enormous implications, particularly for recent immigrants or for students whose home culture is different from that of the teacher. An important consequence of getting to know one's students (Component 1b) is that teachers are able to interact with their students as individuals ("How's your grandma doing?"). In addition, teachers learn to respect the wide variety of backgrounds represented by their students and learn to see the world from their students' perspectives. For some teachers, this requires significant new learning, because ways of showing respect in one culture may be offensive in another.

Teachers create an environment of respect and rapport in their classrooms by the ways they interact with students and by the interaction they encourage and cultivate among students. In a respectful environment, all students feel valued and safe. They know they will be treated with dignity, which encourages them to take intellectual risks. High levels of respect and rapport are sometimes characterized by friendliness and openness, and frequently by humor, but never by teachers forgetting their role as adults. It is essential that teachers not believe that in order to establish good relationships with students they must be seen as a friend or a pal. This is always inappropriate and may undermine the teacher's essential role as an adult.

Some teachers convey their caring for students through a firm demeanor and businesslike atmosphere. Underneath the demeanor, however, is the essential *caring* that teachers exhibit for their students and the caring that students are encouraged to exhibit for one another. That is, students are not offended by teachers whose affect is strict, even stern. Somewhat counterintuitively, students interpret that affect for what it is—teachers caring enough about their students to insist on the highest standards of work and conduct. Parents are known to say to their children, "If I didn't care about you, I would let you stay out all night (or go to an unsupervised party or hang out on the corner with certain friends). It's because I care about you, and your future, that you may not do those things." The same rationale is behind the behavior of some teachers. Students understand caring when they see it and know that it is different from permissiveness. Of course, appropriate interactions are highly dependent on context. What is suitable for kindergarten children is unusual, or even inappropriate, for high school students.

During instruction, an important challenge of a teacher's skill occurs when students offer an idea, or a response to a teacher's question, that is inadequate. How the teacher responds—and how other students are permitted to respond—sets the tone for how students are treated and therefore how they feel about themselves, both as people and as learners. If a student's effort is ridiculed by other students (if they snicker or shoot their hands up to correct the response) or if the teacher responds sarcastically, the student is unlikely to take such a risk again. Much better is a response that recognizes the thinking that prompted the response and steers the student in another direction, such as, "That's an interesting idea, Jimmy, but I wonder whether you have overlooked the fact that . . . ?" Such a response invites another attempt by the student and also shapes the ensuing discussion with the rest of the class.

Of course, respect for others is demonstrated through nonverbal as well as verbal means. When students roll their eyes or when teachers express exasperation in their posture, students quickly pick up the messages. And students are quick to recognize a display of favoritism by the teacher toward some students.

As noted, an important aspect of a teacher's skill in creating an environment of respect and rapport relates to how the students are permitted to treat one another. This is not a trivial matter; how students are treated by their peers can have an enormous influence on their sense of self-worth. Extreme cases of lack of respect lead to bullying, from which some students never fully recover. Furthermore, popular American culture, as reflected in television sitcoms, provides continuous models of the "humorous" put-down, the scoring of cheap points by one person over another. And as any parent knows, children are not born being nice to one another; this is a *learned* skill.

Some teachers are reluctant to have their own performance judged by an aspect of their classroom over which, they maintain, they have little control, because so many of students' patterns of interaction with other students are formulated by their patterns of behavior at home and in the larger community. On the other hand, establishing ground rules for interaction is as important as establishing standards of conduct or routines for activities such as sharpening pencils—aspects of creating a learning community that no experienced teacher would over-look at the outset of a school year. Patterns of student interaction are critical to the overall tone of a class. So although it is true that students observe many models of how people treat one another (some of them negative), promoting positive interactions among students is a critical aspect of teaching. As Anna Quindlen put it in a commencement address in 2002: "People will forget what you said. They will forget what you did. But they will never forget how you made them feel."

Demonstration

Teachers demonstrate skill in establishing an environment of respect and rapport through their words and actions in the classroom. Occasionally, interaction with a student, or student interactions with one another, may require that a teacher offer an explanation so that an observer can fully understand the teacher's actions. Such explanations can take place in a discussion following the class. (See Figure 4.7.)

FIGURE 4.7

DOMAIN 2: THE CLASSROOM ENVIRONMENT
Component 2a: Creating an Environment of Respect and Rapport
Elements: Teacher interaction with students • Student interactions with other students

	LEVEL OF PERFORMANCE			
ELEMENT	UNSATISFACTORY	BASIC	PROFICIENT	DISTINGUISHED
Teacher interaction with students	Teacher interaction with at least some students is negative, demeaning, sarcastic, or inappropriate to the age or culture of the students. Students exhibit disrespect for the teacher.	Teacher-student interactions are generally appropriate but may reflect occasional inconsistencies, favoritism, or disregard for students' cultures. Students exhibit only minimal respect for the teacher.	Teacher-student interactions are friendly and demonstrate general caring and respect. Such interactions are appropriate to the age and cultures of the students. Students exhibit respect for the teacher.	Teacher interactions with students reflect genuine respect and caring for individuals as well as groups of students. Students appear to trust the teacher with sensitive information.
Student interactions with other students	Student interactions are characterized by conflict, sarcasm, or put-downs.	Students do not demonstrate disrespect for one another.	Student interactions are generally polite and respectful.	Students demonstrate genuine caring for one another and monitor one another's treatment of peers, correcting classmates respectfully when needed.

COMPONENT 2B: ESTABLISHING A CULTURE FOR LEARNING

Rationale and Explanation

"A culture for learning" refers to the atmosphere in the classroom that reflects the importance of the work undertaken by both students and teacher. It describes the norms that govern the interactions among individuals about the activities and assignments, the look of the classroom, and the general "tone" of the class.

In classrooms with a strong culture for learning, everyone, including the teacher, is engaged in pursuits of value. Rather than an atmosphere of "getting by" or "punching the time clock," both students and teachers take pride in their work and give it their best effort. In such classrooms, it is "cool" to be smart, and good ideas are valued. The classroom is characterized by high energy, by a sense that what is happening there is important and that it is essential to get it right. Reinforcing the notion that a primary purpose of school is for students to develop conceptual understanding of complex material, the teacher conveys that it is not sufficient for students to be able to go through the motions, to follow a procedure without understanding why. No—they must develop conceptual understanding; it must build from one idea to another, and students should be able to explain to the teacher, or to another student, why something is the way it is.

A culture for learning implies high expectations for all students and is closely related to Component 2a, Creating an Environment of Respect and Rapport. Students experience a safe environment for taking risks. They know that they do not have

to fear ridicule when they advance an idea and that their teacher will ensure that their ideas receive a thoughtful reception. Moreover, students know that their teacher has a high regard for their abilities; this strengthens their commitment to high-quality work. These high expectations, which students internalize, are at the heart of a culture for learning. When students believe that their teacher has confidence in their abilities, they are willing to work hard to live up to those expectations. They put forth effort, and that effort is rewarded.

Classrooms without a culture for learning are characterized by an atmosphere where no one—teacher or students—cares about the content to be learned. Teachers may even indirectly blame the textbook, the administration, the state, or the district for a curriculum that they don't think has much value. Or, more insidiously, they may communicate to students a belief that the material is beyond the reach of most of the students in the class. Alternatively, because of low expectations of student capabilities, the teacher may have so watered down the material to be learned that it is trivial and boring. Students quickly pick up on such manifestations of teacher beliefs; they are lethargic or alienated, do not invest energy in their work, and appear motivated by the desire to get by, preferably with as little effort as possible.

On the other hand, classrooms with a culture for learning are cognitively busy places. Students have clearly accepted the notion that important outcomes can be achieved only by hard work, and they invest energy in their activities and assignments, persevering to overcome temporary setbacks. The teacher insists on, and students accept, the obligation for students to expend their best efforts. Both students and teacher see the content as important, and students take obvious pride in their work. Student work may be displayed, but whether it is on the wall or in a portfolio, students are eager to explain it to a visitor.

A culture for learning is also evident—or not—in the school as a whole. In many schools, particularly at the secondary level, athletes receive the most recognition for their accomplishments. The school's athletic trophy case is mounted in the front hall, and sports letters are awarded in an assembly. No such acknowledgment is generally given to the editors of the literary magazine; students who participate in and excel at other activities, such as music, drama, or writing, receive little public acknowledgment for their work. Students who represent the school in the "Math Olympics" or the state chess tournament may labor in obscurity. And students whose grades place them on the honor roll or dean's list may actually be ridiculed by other students, referred to as "nerds" or "geeks." Alternatively, schools with a culture for learning are purposeful and exciting places. Such schools demonstrate high levels of intellectual energy, extending beyond the specific demands of the school curriculum.

Of course, school cultures can be changed; there are schools where the academic trophies enjoy prominent space in the school's main entrance corridor, with the athletic trophies in an attractive and important location near the gym. Students whose grades place them on the honor roll or who demonstrate other important academic qualifications, such as hard work or significant improvement, are acknowledged publicly.

But even if the school culture does not support such recognition, every teacher has an important role to play within his or her classroom. High-quality work can and must be valued; students must recognize that what they do in their classes, every

day, will influence their futures. The fact that such a culture for learning is difficult to effect in some situations does not mean it is not an important responsibility of every teacher. And when working with students whose families do not value education, the teacher's work is correspondingly more challenging.

But the benefits are palpable. When a culture for learning has been established, other aspects of teaching become easier and more rewarding. Students enter the classroom ready to get to work; they assume responsibility for their learning; they have confidence in their abilities. Students come to recognize important academic learning, and the intellectual challenges that accompany it, as fun. And when they master complex material, they enjoy the satisfaction that comes only from demonstrated competence in important work.

Demonstration

Evidence of a culture for learning is found primarily in the classroom itself, where it's evident from the look of the room (which may display student work), the nature of the interactions, and the tone of the conversations. The teachers' instructional outcomes and activities, as described in their planning documents, also demonstrate high expectations of all students for learning. Conversations with students reveal that they value learning and hard work. (See Figure 4.8.)

COMPONENT 2C: MANAGING CLASSROOM PROCEDURES

Rationale and Explanation

For new teachers, the challenge of managing the activities of a large number of students is a daunting one; there is only

FIGURE 4.8

DOMAIN 2: THE CLASSROOM ENVIRONMENT
Component 2b: Establishing a Culture for Learning
Elements: Importance of the content • Expectations for learning and achievement • Student pride in work

ELEMENT	LEVEL OF PERFORMANCE			
	UNSATISFACTORY	BASIC	PROFICIENT	DISTINGUISHED
Importance of the content	Teacher or students convey a negative attitude toward the content, suggesting that it is not important or has been mandated by others.	Teacher communicates importance of the work but with little conviction and only minimal apparent buy-in by the students.	Teacher conveys genuine enthusiasm for the content, and students demonstrate consistent commitment to its value.	Students demonstrate through their active participation, curiosity, and taking initiative that they value the importance of the content.
Expectations for learning and achievement	Instructional outcomes, activities and assignments, and classroom interactions convey low expectations for at least some students.	Instructional outcomes, activities and assignments, and classroom interactions convey only modest expectations for student learning and achievement.	Instructional outcomes, activities and assignments, and classroom interactions convey high expectations for most students.	Instructional outcomes, activities and assignments, and classroom interactions convey high expectations for all students. Students appear to have internalized these expectations.
Student pride in work	Students demonstrate little or no pride in their work. They seem to be motivated by the desire to complete a task rather than to do high-quality work.	Students minimally accept the responsibility to do good work but invest little of their energy into its quality.	Students accept the teacher's insistence on work of high quality and demonstrate pride in that work.	Students demonstrate attention to detail and take obvious pride in their work, initiating improvements in it by, for example, revising drafts on their own or helping peers.

one teacher, after all, and there are lots of students. What is to prevent them from "ganging up" on the teacher and simply refusing to cooperate? It is the loss of control—or the failure to ever establish control—that causes novice educators the greatest anxiety.

Their concern is well founded; a smoothly functioning classroom is a prerequisite to good instruction. The best instructional techniques are worthless in a chaotic environment. Therefore, teachers find that they must develop procedures for the smooth operation of the classroom and the efficient use of time before they can focus on instructional techniques. One of the marks of expert teachers is that they take the time required to establish their routines and procedures at the outset of the school year. In fact, when experts take over a class in the middle of a school year, for example, replacing a teacher on leave, they set aside time to get the routines established before embarking on the teaching.

A poorly managed classroom is easy to spot: it is chaotic. Time is wasted on noninstructional matters, students must wait for a teacher's attention, instructional groups are off task, materials are not at hand, and transitions are confused. In a well-managed classroom, procedures and transitions are seamless, and students assume responsibility for the classroom's smooth operation. Instructional groups are engaged at all times, and students function well in those groups. Even when the teacher is not directly monitoring their activities, students working in groups maintain their momentum, seeking help when they need it.

A hallmark of a well-managed classroom is that instructional groups are used efficiently. Most students enjoy small-group work; it permits them to interact with their friends, which for some students is an essential element of school life. And teachers find that by assigning small-group work, they can differentiate instruction while helping students develop important social skills. But a teacher cannot be everywhere at once. If the teacher is working with one group, the others must be able to work independently. Alternatively, if the teacher is circulating among groups, students must wait their turn before the teacher can get to them. Teaching students to work unsupervised is an important aspect of classroom management.

Another important aspect of classroom management relates to how a teacher handles transitions between activities. When skillfully done, the directions are clearly explained, students know what to do and where to go, and momentum is maintained. As a consequence, little time is lost during the lesson. Different activities have clear beginnings and endings, and minimal time is lost as the teacher and students move from one lesson segment to another.

Furthermore, materials and supplies are well managed. They are stored such that traffic patterns are efficient, and students don't interfere with others when obtaining such things as lab chemicals or art supplies. When papers are to be distributed, the teacher has established routines that ensure efficient operation. They may be passed down rows of desks, or, if students are working in small groups, one member of each group might collect the materials for everyone in the group. These procedures have been deliberately established; if asked, students could state them.

Expert teachers make highly efficient use of time in their management of noninstructional tasks. Expert teachers can take attendance in 20 seconds, whereas a novice might need 5 minutes. Actually, an expert teacher might take attendance while the students are engaged in an activity. Other noninstructional activities are accomplished in a similarly efficient manner. Procedures for lunch counts, the return of permission slips for a field trip, or the distribution of newsletters for students to take home are streamlined and carried out with little expenditure of energy. In fact, the procedures for noninstructional duties may have evolved such that students themselves play an important role in carrying them out.

Another aspect of noninstructional tasks relates to teachers' familiarity with and successful execution of school emergency procedures. They know how to handle a fire alarm, a disaster evacuation, or a situation in which strangers are in the building, and they will have practiced with students what to do in such cases. Everyone is familiar with procedures for a school lockdown, should that become necessary.

Not all teachers are so fortunate as to have classroom volunteers and paraprofessionals at their disposal. However, although these assistants greatly enhance the quality of a program, they generally require a considerable amount of supervision before they can make much of a contribution. Experienced teachers devote the necessary time to providing guidance to their assistants. They determine an appropriate role, with written directions if necessary. They might actually teach their assistants skills; as a result, they ensure that those assistants can make a substantial contribution to the class.

Demonstration

Evidence for how teachers manage classroom procedures is obtained through classroom observation. If asked, students would be able to describe the classroom procedures. In addition, teachers can explain their procedures, how they have been developed, and how students were involved in their creation and maintenance. (See Figure 4.9.)

COMPONENT 2D: MANAGING STUDENT BEHAVIOR

Rationale and Explanation

Learning cannot occur in an environment where student behavior is out of control. If students are running around, defying the teacher, or picking fights, they cannot also engage deeply with content. Of course, the reverse is also true: when

students are engaged deeply with content, they are less likely to pick fights, defy a teacher, or run around a classroom.

Most classrooms are crowded places, with students sharing space and materials. This proximity, exacerbated by other elements, can cause students to be disruptive. Students can easily barge into one another, for example, or inadvertently knock a classmate's pottery creation off a table. Therefore, in the event of a classroom conflict, it is essential to establish intent: did the student *mean* to cause harm?

Experienced teachers recognize that much of what appears to be student misbehavior is actually a result of other causes, such as these:

• Students who are not prepared attempt to camouflage their situation by "acting out."

• Students who don't find a task engaging let their attention wander to more interesting matters. For example, high school students pass notes or discuss out-of-class events; a 2nd grader converts his pencil into an imaginary car and runs it around his desk, with appropriate sound effects.

• Students who have poorly developed social skills or low self-esteem find opportunities to initiate oral and physical confrontations with other students, disrupting a class. They might prefer being sent to the office to being ridiculed in front of other students.

A key to efficient and respectful management of student behavior lies in agreed-upon standards of conduct and clear consequences for overstepping the bounds. Such standards may encompass appropriate language (for example, no swearing); attire (for example, no hats); and various procedures, such as procedures for being recognized to speak during a discussion (raise

FIGURE 4.9

DOMAIN 2: THE CLASSROOM ENVIRONMENT
Component 2c: Managing Classroom Procedures

Elements: Management of instructional groups • Management of transitions • Management of materials and supplies •

Performance of noninstructional duties • Supervision of volunteers and paraprofessionals

	LEVEL OF PERFORMANCE			
ELEMENT	UNSATISFACTORY	BASIC	PROFICIENT	DISTINGUISHED
Management of instructional groups	Students not working with the teacher are not productively engaged in learning.	Students in only some groups are productively engaged in learning while unsupervised by the teacher.	Small-group work is well organized, and most students are productively engaged in learning while unsupervised by the teacher.	Small-group work is well organized, and students are productively engaged at all times, with students assuming responsibility for productivity.
Management of transitions	Transitions are chaotic, with much time lost between activities or lesson segments.	Only some transitions are efficient, resulting in some loss of instructional time.	Transitions occur smoothly, with little loss of instructional time.	Transitions are seamless, with students assuming responsibility in ensuring their efficient operation.
Management of materials and supplies	Materials and supplies are handled inefficiently, resulting in significant loss of instructional time.	Routines for handling materials and supplies function moderately well, but with some loss of instructional time.	Routines for handling materials and supplies occur smoothly, with little loss of instructional time.	Routines for handling materials and supplies are seamless, with students assuming some responsibility for smooth operation.
Performance of noninstructional duties	Considerable instructional time is lost in performing noninstructional duties.	Systems for performing noninstructional duties are only fairly efficient, resulting in some loss of instructional time.	Efficient systems for performing noninstructional duties are in place, resulting in minimal loss of instructional time.	Systems for performing noninstructional duties are well established, with students assuming considerable responsibility for efficient operation.
Supervision of volunteers and paraprofessionals	Volunteers and paraprofessionals have no clearly defined duties and are idle most of the time.	Volunteers and paraprofessionals are productively engaged during portions of class time but require frequent supervision.	Volunteers and paraprofessionals are productively and independently engaged during the entire class.	Volunteers and paraprofessionals make a substantive contribution to the classroom environment.

hand or other signal for the discussion leader), for entering and leaving the classroom (lining up or dismissal by rows), for sharpening pencils, for getting materials, and for going to the restroom.

Experienced teachers successfully enlist students in both setting and maintaining standards of conduct. Even very young students know what are reasonable expectations, both for themselves and for what they can expect of other students. Active participation in setting the rules of the classroom contributes to students' feelings of safety in class.

Managing one's own conduct is a difficult skill for most students to learn. It's one thing to say, when the atmosphere is calm, that students should raise their hand to be recognized. But in the middle of a heated discussion, those rules are easily forgotten. Awareness of one's behavior—and being able to change it—requires metacognitive skills that some students may still be developing. Teaching students to engage in such reflection is an important aspect of teachers' responsibilities.

Whatever the details of the standards of conduct, approaches to managing student behavior in well-run classrooms share certain characteristics:

• Expectations are clear to everyone and may be posted in the classroom.
• The standards of behavior are appropriate to the developmental levels of the students and are consistent with the cultural norms of students in the class.
• Expectations are consistently applied—no favoritism.
• Teachers are aware of what is going on; they have "eyes in the backs of their heads." Teachers sometimes influence students' behavior—for example, by calling on a student to redirect the student's attention or by moving nearer to a student.

• Teachers refrain from losing their temper, banging books on a desk, or otherwise demonstrating that they have lost their composure. Students do not fear being physically or orally attacked.
• Any chastisement of conduct focuses on a student's behavior, not on the student. It is carried out so that the classroom rhythm is only minimally disrupted and the student's dignity is maintained.
• Teachers encourage students to monitor their own behavior.

Demonstration

A teacher's skill in managing student behavior can only be observed in the classroom. Standards of conduct, however, must frequently be inferred, because in a smoothly running classroom an observer may not witness explicit attention to those standards. Rather, student behavior indicates that a teacher has established standards at the beginning of the year and has maintained them consistently. Although most teachers can articulate their approach to standards of conduct, implementation is critical. In a well-managed classroom, students themselves will be able to explain the agreed-upon standards of conduct. (See Figure 4.10.)

COMPONENT 2E: ORGANIZING PHYSICAL SPACE

Rationale and Explanation

Use of physical space is important in a total learning environment; the physical surroundings can have a material effect on interactions or the structure of activities. Indeed, one important reason that teachers like to participate in

FIGURE 4.10

DOMAIN 2: THE CLASSROOM ENVIRONMENT
Component 2d: Managing Student Behavior
Elements: Expectations • Monitoring of student behavior • Response to student misbehavior

	LEVEL OF PERFORMANCE			
ELEMENT	UNSATISFACTORY	BASIC	PROFICIENT	DISTINGUISHED
Expectations	No standards of conduct appear to have been established, or students are confused as to what the standards are.	Standards of conduct appear to have been established, and most students seem to understand them.	Standards of conduct are clear to all students.	Standards of conduct are clear to all students and appear to have been developed with student participation.
Monitoring of student behavior	Student behavior is not monitored, and teacher is unaware of what the students are doing.	Teacher is generally aware of student behavior but may miss the activities of some students.	Teacher is alert to student behavior at all times.	Monitoring by teacher is subtle and preventive. Students monitor their own and their peers' behavior, correcting one another respectfully.
Response to student misbehavior	Teacher does not respond to misbehavior, or the response is inconsistent, is overly repressive, or does not respect the student's dignity.	Teacher attempts to respond to student misbehavior but with uneven results, or there are no major infractions of the rules.	Teacher response to misbehavior is appropriate and successful and respects the student's dignity, or student behavior is generally appropriate.	Teacher response to misbehavior is highly effective and sensitive to students' individual needs, or student behavior is entirely appropriate.

meetings in one another's classrooms is so they can find good ideas they might be able to incorporate into their own setting.

Of course, the use of the physical environment will vary depending on context. Elementary teachers establish "reading corners" and separate spaces for noisy and quiet activities, and teachers at all levels arrange furniture to accommodate discus-

sion sessions or group projects. Organization of space sends signals to students about how teachers view learning: "centers" for exploration, desks facing forward for a presentation, chairs in a circle for a group discussion, or a science lab organized for effective work.

One element of a physical environment concerns safety and accessibility to learning. A classroom must be safe—no dangling cords or obstructed exits. Chemicals must be stored in a safe place, and when they are used, they must be handled with care. The traffic flow must be efficient, so that, for example, all students can get to the pencil sharpener. Students, including those with special needs, must have accessibility to the board, the teacher, and other learning resources. This may mean that a student with impaired vision or hearing will sit near the front of the room, or a student with a learning disability will be seated so that an accompanying aide can be of assistance without calling undue attention to the student's condition. Such accommodations by the teacher signal respect for the learning needs of all students and a willingness to make necessary adjustments to ensure success.

A second element involves the arrangement of furniture. In today's classrooms, few desks are bolted to the floor, although many teachers still choose to arrange the chairs or desks in rows. For a presentation to the entire class by the teacher, by a visiting expert, or by other students, that may be the best arrangement. But for other types of student activity, such an arrangement may not be optimal. For group work, tables or desks arranged in blocks may be preferable. And if students are expected to discuss ideas, they need to be able to see one another. For a class discussion, desks or chairs arranged in a circle or two parallel horseshoes may be the best arrangement.

Many classrooms are equipped with computers for student use. The placement of these, and student accessibility to them, can have a significant impact on the success of the physical space for learning. It is desirable that they be placed out of the main traffic flow so students can get to them without disrupting other students at work.

A final element is teachers' use of physical resources. Teaching aids such as boards, flip charts, overhead projectors, computers and projection devices, and VCRs may be skillfully or poorly used. When used well, they enhance learning and contribute to effective instruction. When used poorly, they detract from learning. Machines that don't work mean that transparencies are out of focus or can't be read, Internet access is disrupted, or videos can't be viewed.

When a classroom is a true community of learners, students themselves become involved in the physical environment and take initiative in making it effective. They may, for example, plan a display of work, move furniture to facilitate a group project, or shift supplies to improve traffic flow. They may lower the shades to block the sun from a classmate's eyes or shut the door to keep out hall noise. It is their room, and they make it work. Naturally, such student involvement can only occur when the teacher cultivates and encourages student participation in establishing the environment.

Some teachers, such as those who move from room to room, have only limited control over the physical environment in which they teach. When teachers teach from a cart, or when they share space with another teacher, they can influence the physical environment far less than teachers who have their own rooms. All teachers must be responsible for a safe environment, but they cannot be held accountable for those aspects of teaching that they cannot control.

Demonstration

Teachers' use of the physical environment can be observed or illustrated on a sketch of the classroom. Teachers may be able to explain how they enhance the physical environment and use it as a resource for learning, but implementation is essential. (See Figure 4.11.)

FIGURE 4.11

DOMAIN 2: THE CLASSROOM ENVIRONMENT
Component 2e: Organizing Physical Space

Elements: Safety and accessibility • Arrangement of furniture and use of physical resources

ELEMENT	LEVEL OF PERFORMANCE			
	UNSATISFACTORY	BASIC	PROFICIENT	DISTINGUISHED
Safety and accessibility	The classroom is unsafe, or learning is not accessible to some students.	The classroom is safe, and at least essential learning is accessible to most students.	The classroom is safe, and learning is equally accessible to all students.	The classroom is safe, and students themselves ensure that all learning is equally accessible to all students.
Arrangement of furniture and use of physical resources	The furniture arrangement hinders the learning activities, or the teacher makes poor use of physical resources.	Teacher uses physical resources adequately. The furniture may be adjusted for a lesson, but with limited effectiveness.	Teacher uses physical resources skillfully, and the furniture arrangement is a resource for learning activities.	Both teacher and students use physical resources easily and skillfully, and students adjust the furniture to advance their learning.

DOMAIN 3: INSTRUCTION

Domain 3 is the heart of the framework for teaching; it describes, after all, the critical interactive work that teachers undertake when they bring complex content to life for their students. And the heart of Domain 3 is engaging students in learning; all the other aspects of the framework serve the purpose of engagement, because it is engagement that ensures learning.

However, the other components of Domain 3 play an important supporting role in promoting learning. Teachers must provide clear directions and explanations; their work is enhanced through the skillful use of questioning and discussion and through the integration of assessment strategies into instruction. Furthermore, only when teachers demonstrate flexibility and responsiveness can they maximize opportunities for learning by their students. So although engagement in learning is the centerpiece of Domain 3, the other components play an important role in making that engagement possible.

COMPONENT 3A: COMMUNICATING WITH STUDENTS

Rationale and Explanation

For students to become engaged in learning, they must receive clear directions and explanations. Because teachers communicate with students largely through language, that language must be audible and legible. When teachers speak, students must be able to hear and understand them. When teachers distribute written directions, students must be able to read and understand them. When teachers offer an explanation, it should aid in learning. In addition, a teacher's use of vivid and expressive language can enhance a learning experience.

Clear and accurate communication has several elements. The first is expectations for learning. A fundamental assumption of the framework for teaching is that teaching is purposeful; that purpose should be clear to students. The teacher should convey what the students will be learning, why it is important, and what the students will be doing to achieve the goals. Students should be able to explain to a visitor, if asked, what the topic for a lesson is and where it fits in the larger context of what they are learning.

This aspect of teaching has long been recognized. In fact, in the 1970s, teachers were evaluated on whether they had written the day's learning objectives on the board. Most educators now take a more flexible view; there are many techniques that teachers can use to convey their purposes to students, but they should do so in one way or another. Part of running a businesslike classroom is that everyone involved, students and teacher alike, know they are engaged in important work. This is not to say that the atmosphere is somber, or that there is no place for laughter or playfulness; but even when lighthearted, the atmosphere must be purposeful.

Of course, there are situations in which a teacher might not reveal the exact purpose of an activity at the outset of a lesson. For example, if the teacher wants to engage students in discovering a scientific principle, announcing it at the beginning would spoil the activity. However, students should not be kept in the dark for long; by the end of the session, they should know clearly why they were asked to do a certain task and what concept it has illuminated.

Another element of communication with students is clarity of directions and procedures. When students work independently or in small groups, the information they receive must be clear. Otherwise, valuable time is lost because they are confused or are engaged in the wrong activity. Clear directions may be oral, written, or a combination of the two. When students are determining their own procedures or activities—for example, in an art project—a teacher should make clear any limits to their choices. Some teachers use the board or a projection device to good effect in this regard. When the directions are clearly written and displayed, students, when not sure, can refer to them without requiring the teacher's attention.

Next, all teachers face the challenge of helping students understand new content. The new content may consist of concepts (for example, buoyancy and density, or place value), skills (for example, a basketball layup), or relationships (for example, the role of the Renaissance in the development of art in Europe). How this content is presented to students has enormous bearing on their understanding. Many teachers are remembered years later for skill in this area—the clarity of their explanations, their use of analogies to convey a concept, their stories to illustrate a point.

Skilled teachers select examples and metaphors that illuminate the new ideas or skills, connecting new content to students' backgrounds, knowledge, and interests and to a school's culture. For example, in explaining the Trojan horse, a teacher may liken it to a possible (or actual) infiltration of a high school's football team by the opposition. Presentation of content can take the form of oral description, visual representation (through some type of graphic organizer), or teacher-led discussion. Furthermore, the language and concepts used must be appropriate to the age and backgrounds of the students, and the words used should reflect vocabulary suitable to the specific language of a discipline.

Many students model their use of language on that of their teachers; they acquire new words and rich nuances from how their teachers use the language. Consequently, teachers' language should reflect correct usage and contain expressive vocabulary. And teachers have many informal opportunities to offer little vocabulary lessons while they are teaching a concept; such incidental learning may make a large difference to students, particularly to those who are not exposed to rich language at home or whose first language is not English.

Not all oral communication needs to be expressed formally at all times; more informal speech is sometimes appropriate. Some students, in their home environments, communicate with family and friends in a version of English that, while rich and expressive, does not represent standard (or formal) usage. This situation may present teachers with a dilemma. On the one hand, they do not want to convey disrespect for the language of students' families and neighborhoods, which means that they don't want to criticize such language simply as a matter of course. On the other hand, academic and economic success depends on students' learning to communicate, and communicate well, using standard English. Furthermore, in learning to read, students from backgrounds in which standard English is not the norm are confronted with a difficult challenge; they may be trying to learn to read in what is, for them, the equivalent of a second language.

Many teachers address this situation by making a clear distinction between "home" language and "school" language. They let students know, often informally, that their home language is a complete language, with its own vocabulary and syntax. That is, it is worthy of respect. However, it is also important for students to learn to speak and understand "school" English, which they also hear in most television broadcasts. Such students become, in effect, bilingual in English, and they are able to communicate effectively in either environment as appropriate.

Demonstration

Teachers demonstrate the clarity and accuracy of their communication primarily through classroom performance. The evidence is not, of course, whether an explanation, for example, is clear to an observer; it must be clear to the students. Watching the students' reactions provides the best indication of whether that goal has been achieved. (See Figure 4.12.)

COMPONENT 3B: USING QUESTIONING AND DISCUSSION TECHNIQUES

Rationale and Explanation

A teacher's skill in questioning and in leading discussions makes a powerful contribution to student learning and is valuable for many instructional purposes: exploring new concepts, eliciting evidence of student understanding, and promoting deeper student engagement.

Before teachers have acquired skill in questioning and discussion, they tend to pose primarily rapid-fire, short-answer, low-level questions to their students, using the questions as a vehicle for students to demonstrate their knowledge. Such questioning is better labeled "recitation" than "discussion," because the questions are not true questions but rather form a quiz in which teachers elicit from students their knowledge on a particular topic, or perhaps evidence that they have completed reading that was assigned for homework.

Poor questions may be those that are boring, comprehensible to only a few students, or narrow—the teacher has a single answer in mind even when other options are possible. Good questions, on the other hand, tend to be divergent rather than convergent, framed in such a way that they invite students to formulate hypotheses, make connections, or challenge previously held views. High-quality questions, in other words, promote thinking by students, encouraging them to make connections among previously believed, unrelated concepts or events and to arrive at new understandings of complex material. Even when a question has a limited number of correct responses—for example, a question for 1st graders as to the different coins they could use to make 23 cents—the question, being nonformulaic, is likely to promote thinking by students.

When teachers use questions skillfully, they engage their students in an exploration of content. Carefully framed questions enable students to reflect on their understanding and consider new possibilities. The questions rarely require a simple yes/no response and may have many possible correct answers. Experienced teachers allow students time to think before they must respond to a question and encourage all students to participate. Teachers often probe a student's answer, seeking clarification or elaboration through such questions as "Could you give an example of that?" or "Would you explain further what you mean?" Such interactions, in addition to encouraging deeper understanding, convey respect for students and their thinking.

Moreover, teachers make good use of questioning and discussion as an instructional skill by teaching their students how to

FIGURE 4.12

DOMAIN 3: INSTRUCTION
Component 3a: Communicating with Students

Elements: Expectations for learning • Directions and procedures • Explanations of content • Use of oral and written language

ELEMENT	LEVEL OF PERFORMANCE			
	UNSATISFACTORY	BASIC	PROFICIENT	DISTINGUISHED
Expectations for learning	Teacher's purpose in a lesson or unit is unclear to students.	Teacher attempts to explain the instructional purpose, with limited success.	Teacher's purpose for the lesson or unit is clear, including where it is situated within broader learning.	Teacher makes the purpose of the lesson or unit clear, including where it is situated within broader learning, linking that purpose to student interests.
Directions and procedures	Teacher's directions and procedures are confusing to students.	Teacher's directions and procedures are clarified after initial student confusion.	Teacher's directions and procedures are clear to students.	Teacher's directions and procedures are clear to students and anticipate possible student misunderstanding.
Explanations of content	Teacher's explanation of the content is unclear or confusing or uses inappropriate language.	Teacher's explanation of the content is uneven; some is done skillfully, but other portions are difficult to follow.	Teacher's explanation of content is appropriate and connects with students' knowledge and experience.	Teacher's explanation of content is imaginative and connects with students' knowledge and experience. Students contribute to explaining concepts to their peers.
Use of oral and written language	Teacher's spoken language is inaudible, or written language is illegible. Spoken or written language contains errors of grammar or syntax. Vocabulary may be inappropriate, vague, or used incorrectly, leaving students confused.	Teacher's spoken language is audible, and written language is legible. Both are used correctly and conform to standard English. Vocabulary is correct but limited or is not appropriate to the students' ages or backgrounds.	Teacher's spoken and written language is clear and correct and conforms to standard English. Vocabulary is appropriate to the students' ages and interests.	Teacher's spoken and written language is correct and conforms to standard English. It is also expressive, with well-chosen vocabulary that enriches the lesson. Teacher finds opportunities to extend students' vocabularies.

frame good questions. They may provide an initial experience—for example, a brief but anomalous demonstration in science, or some primary source material in history—and invite students to ask questions about what they have seen. Teachers show students how to frame questions of high cognitive challenge and how to use the questions to extend learning. A well-run discussion uses questions posed by the students. The formulation of questions requires that students engage in analytical thinking and motivates them more than questions presented by the teacher.

Experienced teachers also cultivate their skills in leading discussions. As a result, class discussions are animated, engaging all students in important questions and using the discussion format as a technique to extend knowledge. In a well-run discussion, a teacher does not hold center stage but rather encourages students to comment on one another's answers and request further elaboration. In classes accustomed to discussion, students assume considerable responsibility for the depth and breadth of the conversation.

In a well-run discussion, all students are engaged. The dialogue is not dominated by a few "star" students, and the teacher is not simply waiting for someone to provide the answer he has been looking for. Rather, *all* students are drawn into the conversation; the perspectives of *all* students are sought, and *all* voices are heard. The students themselves ensure high levels of participation.

One mark of skill in leading discussions is a teacher's response when a student proposes an interesting but irrelevant tangent. Young children may innocently find something interesting and worthy of exploration. Older students, on the other hand, may do it deliberately to manipulate a situation: "Let's see how long we can get him talking about the '70s today!" Accomplished

teachers are able to pull the group back to the topic, while conveying respect for the students and their interests. Others are able to incorporate the students' ideas into the discussion, thereby enhancing those students' commitment to the topic at hand.

In a classroom where a teacher uses questions and discussions to enhance learning, the teacher may pose a single, well-crafted question and then wait for a thoughtful response. Follow-up questions like "Does anyone see another possibility?" or "Who would like to comment on Jerry's idea?" may provide a focus for an entire class period. The teacher gradually moves from the center to the side of the discussion and encourages students to maintain the momentum. At times the teacher may find it necessary to rephrase the question to refocus group attention on the topic. But in the hands of a skilled teacher, discussion becomes a vehicle for deep exploration of content.

Naturally, some disciplines present more opportunities than do others for teachers to use questioning and discussion techniques. Discussions in literature and history can be rich, with students hearing different perspectives on shared information. Although used less frequently in mathematics and science, discussion can nevertheless greatly enliven student engagement with important concepts. Students may be asked how they could test a theory in science or a procedure in mathematics—how would they proceed? The ensuing discussion serves to both deepen student understanding and to reveal, where appropriate, student misconceptions.

Demonstration

Teachers demonstrate their skill in questioning and discussion techniques almost exclusively in classroom observation. The initial questions used to frame a discussion should be planned in advance, however, and will be part of planning documents. (See Figure 4.13.)

COMPONENT 3C: ENGAGING STUDENTS IN LEARNING

Rationale and Explanation

If one component of the framework for teaching can claim to be the most important, it is student engagement. Engaging students in learning is the raison d'être of schools; it is through active engagement that students learn complex content. All the rest of the framework is in the service of student engagement, from planning and preparation, to establishing a supportive environment, to reflecting on classroom events. Lack of engagement is generally easy to spot, manifesting itself when students doodle on their notebooks, pass notes, or gaze out the window. Occasionally, lack of engagement takes more aggressive forms, creating serious discipline problems. Of

---

FIGURE 4.13

DOMAIN 3: INSTRUCTION
Component 3b: Using Questioning and Discussion Techniques
Elements: Quality of questions • Discussion techniques • Student participation

ELEMENT	LEVEL OF PERFORMANCE			
	UNSATISFACTORY	BASIC	PROFICIENT	DISTINGUISHED
Quality of questions	Teacher's questions are virtually all of poor quality, with low cognitive challenge and single correct responses, and they are asked in rapid succession.	Teacher's questions are a combination of low and high quality, posed in rapid succession. Only some invite a thoughtful response.	Most of the teacher's questions are of high quality. Adequate time is provided for students to respond.	Teacher's questions are of uniformly high quality, with adequate time for students to respond. Students formulate many questions.
Discussion techniques	Interaction between teacher and students is predominantly recitation style, with the teacher mediating all questions and answers.	Teacher makes some attempt to engage students in genuine discussion rather than recitation, with uneven results.	Teacher creates a genuine discussion among students, stepping aside when appropriate.	Students assume considerable responsibility for the success of the discussion, initiating topics and making unsolicited contributions.
Student participation	A few students dominate the discussion.	Teacher attempts to engage all students in the discussion, but with only limited success.	Teacher successfully engages all students in the discussion.	Students themselves ensure that all voices are heard in the discussion.

course, some students do their best thinking while gazing out the window, and others can mimic attentive listening to a teacher while actually thinking about other things. Therefore, student engagement is not always easily identified; sophisticated observation is essential.

The quality of student engagement is the result of careful planning of learning experiences (Component 1e.) When a lesson is carefully designed and the instructional methods and student activities are structured to maximize student learning, the result is evident in the classroom. All students are mentally involved in understanding important content; they are actively participating and are making genuine contributions to the effort.

Student engagement is not the same as "busy" or "time on task," concepts that refer to student involvement in instructional activities. Students may be completing a worksheet (rather than talking or passing notes) and therefore be "on task," even if the worksheet does not engage them in significant learning. Perhaps the worksheet requires skills and knowledge that they do not yet have, or it represents concepts that, because the students learned them long ago, constitute no challenge. Mere activity, then, is inadequate for engagement. Nor is simple participation sufficient. The activity should represent new learning. What is required for student engagement is *intellectual involvement* with the content or active construction of understanding.

Physical materials may enhance student engagement in learning. Many elementary-level mathematics concepts, such as place value, are best explained using and explored through physical representations. When students use physical materials, they are more likely to be actively involved than if they don't use them. But physical materials are no guarantee of engagement—students can mess around unproductively

with manipulatives, learning nothing. What is required is *mental engagement,* which may or may not involve physical activity. Hands-on activity is not enough; it must also be "minds on." School, in other words, is not a spectator sport. Successful instruction requires the active and invested participation of all parties.

Students can be engaged in multiple ways, reflecting the complex nature of mental engagement. For example, a teacher might be introducing the concept of symbolism in literature or explaining the difference between active and passive solar energy. The method for presenting information may be reading, followed by small-group discussion; or a teacher-led mini-presentation, followed by discussion or an individual activity. If the instructional purposes relate to thinking and reasoning skills, such as the collection and analysis of data, the preferred approach may be independent student investigations, conducted either individually or in small groups. Even if the instructional outcomes relate to information that must eventually be learned by rote—for example, multiplication facts—the activities can still engage students intellectually, such as searching for patterns in the numbers or devising techniques to enhance memorization.

Student engagement consists of several distinct, though related, elements, as described in the following paragraphs.

Activities and assignments. When students are actively engaged in learning, their activities and assignments (including homework) challenge them to think broadly and deeply, to solve a problem, or to otherwise engage in nonroutine thinking. There is nothing mechanical about what students are asked to do; the cognitive challenge, in other words, is appropriately high.

An important technique for determining the level of student engagement in the activities and assignments in a class is to examine not only the directions for the activities and assignments themselves, but the quality of student work in response to the directions. When students are not engaged, they will "blow it off," whereas when they are engaged in the task, their work, even when incorrect, reflects serious thinking.

Grouping of students. Students may be grouped in many different ways to enhance their level of engagement: in a single, large group, led by either the teacher or another student; in small groups, either working on their own or in an instructional activity with a teacher; or independently. In small groups, the students' ability level and skill in an area can be homogeneous or heterogeneous. Grouping can be in pairs, in triads, or in other configurations that the students or teachers establish.

A teacher's decisions about student grouping are based on a number of considerations. Most important, the type of instructional group should reflect what a teacher is trying to accomplish and should serve that purpose. In some cases, homogeneous groups working on their own will be the most effective; at other times a large-group presentation, followed by heterogeneous groups, may be appropriate.

It should be noted that teachers typically vary the instructional groupings within a single lesson, and they most assuredly vary them from one day to the next. Small-group work, although an effective strategy for many purposes, would become tedious if used exclusively.

Instructional materials and resources. Instructional materials can include any items that help students engage with content: textbooks, readings, lab equipment, maps, charts, the Internet, films, videos, and math manipulatives, for example. Resources might include an outside visitor or material from a local museum. Instructional materials and resources are not, in themselves, engaging or unengaging; rather, it is a teacher's and students' use of the materials that is the determinant. It is essential that they be suitable for the students and applicable to the instructional outcomes. For instance, students can use laboratory materials to formulate and test hypotheses about a phenomenon, or a teacher can use them to present an experiment, with students as simply observers.

Structure and pacing. A well-designed lesson has a defined structure, and students know where they are in that structure. Some lessons have a recognizable beginning, middle, and end, with a clear introduction and closure. Others consist more of a working session—for example, in an art studio. In either case, there is a structure to what happens, and that structure has been created through the teacher's design. Pacing is related to structure. In classrooms characterized by student engagement, pacing is appropriate to the students and to the content, and suitable opportunities for closure are provided. Students do not feel rushed in their work, nor does time drag while some students are completing their work.

Demonstration

Teachers demonstrate their skill in engaging students in learning through their conduct of lessons, which may be observed live or via videotape. In addition, the degree of student engagement is revealed through the analysis of student work in response to a well-designed assignment. (See Figure 4.14.)

FIGURE 4.14

DOMAIN 3: INSTRUCTION
Component 3c: Engaging Students in Learning

Elements: Activities and assignments • Grouping of students • Instructional materials and resources • Structure and pacing

ELEMENT	LEVEL OF PERFORMANCE			
	UNSATISFACTORY	BASIC	PROFICIENT	DISTINGUISHED
Activities and assignments	Activities and assignments are inappropriate for students' age or background. Students are not mentally engaged in them.	Activities and assignments are appropriate to some students and engage them mentally, but others are not engaged.	Most activities and assignments are appropriate to students, and almost all students are cognitively engaged in exploring content.	All students are cognitively engaged in the activities and assignments in their exploration of content. Students initiate or adapt activities and projects to enhance their understanding.
Grouping of students	Instructional groups are inappropriate to the students or to the instructional outcomes.	Instructional groups are only partially appropriate to the students or only moderately successful in advancing the instructional outcomes of the lesson.	Instructional groups are productive and fully appropriate to the students or to the instructional purposes of the lesson.	Instructional groups are productive and fully appropriate to the students or to the instructional purposes of the lesson. Students take the initiative to influence the formation or adjustment of instructional groups.
Instructional materials and resources	Instructional materials and resources are unsuitable to the instructional purposes or do not engage students mentally.	Instructional materials and resources are only partially suitable to the instructional purposes, or students are only partially mentally engaged with them.	Instructional materials and resources are suitable to the instructional purposes and engage students mentally.	Instructional materials and resources are suitable to the instructional purposes and engage students mentally. Students initiate the choice, adaptation, or creation of materials to enhance their learning.
Structure and pacing	The lesson has no clearly defined structure, or the pace of the lesson is too slow or rushed, or both.	The lesson has a recognizable structure, although it is not uniformly maintained throughout the lesson. Pacing of the lesson is inconsistent.	The lesson has a clearly defined structure around which the activities are organized. Pacing of the lesson is generally appropriate.	The lesson's structure is highly coherent, allowing for reflection and closure. Pacing of the lesson is appropriate for all students.

COMPONENT 3D: USING ASSESSMENT IN INSTRUCTION

Rationale and Explanation

Assessment has, for many years, played a critical role in teaching. Tests and other forms of assessment have been used to determine the extent to which students have mastered important content; when used in a high-stakes manner, such assessments can certify individuals for promotion to a higher grade, for passing a course, or for admission to college. And collectively, student assessment is used for both program improvement and accountability of institutions. That is, assessment has come to signal the *end* of instruction, the time at which results are known.

But more recently, educators have come to recognize that assessment can play an even larger role in teaching than was previously recognized. Rather than signaling the *end* of instruction, it has become incorporated as an integral *part of* instruction. Teachers have found that assessment is a highly valuable tool in their instructional repertoire; through a skillful use of formative assessment, teachers promote learning.

As a lesson progresses, teachers engage in continuous monitoring. They monitor everything going on in the class: student engagement in the activities, the appropriateness of the materials and groupings, and the extent to which students are actually learning what the teacher intended. Of these, the last is, in the end, the most important; that is, the learning activities, the materials, and the student groups are means the teacher has designed to effect student learning. Whether or not the students are, in fact, learning is essential information for teachers and permits them to make midcourse corrections. And as students assume increasing responsibility for their own learning, they are able to monitor their own progress and take corrective action.

Teacher monitoring, feedback to students, and student self-regulation can operate effectively only within an environment of clear outcomes for learning. For example, student writing will improve if the standards for good writing have been clearly explained and strengthened by actual samples of student work. Or, if it is problem solving that a teacher is trying to encourage, clear descriptions of what that means (a systematic strategy, for example) will help students meet the standards. Clear criteria, then, are a critical component of a teacher's strategy for promoting student learning.

As part of their lesson design, teachers will have prepared specific techniques (questions, activities, and the like) to elicit from students evidence of their learning so that corrective action can be taken when needed. These devices are planned so that they provide diagnostic information; that is, a student's wrong answer to a question may indicate merely that the student doesn't "get it." That is important information, but not very useful information. It is far better if the teacher can determine, from the student's wrong answer, information about what the student does not understand and therefore how the situation can be remedied. Therefore, careful attention to student work and student responses in class, particularly if the questions and prompts have been specifically designed to supply diagnostic information, provides valuable information to a teacher as to how to proceed. Experienced teachers, then, carefully watch and listen to students, who reveal their level of understanding through the questions they ask, the responses they give, their approaches to projects and assignments, and the work they produce.

Providing feedback to students is an important aspect of using assessment as part of instruction. In reviewing feedback, such as comments on a piece of writing or an explanation of how the process used in a math problem was misguided, students may advance their understanding. The process of feedback individualizes instruction. Even when instructional goals and learning activities are common to an entire class, the experience of individual students is distinct; feedback ensures that each student knows the extent to which her performance meets the required standards.

Teachers continuously provide feedback to students on their learning—sometimes subtly and informally, through, for example, a quizzical look as a student attempts an explanation or nods of encouragement as a student works through a math problem. Other forms of feedback are more formal and systematic, such as comments on student papers or individual conferences with students. It is essential that teachers provide feedback equitably, that *all* students receive feedback on their work. It is not equitable for a few star pupils to receive detailed and constructive suggestions on their papers, while others receive only negative feedback or little attention to their work.

But teachers are not the only source of feedback to students. Feedback may also be provided through the following means:

- Instructional activities—for example, when students discover from a science experiment that their understanding was incorrect because the experiment does not yield the expected result.
- Materials—for example, the answers to math problems in the back of a textbook.
- Problems—for example, when a solution to a math problem does not "check out."
- Computer programs—for example, those designed to generate a varied sequence of steps or actions depending on a student's responses.
- Other students—for example, peer review of a writing assignment.

To be effective, feedback should be accurate, constructive, substantive, specific, and timely. Global comments such as "very good" do not qualify as feedback, nor do comments to an entire class about the weaknesses of a few students. Feedback must be informational, drawing students' attention to errors they can correct, and with sufficient distance between current and desired performance such that students have a reasonable expectation of being able to achieve the goal. It must also be timely; returning papers three weeks after students handed them in—regardless of the quality of the comments—is not timely and will not be valuable to students.

Peer feedback may be helpful if students have been taught how to provide suggestions in a supportive manner. When used well, peer feedback is extremely powerful; students respect the opinions of their peers. But if students have not learned the skills of providing feedback, it may not be accurate or supportive; feedback that undercuts a student's sense of value does not promote learning.

Regardless of the quality of feedback, it is of little value if students do not use it in their learning. And the degree to which students use feedback well is highly related to their level of confidence. Many teachers have experienced the phenomenon of high-performing students who are surprised at poor performance on a test—for example, reading the teacher's comments thoroughly and vowing that "*that* won't happen again!"

Other students, in contrast, who might have less experience with school success, respond differently; when they have a paper returned with lots of corrections, they take a quick look, crumple it up, and throw it in the trash can. If students don't even read a teacher's comments, they can't learn from them.

Lastly, students take responsibility for their learning when they engage in self-assessment against the criteria for success and take steps to narrow the gap. This kind of self-assessment can take many forms, depending on the subject; it includes sample tests and quizzes, problem sets that allow students to look up the answers, and soliciting feedback on their work.

Demonstration

A teacher's use of assessment in instruction is sometimes evident during a classroom observation, depending on the activities planned for a lesson. Moreover, in discussing a lesson, teachers will be able to explain the point at which they knew that a student was confused, and how they responded. Feedback may be demonstrated through samples of student work with teacher or peer comments. The timeliness of feedback and student use of feedback to engage in further learning can also be revealed through student responses to a questionnaire, particularly at the secondary level. (See Figure 4.15.)

COMPONENT 3E: DEMONSTRATING FLEXIBILITY AND RESPONSIVENESS

Rationale and Explanation

Teachers make literally hundreds of decisions daily. Some decisions are small and trivial; most are not. The most difficult decisions have to do with adjusting a lesson plan in midstream, when it is apparent that such adjustments will improve students' experience. For example, an activity may be confusing to students or require understanding they have not yet acquired. Alternatively, a planned activity may be suitable for only some students in a class, requiring adjustments for others.

Teachers can demonstrate flexibility and responsiveness in three types of situations. One is an instructional activity that is not working. If students are not familiar with a phenomenon on which a teacher is basing an entire explanation, the teacher may need to back up and offer an explanation. Alternatively, if an activity is not appropriate for students, the teacher may choose to abandon the activity or to modify it significantly. Sometimes such adjustments involve a major change. At other times the shift is more modest. Occasionally a change in pace is all that is required; students are lethargic when a pace is too slow, but they become reengaged when the pace picks up. Alternatively, a fast-paced lesson may leave some students perplexed; in those situations, the teacher must return to the point of confusion and revisit some aspect of the lesson.

The second situation that happens occasionally is a spontaneous event that provides an opportunity for valuable learning. For example, a 2nd grader might arrive at school with a caterpillar that immediately captures the interest of the entire class. Events at the secondary level, such as an athletic contest or a schoolwide conflict, can divert the attention of the entire school. Handling such events is a challenge every teacher faces, perhaps offering a "teachable moment" and a springboard for an important and memorable intellectual experience. Teachers demonstrate flexibility when they seize upon a major event and adapt their lesson to it, fulfilling their instructional

FIGURE 4.15

DOMAIN 3: INSTRUCTION
Component 3d: Using Assessment in Instruction

Elements: Assessment criteria • Monitoring of student learning • Feedback to students • Student self-assessment and monitoring of progress

ELEMENT	LEVEL OF PERFORMANCE			
	UNSATISFACTORY	BASIC	PROFICIENT	DISTINGUISHED
Assessment criteria	Students are not aware of the criteria and performance standards by which their work will be evaluated.	Students know some of the criteria and performance standards by which their work will be evaluated.	Students are fully aware of the criteria and performance standards by which their work will be evaluated.	Students are fully aware of the criteria and performance standards by which their work will be evaluated and have contributed to the development of the criteria.
Monitoring of student learning	Teacher does not monitor student learning in the curriculum.	Teacher monitors the progress of the class as a whole but elicits no diagnostic information.	Teacher monitors the progress of groups of students in the curriculum, making limited use of diagnostic prompts to elicit information.	Teacher actively and systematically elicits diagnostic information from individual students regarding their understanding and monitors the progress of individual students.
Feedback to students	Teacher's feedback to students is of poor quality and not provided in a timely manner.	Teacher's feedback to students is uneven, and its timeliness is inconsistent.	Teacher's feedback to students is timely and of consistently high quality.	Teacher's feedback to students is timely and of consistently high quality, and students make use of the feedback in their learning.
Student self-assessment and monitoring of progress	Students do not engage in self-assessment or monitoring of progress.	Students occasionally assess the quality of their own work against the assessment criteria and performance standards.	Students frequently assess and monitor the quality of their own work against the assessment criteria and performance standards.	Students not only frequently assess and monitor the quality of their own work against the assessment criteria and performance standards but also make active use of that information in their learning.

goals but in a manner that is different from what they had originally planned. However, sometimes what appeared to be a valuable teachable moment cannot be related to the subject at hand, and, after pausing long enough to acknowledge the outside event, the teacher returns to the original plan.

The third manifestation of flexibility and responsiveness relates to a teacher's sense of efficacy and commitment to the learning of all students. When some students experience difficulty in learning, a teacher who is responsive and flexible persists in the search for alternative approaches, not blaming the students, the home environment, or the larger culture for the deficiency. It is possible that the optimal approach for a student will be to call on resources outside the classroom, but most teachers initially try other approaches in their own class.

Of course, when a lesson is very well planned, there may be no need for changes during the course of the lesson itself. Shifting the approach in midstream is not always necessary; in fact, with experience comes skill in accurately predicting how a lesson will go and being prepared for different possible scenarios. But even the most skilled and best-prepared teachers will on occasion find either that a lesson is not going as they would like or that a teachable moment has presented itself. They are ready for such situations.

In general, flexibility and responsiveness are the mark of experience. Novice teachers rarely have the instructional repertoire or the confidence to abandon a lesson plan in midstream and move in a new direction. Such a response requires both courage and confidence, which come with experience. Furthermore, it is only when teachers develop expertise and have incorporated large portions of their practice into a routine that they are able to attend to the multiple dimensions of

teaching—and to even recognize that an adjustment is needed. Such flexibility is, indeed, a high-level skill.

Teachers demonstrate lack of flexibility and responsiveness when they stick to a plan even when the plan is clearly not working, when they brush aside a student's comment or question, or when they quickly dismiss the caterpillar (from the earlier example) in the interests of returning to "real work." Or a teacher may stay with an approach even when it is clearly inappropriate for some students. Such decisions are, indeed, tricky. Sometimes the instructional goals of the day simply cannot accommodate the caterpillar, or the students are not really that interested. But when the conditions are right, flexibility can enrich students' experience. Not every episode in a classroom represents a spontaneous opportunity for learning. But many do, and with experience, teachers become more skilled at exploiting them while still achieving their instructional purposes.

Every teacher should, over time, acquire the skills of adjusting a lesson when it becomes necessary. Rigid adherence to a plan in the face of lack of student understanding is stubbornness; the teacher's first obligation is to ensure the learning of all students. Ensuring learning requires paying close attention to how things are going and being prepared to act accordingly. This applies also when it is just one student, or a few students, who are struggling; an experienced and conscientious teacher will find ways to ensure that *all* students learn.

Demonstration

Flexibility and responsiveness can be observed when they occur in a classroom. In addition, a teacher may describe such an event when discussing a lesson after the event. Of course, in many lessons, no such opportunities arise. Their absence is not necessarily a sign of rigidity; rather, it may simply reflect either successful planning or a lack of opportunity. (See Figure 4.16.)

FIGURE 4.16

DOMAIN 3: INSTRUCTION
Component 3e: Demonstrating Flexibility and Responsiveness
Elements: Lesson adjustment • Response to students • Persistence

ELEMENT	LEVEL OF PERFORMANCE			
	UNSATISFACTORY	BASIC	PROFICIENT	DISTINGUISHED
Lesson adjustment	Teacher adheres rigidly to an instructional plan, even when a change is clearly needed.	Teacher attempts to adjust a lesson when needed, with only partially successful results.	Teacher makes a minor adjustment to a lesson, and the adjustment occurs smoothly.	Teacher successfully makes a major adjustment to a lesson when needed.
Response to students	Teacher ignores or brushes aside students' questions or interests.	Teacher attempts to accommodate students' questions or interests, although the pacing of the lesson is disrupted.	Teacher successfully accommodates students' questions or interests.	Teacher seizes a major opportunity to enhance learning, building on student interests or a spontaneous event.
Persistence	When a student has difficulty learning, the teacher either gives up or blames the student or the student's home environment.	Teacher accepts responsibility for the success of all students but has only a limited repertoire of instructional strategies to draw on.	Teacher persists in seeking approaches for students who have difficulty learning, drawing on a broad repertoire of strategies.	Teacher persists in seeking effective approaches for students who need help, using an extensive repertoire of strategies and soliciting additional resources from the school.

DOMAIN 4: PROFESSIONAL RESPONSIBILITIES

Domain 4, together with Domain 1 (Planning and Preparation) represents "behind the scenes" work associated with teaching. Through their skill in Domain 4, teachers demonstrate their commitment to high ethical and professional standards and seek to improve their practice. The components of Domain 4 encompass the range of teacher professionalism.

COMPONENT 4A: REFLECTING ON TEACHING

Rationale and Explanation

Educators, as well as researchers, recognize that the ability to reflect on teaching is the mark of a true professional. It is through critical reflection that teachers are able to assess the effectiveness of their work and take steps to improve it. By trying to understand the consequences of their actions and by contemplating alternative approaches, teachers expand their repertoire of practice. The importance of reflection on practice is governed by the belief that teaching, given its complexity, can never be perfect. That is, no matter how good a lesson was, it can always be improved. This is not to suggest that the teaching was of poor quality and must be "fixed"; rather, it is because teaching is so *hard* that some aspect of it can always be improved.

Reflecting on teaching includes the thinking that follows any instructional event. During that follow-up thinking, teachers consider if their goals were met and if a lesson "worked." Awareness of the engagement of students—in both quantity and

quality—helps teachers know to what extent the approach used was appropriate or if an alternative approach would have been more effective. Of course, it often takes a few days for students to demonstrate their learning; therefore teachers frequently don't know whether a lesson was successful for several days. But by considering each of the elements of a lesson, teachers can decide where to focus their efforts in revising their strategies.

Reflection on practice is a natural activity by all professionals. They know that in the course of their day they have made hundreds of decisions; they wonder whether any of them, if made differently, could have yielded better results. Some teachers use their commuting time to and from school to think through their lessons, to "replay the tape" of the day, and to identify points at which they could have taken a class in a different direction.

However, although reflection on practice is a natural activity for all professionals, doing it *well* is a learned skill. Novices tend to make very global judgments, reporting that a lesson was "fine" if the students were busy throughout the lesson and if they themselves survived the day. Alternatively, a new teacher might say to a mentor that the lesson was "terrible" or that it "bombed," with no analysis of what about it was terrible. With no deeper thinking, the next lesson might be "terrible" for the same reasons, because the teacher does not know what those reasons were.

With experience, teachers become more discerning and can evaluate both their successes and their errors. Accuracy in these judgments helps teachers refine their approach the next time, improving their practice. This contribution to ongoing improvement is the true benefit of reflection, enabling teachers to focus on those aspects of their teaching that can be strengthened.

Mentors and coaches play a critical role with new teachers in acquiring the skill of reflection on practice. Through skilled questioning and probing, they can help those new to the profession become more accurate, more analytic, and more insightful about their practice. A structured protocol can assist with this process, so mentors and coaches have guidance as to how to organize the conversation. As a result, instead of simply responding "fine" when asked about a lesson, the teacher, after thinking about specific aspects of the lesson, can make more nuanced judgments. And in conducting these conversations, mentors and coaches frequently ask the essential question: "If you had the chance to do this again, with the same group of students, would you do it the same way, or would you do it differently? How?"

Thus, when asked whether the activity was effective, whether it helped achieve the desired goals, the teacher might respond, "Yes, it worked pretty well, but now that I think about it, the directions for the activity weren't completely clear. I think I'll improve those before I use it again." Or when asked about the instructional groups, the teacher might respond, "I don't think I'll put *those* two students together again!" That is, when designing lessons, teachers make multiple decisions involving complex trade-offs. Through supportive and deep questioning, teachers become more skilled in analyzing their own practice. Before long, this way of thinking becomes incorporated into the teacher's normal activity and becomes a habit of mind. So although the teacher is unlikely to engage in a complete analysis following every lesson, she may well run down the elements of the lesson design (activities, materials, grouping, and so on) and identify those that could have been organized differently—and better.

Skilled reflection is characterized by accuracy, specificity, and ability to use the analysis in future teaching. Novices may report that a lesson was "fine" even when it was not. Of course, the culture of the school must be such that it is safe for a teacher to acknowledge that a lesson was less than "fine." But even when such an admission is safe, the teacher may actually believe that the lesson *was* fine. To suggest that a lesson could be improved is not to imply that a teacher's work is deficient; instead, it is to engage a teacher in the work of every professional—namely, analysis and improvement.

As they become more skilled at reflection, teachers are able to cite specific examples from a lesson to support their assessment of an event, whether it was successful or not. That is, they can refer to a student's question, or an interruption, as a point at which a different response might have been better. Furthermore, expert teachers are able to suggest specific remedies and, because of their experience, are able to predict the likely consequences of incorporating them into their practice. Novice teachers, as they acquire the skill of reflection, have the opportunity to develop this skill.

In addition to making accurate judgments, teachers must use these reflections in practice. Most teachers have an opportunity to teach the same topic another year, or even the next class period. By reflecting on what went well and what could have been strengthened, teachers are able to improve their next experience with a topic. And because many of the principles they learn from reflecting on practice apply to many instructional settings, their overall teaching generally improves.

Demonstration

Teachers demonstrate their skill in reflection through professional conversation with colleagues. In some situations, a written reflection may encourage more thoughtful results. (See Figure 4.17.)

FIGURE 4.17

DOMAIN 4: PROFESSIONAL RESPONSIBILITIES
Component 4a: Reflecting on Teaching
Elements: Accuracy • Use in future teaching

ELEMENT	LEVEL OF PERFORMANCE			
	UNSATISFACTORY	BASIC	PROFICIENT	DISTINGUISHED
Accuracy	Teacher does not know whether a lesson was effective or achieved its instructional outcomes, or teacher profoundly misjudges the success of a lesson.	Teacher has a generally accurate impression of a lesson's effectiveness and the extent to which instructional outcomes were met.	Teacher makes an accurate assessment of a lesson's effectiveness and the extent to which it achieved its instructional outcomes and can cite general references to support the judgment.	Teacher makes a thoughtful and accurate assessment of a lesson's effectiveness and the extent to which it achieved its instructional outcomes, citing many specific examples from the lesson and weighing the relative strengths of each.
Use in future teaching	Teacher has no suggestions for how a lesson could be improved another time the lesson is taught.	Teacher makes general suggestions about how a lesson could be improved another time the lesson is taught.	Teacher makes a few specific suggestions of what could be tried another time the lesson is taught.	Drawing on an extensive repertoire of skills, teacher offers specific alternative actions, complete with the probable success of different courses of action.

COMPONENT 4B: MAINTAINING ACCURATE RECORDS

Rationale and Explanation

One consequence of the complexity of teaching is the need for teachers to keep accurate records of routine classroom events, of student progress, of noninstructional matters. In fact, many teachers bemoan all the "paperwork" that is an integral part of their job. However, it is clearly essential; although not an inherent part of interaction with students, such records inform those interactions and enable teachers to respond to individual needs. A mark of truly experienced and expert teachers is that they have made their record keeping a routine procedure that no longer requires much extra effort. When teachers make assignments, particularly those with important deadlines, they must keep track of which students have completed which assignments, fully or in part. Few shortcomings of teachers are more irritating to students—particularly at the secondary level—than a habit of losing or otherwise not registering student work. A well-designed system for assignments enables both teacher and students to know at all times which assignments have been completed and which are still outstanding. Students themselves can contribute to the design and implementation of such a system. They are well aware of how a good system should function, and they will have experienced, in their years as a student, many different approaches.

Increasingly, it is essential for teachers to keep track of student learning so that they know which parts of the curriculum students have learned and which they have not. Such tracking may take the form of skills checklists, records of competencies that are demonstrated, and portfolios of student work. A system for monitoring student progress must align with a teacher's approach to assessment (Component 1f). For example, if performance tasks are used to evaluate student understanding, then the records must include the level of student success on those tasks and provide the information for feedback to students (Component 3d). Similarly, records of student progress enable a teacher to provide information to families (Component 4c).

It should be noted that the records of student learning need not reflect only formal assessment strategies. Some of the most accurate records are teachers' anecdotal notes. The challenge with those is to incorporate them into a more comprehensive system, including everything that is viewed as important to both the teacher and to the school's accountability system.

Again, students are important resources in designing effective systems for recording their levels of mastery of the curriculum. Particularly when the system includes portfolios of student work, students can use the items in the portfolio to maintain ongoing evidence of their increasing skill, especially in areas of complex learning, such as writing, mathematical problem solving, or the design of scientific experiments.

Lastly, records must also be maintained on the noninstructional activities that are essential to a school's smooth operation. For example, records of which students have returned their signed permission slips for a field trip and records of which students regularly buy milk for lunch all need to be kept accurately. New teachers frequently don't appreciate the importance of accuracy in these matters, resulting in random little notes covering their desk or arriving at school on the day of a field trip only to discover that some students have not turned in their permission slips. If alternate arrangements must be made for those students, the consequence is, at the least, higher levels of stress. It can also irritate one's colleagues, who are obliged to help out at the last minute.

Some noninstructional records involve money—for example, when parents elect to purchase school pictures. In such situations, of course, it is absolutely essential that the system be effective and that the records be accurate. If they are not, teachers may be accused of carelessness or, much worse, actual embezzlement.

Teachers are also required to complete and submit certain paperwork, such as supply orders and inventories of furniture and equipment, in an accurate and timely fashion. Although some teachers resent the time that such requirements consume, they recognize that they are, in truth, the most knowledgeable individuals with regard to the equipment they have and the supplies they need. Again, efficiency of operation is the key, and well-designed systems require very little ongoing maintenance.

Many successful record-keeping methods are managed as paper-and-pencil systems. However, as more teachers become proficient in the use of databases and spreadsheets, they have discovered that electronic approaches, for at least some records, can be both more accurate and less time-consuming.

Demonstration

Teachers demonstrate their skill in maintaining accurate records through artifacts, such as a grade book, skills inventories, results of student assessments, and records of classroom noninstructional activities. (See Figure 4.18.)

COMPONENT 4C: COMMUNICATING WITH FAMILIES

Rationale and Explanation

As the African proverb reminds us, "It takes a village to raise a child." Educators have long recognized that when they can enlist the participation of students' families in the educational process, student learning is enhanced. Although parents and guardians vary enormously in how active a part they can take in their children's learning, most parents care deeply about the progress of their children and appreciate meaningful participation. The relationship between parents and teachers also depends on the age of the children; most kindergarten teachers have far greater contact with the families of their students than do high school teachers.

Communication with families involves keeping them informed about how a class is run. Just as students should never be surprised by the way their work is assessed or the rules governing such things as coming to class on time or bringing pencils, parents also need information about the teacher's approach to the class. Many strategies are useful for such communication; teachers can send written information home via students (the lunchbox express) or put it on their Web site. Most schools schedule a back-to-school night early in the year so that teachers can touch base with parents and explain the goals for the year, the curriculum, and class procedures. Other important purposes can be achieved during these opportunities as well; parents may want to have a brief conversation with the teacher to convey information about their child that would not warrant a full conference. By meeting the parents of their students, teachers have an opportunity to understand their students more fully.

Furthermore, if teachers are using instructional strategies in their class that may be unfamiliar to parents, such as an inquiry approach to teaching elementary mathematics, it is critical that parents understand it. Some teachers find that engaging parents in a typical (but brief) instructional activity during back-to-school night is helpful. By placing parents in the role of students learning something unfamiliar, such as deriving the principles that underlie a nondecimal numeration system based on place value, the parents may come to appreciate the complexities of what their children are learning. Then, when students bring home assignments that might otherwise appear strange to their parents, the parents will have a greater understanding of the instructional program.

Many teachers, particularly at the elementary level, send home a regular newsletter that includes information on

FIGURE 4.18

DOMAIN 4: PROFESSIONAL RESPONSIBILITIES
Component 4b: Maintaining Accurate Records
Elements: Student completion of assignments • Student progress in learning • Noninstructional records

ELEMENT	LEVEL OF PERFORMANCE			
	UNSATISFACTORY	BASIC	PROFICIENT	DISTINGUISHED
Student completion of assignments	Teacher's system for maintaining information on student completion of assignments is in disarray.	Teacher's system for maintaining information on student completion of assignments is rudimentary and only partially effective.	Teacher's system for maintaining information on student completion of assignments is fully effective.	Teacher's system for maintaining information on student completion of assignments is fully effective. Students participate in maintaining the records.
Student progress in learning	Teacher has no system for maintaining information on student progress in learning, or the system is in disarray.	Teacher's system for maintaining information on student progress in learning is rudimentary and only partially effective.	Teacher's system for maintaining information on student progress in learning is fully effective.	Teacher's system for maintaining information on student progress in learning is fully effective. Students contribute information and participate in interpreting the records.
Noninstructional records	Teacher's records for noninstructional activities are in disarray, resulting in errors and confusion.	Teacher's records for noninstructional activities are adequate, but they require frequent monitoring to avoid errors.	Teacher's system for maintaining information on noninstructional activities is fully effective.	Teacher's system for maintaining information on noninstructional activities is highly effective, and students contribute to its maintenance.

upcoming school and classroom events. Such publications can also be a vehicle to recognize exemplary student work or to call attention to a visitor to the class. Students themselves, of course, will frequently be able to contribute to such communications.

In some communities, parents—possibly because of their own negative school experiences—are reluctant to come to the school. For them, the school may represent an unfamiliar and unwelcoming culture. Alternatively, they may have young children at home, with the added complication of arranging child care. In these situations, the school, and possibly individual teachers, must undertake a program of deliberate outreach, carried out with sensitivity and goodwill. And it may be necessary to arrange, during back-to-school-night activities, a babysitting room so parents can bring their younger children along and know they will be safe.

As an essential component of any program of parent communication, teachers must keep parents informed about the academic and social progress of their children. Schools have formalized procedures for reporting to parents, including parent conferences and report cards. However, many teachers choose to supplement these systems with additional information. For example, they might make frequent telephone calls (with positive as well as negative information), send notes home with students, and send e-mails when possible. They institute a system of reaching out to the parents of every child, on a rotating basis, ensuring that every parent receives a routine update. Particularly when either the parents or the teacher is concerned about a student, frequent communication is essential so problems don't build up to the point where a major issue must be addressed. In those cases, it may be necessary to schedule individual conferences more frequently than those arranged by the school.

When parents express specific concerns about their children in school, it is because they care deeply about their children's progress. Any response should be handled with empathy and respect. And, in particular, the response must be sensitive to the cultural norms of the family and community. What might be acceptable in one situation could be offensive in another. One of the many responsibilities of teachers is to be aware of these subtleties.

Although sometimes difficult to achieve, communicating honestly with parents about their children's learning is essential for teachers. No one is well served when a teacher, however well intentioned, conveys to a parent that a student is "doing fine" when in fact the student is struggling. Parents want to know how their children are *really* doing; pretending that a child is making good progress when he is not does no one a favor. Of course, reports of progress are specific to the individual history of each child. What is inadequate progress for one student might represent significant learning for another; reports of student learning must reflect these differences.

Naturally, communication with families about individual students is best when it is two-way; parents should feel that they are invited, indeed encouraged, to contact the teacher at any time. In fact, one of the most important measures by which parents decide whether a teacher deserves respect concerns this issue of responsiveness; when teachers don't return phone calls or are otherwise inaccessible, parents conclude that they are less than professional.

Many teachers find ways to engage parents in the actual instructional program. Even though this area of communicating with families varies a good deal with the age of the students and the subjects taught, much communication is possible. For example, primary-grade teachers can send home books that are suitable for bedtime reading or suggestions of activities for parents to do with their children. Older students can be asked to interview an older relative. Many teachers find that when students take a portfolio of their work home and explain the contents to family members, both their pride and their family's understanding are enhanced. Teachers find, therefore, that when they can engage the families in the actual learning process, all areas of communication are improved.

Furthermore, parents are essential partners with teachers in ensuring that students devote sufficient time and energy to work that they do at home. Homework should have a clear purpose, and when well designed, it can extend learning time. When it is perceived as busy work, when students don't have the skills they need to complete it, or when too much is assigned for the age of the students, home-school relations are damaged. But when homework serves a valuable educational purpose, parents can help ensure that students take pride in their work and that they devote their attention to it, undistracted by television or video games. Furthermore, parents can establish a protected space and time for homework and contribute to the culture in which students accept the need to study for tests; they can even be a resource to their children as they work to master basic information (for example, the multiplication facts or foreign language vocabulary words.)

Demonstration

Teachers can demonstrate their communication with families in many ways, such as by keeping copies of such things as class newsletters, handouts for back-to-school night, or descriptions of a new program. This collection could include guidelines for parents on how to review a child's portfolio or how to encourage responsible completion of homework. In addition, the teacher might maintain a log of phone and personal contacts with families. (See Figure 4.19.)

COMPONENT 4D: PARTICIPATING IN A PROFESSIONAL COMMUNITY

Rationale and Explanation

Just as schools are complex social organizations for students, so, too, are they for teachers. One's professional colleagues are a rich resource regarding teaching. In addition, the challenge of running schools requires the participation of all members of the professional community.

Therefore, whether they like it or not, most teachers' duties extend beyond their classroom doors. Educators, either by contractual agreement or by a sense of professional responsibility, find that their days contain such activities as committee meetings, rehearsals for the school play, assistance with family math night, or participation in a districtwide examination of some important aspect of the educational program. In addition, professional educators know that their instruction is enhanced when they take advantage of the expertise of their colleagues.

Relationships with colleagues are an important element of teachers' participation in a professional community. Teachers enjoy extensive and highly professional relationships with their colleagues, and the tone of the school is one of mutual support and enhancement. Furthermore, when novice teachers join the faculty, more experienced faculty members assume the essential roles of mentor and coach.

Professional educators are generous with their expertise and willingly share materials and insights, particularly with those less experienced than they. They are supportive and do not try to score points in a faculty meeting at the expense of other teachers or attempt to manipulate the outcome of a discussion for their own benefit. The focus of their work is the school's program and the progress of students, and they collaborate with colleagues to that end. For example, they participate in joint planning of thematic units or coordinate the learning experiences for students with special needs.

Above all, participation in a professional community requires active involvement in a culture of inquiry. An enormous professional resource available in every school is the expertise of its

FIGURE 4.19

DOMAIN 4: PROFESSIONAL RESPONSIBILITIES
Component 4c: Communicating with Families

Elements: Information about the instructional program • Information about individual students • Engagement of families in the instructional program

ELEMENT	LEVEL OF PERFORMANCE			
	UNSATISFACTORY	BASIC	PROFICIENT	DISTINGUISHED
Information about the instructional program	Teacher provides little or no information about the instructional program to families.	Teacher participates in the school's activities for family communication but offers little additional information.	Teacher provides frequent information to families, as appropriate, about the instructional program.	Teacher provides frequent information to families, as appropriate, about the instructional program. Students participate in preparing materials for their families.
Information about individual students	Teacher provides minimal information to families about individual students, or the communication is inappropriate to the cultures of the families. Teacher does not respond, or responds insensitively, to family concerns about students.	Teacher adheres to the school's required procedures for communicating with families. Responses to family concerns are minimal or may reflect occasional insensitivity to cultural norms.	Teacher communicates with families about students' progress on a regular basis, respecting cultural norms, and is available as needed to respond to family concerns.	Teacher provides information to families frequently on student progress, with students contributing to the design of the system. Response to family concerns is handled with great professional and cultural sensitivity.
Engagement of families in the instructional program	Teacher makes no attempt to engage families in the instructional program, or such efforts are inappropriate.	Teacher makes modest and partially successful attempts to engage families in the instructional program.	Teacher's efforts to engage families in the instructional program are frequent and successful.	Teacher's efforts to engage families in the instructional program are frequent and successful. Students contribute ideas for projects that could be enhanced by family participation.

teachers. Therefore, if educators are interested in improving outcomes for students, they must not ignore the expertise within their walls. In addition, to the extent that teaching is a profession, teachers (like other professionals) are obliged to continue their learning for their entire professional lives. As in other fields, the preparation and training of teachers is merely the beginning of professional learning, which can be expected to continue throughout one's career. However, the culture in many schools specifically undermines this expectation. Many schools embody a culture of privacy and autonomy; such a culture makes it virtually impossible for teachers to engage in serious professional discussions with one another.

Professional educators also make many contributions to the life of a school. They assume their share of the duties that help the school function smoothly, whether participating in the PTA, hosting a faculty party, or managing a science fair. These efforts can also include participating in site councils, curriculum committees, and study groups with beginning teachers. Such projects, whether they involve serving on the discipline committee or designing new performance assessments, require a considerable investment of time. In some schools, certain additional roles earn supplementary compensation; in others, it is the faculty's responsibility, working as a team, to divide up the duties. In almost all schools, educators have many opportunities to assume additional responsibilities, thereby enhancing the culture of the entire school.

Schools and districts may undertake major projects that require teacher participation. Professional educators are not content to allow the important decisions to be made by others; they want to help shape, for example, the new reading curriculum to ensure that it reflects current research as to best practice. Such district involvement, of course, imposes burdens on teachers, particularly if it requires absence from one's own classroom. Preparing materials for a substitute teacher is generally more demanding than teaching the classes oneself, and one can't be sure that the plans will be well executed. Therefore, such participation inevitably involves trade-offs between different aspects of one's professional responsibilities.

In general, full participation in the professional community increases with a teacher's level of experience. Novice teachers are fully occupied preparing for their classes each day and have scant time or energy to spare for larger projects. Even collaborating with their colleagues, which results in significant benefits for their daily work, can require an investment of time that they find difficult to make. Expectations must reflect these realities.

A teacher's ability to be an active member of the professional community is, to some extent, a function of events outside school. Making a contribution to the school or to the district can occur in many different ways. At certain times of one's life, family demands are such that teachers have little spare capacity to devote to school and district affairs. Attending to young children or to a parent with a disability can require enormous amounts of time and commitment. Some teachers let it be known that although they must leave school right at the end of the contract day, they can make their contribution through work they do at home, whether it is finding resources on the Internet for a team-teaching project or establishing the roster for students to volunteer at the soup kitchen.

Demonstration

Teachers demonstrate their participation in the professional community through their actions. Some teachers maintain a record of their involvement, and the contributions they have made, in the form of a log. (See Figure 4.20.)

COMPONENT 4E: GROWING AND DEVELOPING PROFESSIONALLY

Rationale and Explanation

Continuing development is the mark of a true professional; it is an ongoing effort that is never completed. Educators committed to attaining and remaining at the top of their profession invest much energy in staying informed and increasing their skills. They are then in a position to exercise leadership among colleagues.

Content knowledge is one area in which educators can always grow and develop professionally. Superficial content knowledge is insufficient for good teaching; deeper understanding is essential. Elementary teachers who provide instruction in all the disciplines face a challenge in understanding them all well enough to design learning experiences and respond to students' questions. Teachers at the secondary level must be experts in their disciplines so they can enable their students to engage with a subject. All teachers can profit from learning more about the subjects they teach.

Although it is important for teachers to continually deepen their content knowledge, the task is challenging because the subjects themselves keep changing. A characteristic of some

fields, particularly in the sciences and computer technology, has been the rapid expansion of knowledge; many teachers find that the subjects themselves have changed considerably from what they learned in college. Continuing education is essential just to stay abreast of the latest developments.

Ongoing developments in pedagogy also create opportunities for educators to improve their practice. Educational research continually discovers new methods to engage students in learning and to advance their understanding. Furthermore, discoveries in related fields—for example, business management and cultural studies—can suggest promising approaches and applications. Most teachers are able to profit from a focus on the latest work in pedagogical research and its applications to classroom practice. Collaborations with universities can help teachers interpret the latest findings.

Expanding developments in information technology are yet another vehicle for intense professional development. With most schools wired to the Internet and many students having access to computers at home, using electronic tools is no longer a choice for teachers; it is a necessity. And it is a moving target; just when a teacher has become proficient in the use of some software, it is changed or made obsolete by the next generation of applications. To keep up, teachers find they need to keep learning, too.

At the outset of their careers and faced with the daunting work of teaching, beginning teachers are engaged in a steep learning curve, confronting challenges for which no teacher training program can offer adequate preparation. It is small wonder that many beginning teachers give up teaching after only a few years; this situation offers a strong argument for a well-designed mentoring and induction program.

FIGURE 4.20

DOMAIN 4: PROFESSIONAL RESPONSIBILITIES
Component 4d: Participating in a Professional Community

Elements: Relationships with colleagues • Involvement in a culture of professional inquiry • Service to the school • Participation in school and district projects

ELEMENT	LEVEL OF PERFORMANCE			
	UNSATISFACTORY	BASIC	PROFICIENT	DISTINGUISHED
Relationships with colleagues	Teacher's relationships with colleagues are negative or self-serving.	Teacher maintains cordial relationships with colleagues to fulfill duties that the school or district requires.	Relationships with colleagues are characterized by mutual support and cooperation.	Relationships with colleagues are characterized by mutual support and cooperation. Teacher takes initiative in assuming leadership among the faculty.
Involvement in a culture of professional inquiry	Teacher avoids participation in a culture of inquiry, resisting opportunities to become involved.	Teacher becomes involved in the school's culture of inquiry when invited to do so.	Teacher actively participates in a culture of professional inquiry.	Teacher takes a leadership role in promoting a culture of professional inquiry.
Service to the school	Teacher avoids becoming involved in school events.	Teacher participates in school events when specifically asked.	Teacher volunteers to participate in school events, making a substantial contribution.	Teacher volunteers to participate in school events, making a substantial contribution, and assumes a leadership role in at least one aspect of school life.
Participation in school and district projects	Teacher avoids becoming involved in school and district projects.	Teacher participates in school and district projects when specifically asked.	Teacher volunteers to participate in school and district projects, making a substantial contribution.	Teacher volunteers to participate in school and district projects, making a substantial contribution, and assumes a leadership role in a major school or district project.

In their quest to constantly improve their practice, some teachers overlook the most obvious and, in some respects, the richest source of all: their own colleagues. In many schools, norms of privacy and autonomy are such that meaningful collaboration among teachers is difficult to implement. For years, teachers have been observed either by supervisors or perhaps by colleagues skilled in cognitive coaching—the observation of teaching and provision of nonjudgmental feedback. In these situations, it is assumed that the beneficiary of the observation is the teacher being observed.

But other situations are possible—indeed, more likely. A high school history teacher might recognize that the discussions in her second-period class are not successful—two students dominate, and the rest are inattentive. She might ask to visit a colleague during third period, because he has some of the same students and she hopes to see a different approach. Or she might sit in on the class of yet another colleague during fourth period, because she has been working on improving her questioning and discussion skills. That is, in these cases the teacher wants to observe her colleagues, not to give them feedback on their teaching but to *learn* from them. The beneficiary of the observation, in other words, is the *observer.*

Schools abound with opportunities for teachers to learn from one another. Joint planning, study groups, and efforts such as lesson study all provide vehicles for professional improvement. The lesson study process was developed in Japan and involves teachers working together to design a lesson, observing one member teach it, working together to review the results and revise the lesson, and observing another teacher present the revised lesson. For more information on lesson study, refer to Richardson (2004). Such efforts have many advantages over more formal approaches, such as attending courses and workshops. Most important, they are concerned with the real work of teaching in one's own classroom. That is, there is no question of "applying" what has been learned in a workshop to one's own situation; the work itself is conducted in the real world of the classroom. And naturally such professional engagement is convenient; it happens right in the school, with one's own colleagues. It is, in the best sense of the word, job embedded.

Professional organizations are another important vehicle for informing educators. Journals written in the language of the practitioner are valuable resources. And conferences, particularly regional ones, are within the reach of most communities. Local universities and state agencies are other valuable resources. All these organizations recognize the complexity of teaching and are committed to helping practitioners be as effective as possible.

Teachers are not only on the receiving end of professional expertise and growth; as they gain experience, educators find ways to make a substantial contribution to the profession, such as the following:

• Conducting research in their classrooms and sharing the results with their colleagues through conference presentations or articles.
• Supervising student teachers and meeting periodically with the student-teacher supervisors.
• Participating in or leading study groups with their colleagues.
• Writing articles for professional publication.

Demonstration

Teachers demonstrate their commitment to ongoing professional learning through the activities they undertake. These may be recorded on a log. The benefit of keeping such a record is that it invites teachers to reflect on how they have used the new knowledge in their teaching. Such a log can, and should, include informal as well as formal activities—for example, observing colleagues or participating in a project with a professor at a local university. (See Figure 4.21.)

FIGURE 4.21

DOMAIN 4: PROFESSIONAL RESPONSIBILITIES
Component 4e: Growing and Developing Professionally

Elements: Enhancement of content knowledge and pedagogical skill • Receptivity to feedback from colleagues • Service to the profession

ELEMENT	LEVEL OF PERFORMANCE			
	UNSATISFACTORY	BASIC	PROFICIENT	DISTINGUISHED
Enhancement of content knowledge and pedagogical skill	Teacher engages in no professional development activities to enhance knowledge or skill.	Teacher participates in professional activities to a limited extent when they are convenient.	Teacher seeks out opportunities for professional development to enhance content knowledge and pedagogical skill.	Teacher seeks out opportunities for professional development and makes a systematic effort to conduct action research.
Receptivity to feedback from colleagues	Teacher resists feedback on teaching performance from either supervisors or more experienced colleagues.	Teacher accepts, with some reluctance, feedback on teaching performance from both supervisors and professional colleagues.	Teacher welcomes feedback from colleagues when made by supervisors or when opportunities arise through professional collaboration.	Teacher seeks out feedback on teaching from both supervisors and colleagues.
Service to the profession	Teacher makes no effort to share knowledge with others or to assume professional responsibilities.	Teacher finds limited ways to contribute to the profession.	Teacher participates actively in assisting other educators.	Teacher initiates important activities to contribute to the profession.

COMPONENT 4F: SHOWING PROFESSIONALISM

Rationale and Explanation

"Professionalism" is an elusive concept that permeates all aspects of a teacher's work. In addition to their technical skills in planning and implementing the instructional program, accomplished teachers display certain professional qualities that help them to serve their students and their profession. Expert teachers display the highest standards of integrity and ethical conduct; they are intellectually honest and conduct themselves in ways consistent with a comprehensive moral code.

A teacher's integrity is demonstrated, most importantly, through honesty. Professional educators can be counted on to do what they said they would do, to maintain confidentiality, to support the best efforts of colleagues. They have a very strong moral compass and are never led astray by the temptations of an easier approach or by convenience. Even if the right thing to do is more difficult, the professional teacher can be counted on to do it anyway and to try to convince others to join in.

Highly professional teachers never forget that schools are not institutions run for the convenience of the adults who work in them; instead, the purpose of schools is to educate students. These educators care deeply for the well-being of their students and mobilize whatever resources are necessary for them to be successful.

Professional educators are keenly alert to the needs of their students and step in on their behalf when needed. They are aware of the signs of physical abuse and of drug and alcohol dependency. They may locate a winter coat for a child or discuss a student's future plans with the student and her parents. They take an interest in their students, and using their familiarity with resources both in the school and in the larger community, they make suggestions to families for student growth. For example, a teacher might be aware that a student has a keen interest in and talent for art. But with budget cutbacks, the school's offerings have been reduced. However, if the teacher knows that, for example, the local Boys and Girls Club offers after-school programs in various sports and artistic media, the teacher would pass this information along to the student and his parents.

Moreover, educators are advocates for their students, particularly those whom the educational establishment has traditionally underserved. They work diligently for their students' best interests, whether that means convincing a colleague that a student deserves an opportunity or supporting a student's efforts at self-improvement. At times, advocating for students requires challenging long-held assumptions of students, other faculty, or administrators. For example, data suggest that girls perform poorly in mathematics and science because they have been led to believe that those are "boys' subjects." Convincing girls and other teachers that girls can do well in those courses may require diligence and patience.

There are other situations in which the school's policies and programs are serving some students poorly or actually doing harm. For example, if an attendance policy mandates that students fail a course if they are absent for more than a certain number of days, a student's illness can have extremely serious consequences. If a student believes, with some justification, that he will never be able to graduate, dropping out of school may seem to be a rational decision. But if what led to that conclusion is the rigid application of a school rule, a concerned teacher will seek greater flexibility to enable the student to reengage with the school.

Furthermore, highly professional teachers demonstrate a commitment to professional standards in problem solving and decision making. Professional educators maintain an open mind and are willing to attempt new approaches to old problems, even if in the short run they are inconvenienced. They base their judgments and recommendations on hard information rather than on hearsay and tradition. They strive to use the best data available to support action. Their recommendations are never merely self-serving; they operate with the best interests of the school, and in particular the students, in mind. The judgments of professional educators with respect to challenging issues such as students' freedom of speech in, for example, the school newspaper, or questions of student privacy in their

lockers, are motivated by a search for the proper balance between conflicting interests, never solely by the dictates of tradition.

Lastly, professional educators comply with school and district regulations and procedures, such as those related to punctuality, dress code, completion of reports, and the like. And when they hear their colleagues complain about the regulations, they use their influence to convince their colleagues of the value of the rules, or they work with their colleagues and administrators, to replace the regulations with other, more reasonable ones.

Demonstration

Teachers display their professional ethics in daily interactions with students and colleagues. (See Figure 4.22.)

FIGURE 4.22

DOMAIN 4: PROFESSIONAL RESPONSIBILITIES
Component 4f: Showing Professionalism

Elements: Integrity and ethical conduct • Service to students • Advocacy • Decision making • Compliance with school and district regulations

	LEVEL OF PERFORMANCE			
ELEMENT	UNSATISFACTORY	BASIC	PROFICIENT	DISTINGUISHED
Integrity and ethical conduct	Teacher displays dishonesty in interactions with colleagues, students, and the public.	Teacher is honest in interactions with colleagues, students, and the public.	Teacher displays high standards of honesty, integrity, and confidentiality in interactions with colleagues, students, and the public.	Teacher can be counted on to hold the highest standards of honesty, integrity, and confidentiality and takes a leadership role with colleagues.

(figure continues)

FIGURE 4.22

DOMAIN 4: PROFESSIONAL RESPONSIBILITIES
Component 4f: Showing Professionalism *(continued)*
Elements: Integrity and ethical conduct • Service to students • Advocacy • Decision making • Compliance with school and district regulations

ELEMENT	LEVEL OF PERFORMANCE			
	UNSATISFACTORY	BASIC	PROFICIENT	DISTINGUISHED
Service to students	Teacher is not alert to students' needs.	Teacher's attempts to serve students are inconsistent.	Teacher is active in serving students.	Teacher is highly proactive in serving students, seeking out resources when needed.
Advocacy	Teacher contributes to school practices that result in some students being ill served by the school.	Teacher does not knowingly contribute to some students being ill served by the school.	Teacher works to ensure that all students receive a fair opportunity to succeed.	Teacher makes a concerted effort to challenge negative attitudes or practices to ensure that all students, particularly those traditionally underserved, are honored in the school.
Decision making	Teacher makes decisions and recommendations based on self-serving interests.	Teacher's decisions and recommendations are based on limited though genuinely professional considerations.	Teacher maintains an open mind and participates in team or departmental decision making.	Teacher takes a leadership role in team or departmental decision making and helps ensure that such decisions are based on the highest professional standards.
Compliance with school and district regulations	Teacher does not comply with school and district regulations.	Teacher complies minimally with school and district regulations, doing just enough to get by.	Teacher complies fully with school and district regulations.	Teacher complies fully with school and district regulations, taking a leadership role with colleagues.

5

FRAMEWORKS FOR
SPECIALIST POSITIONS

The framework for teaching is just that—a framework for *teaching;* it is not a framework for school nurses, school psychologists, or even library or media specialists. Although their responsibilities typically include some teaching, these educators engage in other important activities as well. Librarians, for example, maintain a collection; nurses manage immunization records and dispense medications to students who need them. Therefore, although specialists are typically included in the teachers' bargaining unit and are, in that sense, considered teachers, their positions are essentially different from those of teachers and must be described separately.

This chapter does not include a framework for classroom-based special education teachers; nor is there a separate framework for teachers of physical education, music, or art. This is because the principal responsibility of all those educators is to teach students, typically in a large-group setting.

It is true that teachers of students with special needs may accomplish the components of the framework in ways unique to their situation. For example, teachers of students with behavioral disabilities will include aspects of behavior in their instructional outcomes, and all teachers of special needs students must attend more carefully than others to maintaining accurate records—Individual Education Plans (IEPs)—because these are required by law. Fundamentally, however, they are all teachers of students.

The same reasoning applies to art, music, and physical education teachers. Typically, they organize instruction for large numbers of students—often all the students in an entire school, or even in more than one school. As a result, the degree of their knowledge of individual students, and their interaction with the students' families, is bound to be less than that of classroom teachers, particularly those at the elementary level. However, because these specialists are *teachers,* they do the tasks of teaching as described in the framework for teaching.

The specialist positions described in this chapter, on the other hand, involve many other responsibilities in addition to that of teaching students. In the case of instructional specialists—people who work as instructional coaches, for example—their principal "clients" are other teachers. Although school librarians, nurses, psychologists, and counselors work with students, they do so as part of a larger program that also includes coordinating their work with colleagues and outside agencies to an extent that is not essential for classroom teachers.

The frameworks for specialists have evolved over many years, through the work of educators throughout the United States. Educators in many school districts and, indeed, entire states who have decided to use the framework for teaching as the foundation of their efforts in instructional enhancement have discovered that the work of specialists is not adequately described in the framework for teaching. The state of Delaware, for example, convened statewide committees composed of representatives from many school districts and individuals active in their own professional organizations to develop specialist frameworks. School districts have taken a similar approach; many of them have been willing to share their work.

The frameworks for specialists described here should not be considered the last word on the subject; like the domains and components of the framework for teaching, they may have to be slightly modified to adequately reflect the conditions in any particular location. The frameworks for specialists represent an amalgam of a range of state- and district-developed frameworks but have not drawn extensively on the efforts of any single entity. They reflect, it is hoped, a good first draft that educators can use to formulate their own frameworks.

THE GENERAL FRAMEWORKS FOR SPECIALISTS

The organization of the frameworks for specialists closely follows that of the framework for teaching. Each has four domains, and each domain has the same emphasis as in the framework for teaching:

Planning and Preparation. Each specialist framework includes a domain titled Planning and Preparation. Every specialist must plan and prepare, although some of the details of that planning may differ from that done by a teacher. However, it is primarily a matter of emphasis. For some specialists, the knowledge of resources is critical; it is integral to the work of, for example, a school psychologist.

The Environment. Each specialist framework includes a domain that covers the environment. In some cases—for example, for school counselors or nurses—the environment may principally be an office or a center that students go to and that should be inviting. Librarians typically attend carefully to the environment in the media center, ensuring that it is organized for maximum productivity by both students and teachers. For an instructional specialist, who works primarily with other teachers, the environment may refer to the tone in the room where a workshop is conducted. For those specialists whose responsibilities include teaching students in regular classrooms, the environment includes, as with regular classroom teachers, how they establish an environment conducive to learning.

Delivery of Service. In the specialist frameworks, Delivery of Service is equivalent to Instruction in the framework for teaching. All specialists do important work, but not all of it is actual teaching; in some cases it involves assessing individual student needs or conducting small-group or individual counseling sessions. Specialists in all fields follow the established protocols and best practice of their own organizations; the components of the framework for teaching do not always apply.

Professional Responsibilities. Lastly, all specialists have obligations in the domain of Professional Responsibilities, and many of these are virtually identical to those of classroom teachers. They all reflect on their practice and maintain records. For some of them, communicating with families is an even more significant part of their work than is the case with classroom teachers. Furthermore, all specialists participate in a professional community, and their collaboration with other teachers in the school is absolutely central to their work. So although most of the professional responsibilities are similar to those of classroom teachers, for some specialists they play a critical role.

The rest of this chapter provides frameworks for the following specialists:

- Instructional specialists (instructional coach, for example).
- Library or media specialists.
- School nurses.
- School counselors.
- School psychologists.
- Therapeutic specialists (speech, hearing, occupational, or physical therapists, tutors, and others).

INSTRUCTIONAL SPECIALISTS

Some schools and school districts are able to provide instructional coaches, or support specialists, to teachers. These are individuals with expertise in a particular curricular area or in specific instructional techniques that are deemed of value for the entire faculty.

Arrangements vary widely; some coaches work exclusively in one school, others in several. Some coaches focus on a specific area of teaching, such as literacy; others range more widely, assisting teachers in, for example, instructional planning, classroom-based assessment, or the implementation of differentiated instruction. But common to all instructional specialist roles is that those who fill them are *teachers,* and they play no role in teacher supervision and evaluation.

Instructional coaches do not have classroom responsibilities; they work full-time with their teaching colleagues. Although some instructional specialist positions are permanent appointments, others rotate among different members of the teaching staff, allowing many individuals the opportunity to experience the very different responsibilities of working with faculty as opposed to students.

In some settings, instructional specialists teach model lessons to demonstrate a particular technique or approach; in others, they present workshops to groups of teachers or meet with teachers individually or in groups to plan and reflect on lessons. Their role is facilitative rather than directive. Their aim is to promote improved practice among all teachers in a school, and they tend to be opportunistic, using any strategy that will further that aim.

In some instances an instructional specialist works directly with students. Sometimes such direct work is due to the students' learning needs, such as a reading disability, or because of the demands of a content area, such as mathematics. In some cases the instructional specialist works with students who have developmental lags for whatever reason. When direct teaching is part of the instructional specialist's role, whether such teaching is with individuals, small groups, or the whole class, the original components of the framework for teaching apply.

In performing their work, instructional specialists require advanced understanding and skill; therefore, they typically attend relevant state conferences and may make presentations there. Or they meet with those in similar roles in other schools and districts to compare notes and share practices. Whatever techniques they use, they must themselves remain current in their fields so they can serve as resources to their colleagues.

The domains and components of an instructional specialist's responsibilities are as follows and do not include the components of teaching that may be a part of their work, because these exist already, as previously noted, in the original framework for teaching.

Domain 1: Planning and Preparation

• Demonstrating knowledge of current trends in specialty area and professional development.

• Demonstrating knowledge of the school's program and levels of teacher skill in delivering that program.

• Establishing goals for the instructional support program appropriate to the setting and the teachers served.

• Demonstrating knowledge of resources, both within and beyond the school and district.

• Planning the instructional support program, integrated with the overall school program.

• Developing a plan to evaluate the instructional support program.

Domain 2: The Environment

• Creating an environment of trust and respect.

• Establishing a culture for ongoing instructional improvement.

• Establishing clear procedures for teachers to gain access to instructional support.

• Establishing and maintaining norms of behavior for professional interactions.

• Organizing physical space for workshops or training. This includes the use of training equipment, arrangement of furniture for visual access, traffic flow, and a match between the physical arrangement and workshop activities.

Domain 3: Delivery of Service

• Collaborating with teachers in the design of instructional units and lessons.

• Engaging teachers in learning new instructional skills.

• Sharing expertise with staff. This could include teaching model lessons, presenting workshops, and facilitating study groups.

• Locating resources for teachers to support instructional improvement.

• Demonstrating flexibility and responsiveness.

Domain 4: Professional Responsibilities

• Reflecting on practice.
• Preparing and submitting budgets and reports.
• Coordinating work with other instructional specialists.
• Participating in a professional community.
• Engaging in professional development.
• Showing professionalism, including integrity and confidentiality.

Figures 5.1 through 5.4 present the levels of performance for each component of the four domains.

LIBRARY/MEDIA SPECIALISTS

The work of library/media specialists is integral to the instructional program of a school. Librarians promote information literacy by helping students learn the skills required to access, synthesize, produce, and communicate information. They work with classroom teachers to integrate their mission of information literacy with the academic content that students are pursuing in their various classes. Thus, when classroom teachers ask their students to engage in research on a particular topic, it is frequently the librarian who helps the students actually find the information they will need.

The work of library/media specialists has evolved significantly in recent decades; many libraries (both in schools and in the larger community) no longer have card catalogs. Instead, students locate information by means of an electronic search. Indeed, the ubiquitous nature of the Internet has greatly expanded the reach for information by both students and educators. Learning to use this resource is essential for academic success, and teaching students to do so is at the heart of the work of library/media specialists. And because of the sheer quantity of information available on every conceivable topic, an important aspect of the specialist's role is to assist students in sorting through the volume, to focus their energies so their work yields productive results.

But library/media specialists also have more traditional responsibilities, which they take seriously. They aim to create an inviting physical and emotional environment in which students will choose to spend time when their schedules permit. They organize materials in such a way that when students are investigating one topic, they will encounter other related materials that will pique their interest. Library/media specialists, in other words, attempt to promote a culture for the quest of knowledge that permeates all aspects of the school.

Furthermore, library/media specialists, even more than some other specialists, coordinate their work with classroom teachers and serve as a resource to those teachers. Thus, when a teacher, for example, is embarking on a unit of study with 4th grade students on aviation, the library/media specialist will be able to assemble valuable supplemental materials to enrich the students' learning.

Lastly, an important aspect of a library/media specialist's position is to maintain and to extend the library's collection.

FIGURE 5.1

Domain 1 for Instructional Specialists: Planning and Preparation

COMPONENT	LEVEL OF PERFORMANCE			
	UNSATISFACTORY	BASIC	PROFICIENT	DISTINGUISHED
1a: **Demonstrating knowledge of current trends in specialty area and professional development**	Instructional specialist demonstrates little or no familiarity with specialty area or trends in professional development.	Instructional specialist demonstrates basic familiarity with specialty area and trends in professional development.	Instructional specialist demonstrates thorough knowledge of specialty area and trends in professional development.	Instructional specialist's knowledge of specialty area and trends in professional development is wide and deep; specialist is regarded as an expert by colleagues.
1b: **Demonstrating knowledge of the school's program and levels of teacher skill in delivering that program**	Instructional specialist demonstrates little or no knowledge of the school's program or of teacher skill in delivering that program.	Instructional specialist demonstrates basic knowledge of the school's program and of teacher skill in delivering that program.	Instructional specialist demonstrates thorough knowledge of the school's program and of teacher skill in delivering that program.	Instructional specialist is deeply familiar with the school's program and works to shape its future direction and actively seeks information as to teacher skill in that program.
1c: **Establishing goals for the instructional support program appropriate to the setting and the teachers served**	Instructional specialist has no clear goals for the instructional support program, or they are inappropriate to either the situation or the needs of the staff.	Instructional specialist's goals for the instructional support program are rudimentary and are partially suitable to the situation and the needs of the staff.	Instructional specialist's goals for the instructional support program are clear and are suitable to the situation and the needs of the staff.	Instructional specialist's goals for the instructional support program are highly appropriate to the situation and the needs of the staff. They have been developed following consultations with administrators and colleagues.

FIGURE 5.1

Domain 1 for Instructional Specialists: Planning and Preparation *(continued)*

COMPONENT	LEVEL OF PERFORMANCE			
	UNSATISFACTORY	BASIC	PROFICIENT	DISTINGUISHED
1d: **Demonstrating knowledge of resources, both within and beyond the school and district**	Instructional specialist demonstrates little or no knowledge of resources available in the school or district for teachers to advance their skills.	Instructional specialist demonstrates basic knowledge of resources available in the school and district for teachers to advance their skills.	Instructional specialist is fully aware of resources available in the school and district and in the larger professional community for teachers to advance their skills.	Instructional specialist actively seeks out new resources from a wide range of sources to enrich teachers' skills in implementing the school's program.
1e: **Planning the instructional support program, integrated with the overall school program**	Instructional specialist's plan consists of a random collection of unrelated activities, lacking coherence or an overall structure.	Instructional specialist's plan has a guiding principle and includes a number of worthwhile activities, but some of them don't fit with the broader goals.	Instructional specialist's plan is well designed to support teachers in the improvement of their instructional skills.	Instructional specialist's plan is highly coherent, taking into account the competing demands of making presentations and consulting with teachers, and has been developed following consultation with administrators and teachers.
1f: **Developing a plan to evaluate the instructional support program**	Instructional specialist has no plan to evaluate the program or resists suggestions that such an evaluation is important.	Instructional specialist has a rudimentary plan to evaluate the instructional support program.	Instructional support specialist's plan to evaluate the program is organized around clear goals and the collection of evidence to indicate the degree to which the goals have been met.	Instructional specialist's evaluation plan is highly sophisticated, with imaginative sources of evidence and a clear path toward improving the program on an ongoing basis.

FIGURE 5.2

Domain 2 for Instructional Specialists: The Environment

COMPONENT	LEVEL OF PERFORMANCE			
	UNSATISFACTORY	BASIC	PROFICIENT	DISTINGUISHED
2a: **Creating an environment of trust and respect**	Teachers are reluctant to request assistance from the instructional specialist, fearing that such a request will be treated as a sign of deficiency.	Relationships with the instructional specialist are cordial; teachers don't resist initiatives established by the instructional specialist.	Relationships with the instructional specialist are respectful, with some contacts initiated by teachers.	Relationships with the instructional specialist are highly respectful and trusting, with many contacts initiated by teachers.
2b: **Establishing a culture for ongoing instructional improvement**	Instructional specialist conveys the sense that the work of improving instruction is externally mandated and is not important to school improvement.	Teachers do not resist the offerings of support from the instructional specialist.	Instructional specialist promotes a culture of professional inquiry in which teachers seek assistance in improving their instructional skills.	Instructional specialist has established a culture of professional inquiry in which teachers initiate projects to be undertaken with the support of the specialist.
2c: **Establishing clear procedures for teachers to gain access to instructional support**	When teachers want to access assistance from the instructional specialist, they are not sure how to go about it.	Some procedures (for example, registering for workshops) are clear to teachers, whereas others (for example, receiving informal support) are not.	Instructional specialist has established clear procedures for teachers to use in gaining access to support.	Procedures for access to instructional support are clear to all teachers and have been developed following consultation with administrators and teachers.

FIGURE 5.2

Domain 2 for Instructional Specialists: The Environment *(continued)*

COMPONENT	LEVEL OF PERFORMANCE			
	UNSATISFACTORY	BASIC	PROFICIENT	DISTINGUISHED
2d: **Establishing and maintaining norms of behavior for professional interactions**	No norms of professional conduct have been established; teachers are frequently disrespectful in their interactions with one another.	Instructional specialist's efforts to establish norms of professional conduct are partially successful.	Instructional specialist has established clear norms of mutual respect for professional interaction.	Instructional specialist has established clear norms of mutual respect for professional interaction. Teachers ensure that their colleagues adhere to these standards of conduct.
2e: **Organizing physical space for workshops or training**	Instructional specialist makes poor use of the physical environment, resulting in poor access by some participants, time lost due to poor use of training equipment, or little alignment between the physical arrangement and the workshop activities.	The physical environment does not impede workshop activities.	Instructional specialist makes good use of the physical environment, resulting in engagement of all participants in the workshop activities.	Instructional specialist makes highly effective use of the physical environment, with teachers contributing to the physical arrangement.

FIGURE 5.3

Domain 3 for Instructional Specialists: Delivery of Service

COMPONENT	LEVEL OF PERFORMANCE			
	UNSATISFACTORY	BASIC	PROFICIENT	DISTINGUISHED
3a: **Collaborating with teachers in the design of instructional units and lessons**	Instructional specialist declines to collaborate with classroom teachers in the design of instructional lessons and units.	Instructional specialist collaborates with classroom teachers in the design of instructional lessons and units when specifically asked to do so.	Instructional specialist initiates collaboration with classroom teachers in the design of instructional lessons and units.	Instructional specialist initiates collaboration with classroom teachers in the design of instructional lessons and units, locating additional resources from sources outside the school.
3b: **Engaging teachers in learning new instructional skills**	Teachers decline opportunities to engage in professional learning.	Instructional specialist's efforts to engage teachers in professional learning are partially successful, with some participating.	All teachers are engaged in acquiring new instructional skills.	Teachers are highly engaged in acquiring new instructional skills and take initiative in suggesting new areas for growth.
3c: **Sharing expertise with staff**	Instructional specialist's model lessons and workshops are of poor quality or are not appropriate to the needs of the teachers being served.	The quality of the instructional specialist's model lessons and workshops is mixed, with some of them being appropriate to the needs of the teachers being served.	The quality of the instructional specialist's model lessons and workshops is uniformly high and appropriate to the needs of the teachers being served.	The quality of the instructional specialist's model lessons and workshops is uniformly high and appropriate to the needs of the teachers being served. The instructional specialist conducts extensive follow-up work with teachers.

FIGURE 5.3

Domain 3 for Instructional Specialists: Delivery of Service *(continued)*

COMPONENT	LEVEL OF PERFORMANCE			
	UNSATISFACTORY	BASIC	PROFICIENT	DISTINGUISHED
3d: **Locating resources for teachers to support instructional improvement**	Instructional specialist fails to locate resources for instructional improvement for teachers, even when specifically requested to do so.	Instructional specialist's efforts to locate resources for instructional improvement for teachers are partially successful, reflecting incomplete knowledge of what is available.	Instructional specialist locates resources for instructional improvement for teachers when asked to do so.	Instructional specialist is highly proactive in locating resources for instructional improvement for teachers, anticipating their needs.
3e: **Demonstrating flexibility and responsiveness**	Instructional specialist adheres to his plan, in spite of evidence of its inadequacy.	Instructional specialist makes modest changes in the support program when confronted with evidence of the need for change.	Instructional specialist makes revisions to the support program when it is needed.	Instructional specialist is continually seeking ways to improve the support program and makes changes as needed in response to student, parent, or teacher input.

FIGURE 5.4				
Domain 4 for Instructional Specialists: Professional Responsibilities				
	LEVEL OF PERFORMANCE			
COMPONENT	UNSATISFACTORY	BASIC	PROFICIENT	DISTINGUISHED
4a: **Reflecting** **on practice**	Instructional specialist does not reflect on practice, or the reflections are inaccurate or self-serving.	Instructional specialist's reflection on practice is moderately accurate and objective without citing specific examples and with only global suggestions as to how it might be improved.	Instructional specialist's reflection provides an accurate and objective description of practice, citing specific positive and negative characteristics. Instructional specialist makes some specific suggestions as to how the support program might be improved.	Instructional specialist's reflection is highly accurate and perceptive, citing specific examples. Instructional specialist draws on an extensive repertoire to suggest alternative strategies, accompanied by a prediction of the likely consequences of each.
4b: **Preparing and** **submitting budgets** **and reports**	Instructional specialist does not follow established procedures for preparing budgets and submitting reports. Reports are routinely late.	Instructional specialist's efforts to prepare budgets are partially successful, anticipating most expenditures and following established procedures. Reports are sometimes submitted on time.	Instructional specialist's budgets are complete, anticipating all expenditures and following established procedures. Reports are always submitted on time.	Instructional specialist anticipates and responds to teacher needs when preparing budgets, following established procedures and suggesting improvements to those procedures. Reports are submitted on time.
4c: **Coordinating work** **with other instructional** **specialists**	Instructional specialist makes no effort to collaborate with other instructional specialists within the district.	Instructional specialist responds positively to the efforts of other instructional specialists within the district to collaborate.	Instructional specialist initiates efforts to collaborate with other instructional specialists within the district.	Instructional specialist takes a leadership role in coordinating projects with other instructional specialists within and beyond the district.

FIGURE 5.4

Domain 4 for Instructional Specialists: Professional Responsibilities (continued)

COMPONENT	LEVEL OF PERFORMANCE			
	UNSATISFACTORY	BASIC	PROFICIENT	DISTINGUISHED
4d: **Participating in a professional community**	Instructional specialist's relationships with colleagues are negative or self-serving, and the specialist avoids being involved in school and district events and projects.	Instructional specialist's relationships with colleagues are cordial, and the specialist participates in school and district events and projects when specifically requested.	Instructional specialist participates actively in school and district events and projects and maintains positive and productive relationships with colleagues.	Instructional specialist makes a substantial contribution to school and district events and projects and assumes a leadership role with colleagues.
4e: **Engaging in professional development**	Instructional specialist does not participate in professional development activities, even when such activities are clearly needed for the enhancement of skills.	Instructional specialist's participation in professional development activities is limited to those that are convenient or are required.	Instructional specialist seeks out opportunities for professional development based on an individual assessment of need.	Instructional specialist actively pursues professional development opportunities and makes a substantial contribution to the profession through such activities as participating in state or national conferences for other specialists.
4f: **Showing professionalism, including integrity and confidentiality**	Instructional specialist displays dishonesty in interactions with colleagues and violates norms of confidentiality.	Instructional specialist is honest in interactions with colleagues and respects norms of confidentiality.	Instructional specialist displays high standards of honesty and integrity in interactions with colleagues and respects norms of confidentiality.	Instructional specialist can be counted on to hold the highest standards of honesty and integrity and takes a leadership role with colleagues in respecting the norms of confidentiality.

Every year, authors write new literature. Although annual prizes can guide librarians in making their selections, excellent literature does not always result in public recognition, leaving it to the librarian to make decisions as to the best choices for students. And there is all of the nonfiction collection to consider; with limited resources (a situation that all librarians must contend with), it is critical to make wise choices.

The library/media specialist's role, then, is complex and wide-ranging. In many schools, the media center is physically situated in the center of the building, both to be accessible to students and to serve as a statement about the essential role of information and research in the school's program.

The domains and components of a library/media specialist's responsibilities are as follows:

Domain 1: Planning and Preparation

- Demonstrating knowledge of literature and current trends in library/media practice and information technology.
- Demonstrating knowledge of the school's program and student information needs within that program.
- Establishing goals for the library/media program appropriate to the setting and the students served.
- Demonstrating knowledge of resources, both within and beyond the school and district, and access to such resources as interlibrary loan.
- Planning the library/media program integrated with the overall school program. This includes schedules for individual classes to visit the library and events such as book fairs, work in classrooms, and time for locating resources.
- Developing a plan to evaluate the library/media program.

Domain 2: The Environment

- Creating an environment of respect and rapport.
- Establishing a culture for investigation and love of literature.
- Establishing and maintaining library procedures. This includes supervising library assistants.
- Managing student behavior.
- Organizing physical space to enable smooth flow. This includes clear signage, adequate space for different activities, and attractive displays.

Domain 3: Delivery of Service

- Maintaining and extending the library collection in accordance with the school's needs and within budget limitations. This includes a periodic inventory, repairs, and weeding out.
- Collaborating with teachers in the design of instructional units and lessons.
- Engaging students in enjoying literature and in learning information skills.
- Assisting students and teachers in the use of technology in the library/media center.
- Demonstrating flexibility and responsiveness.

Domain 4: Professional Responsibilities

- Reflecting on practice.
- Preparing and submitting reports and budgets.
- Communicating with the larger community.
- Participating in a professional community.
- Engaging in professional development.
- Showing professionalism. This includes integrity, advocacy, maintaining confidentiality, and observing copyright laws.

Figures 5.5 through 5.8 present the levels of performance for each component of the four domains.

SCHOOL NURSES

School nurses help ensure that students are healthy and prepared to participate actively in learning activities. They maintain immunization records and administer medications to students when needed. The school nurse is aware of state and district regulations concerning health matters and ensures that the school complies with all provisions. Frequently these regulations encompass controversial topics such as birth control information, services to pregnant teens, and drug abuse services and counseling, all of which add to the sensitivity of the nurse's role.

But beyond those responsibilities, school nurses also contribute to an environment of wellness throughout the school. In some settings, they teach health classes; in others, their responsibilities are exercised through the health office. Nurses identify and address individual student needs through screening and nursing interventions. As the resident medical consultant, school nurses serve a critical consulting role for the entire school, for teachers as well as students.

The domains and components of a school nurse's responsibilities are as follows:

Domain 1: Planning and Preparation
- Demonstrating medical knowledge and skill in nursing techniques.
- Demonstrating knowledge of child and adolescent development.
- Establishing goals for the nursing program appropriate to the setting and the students served.
- Demonstrating knowledge of government, community, and district regulations and resources.
- Planning the nursing program for both individuals and groups of students, integrated with the regular school program.
- Developing a plan to evaluate the nursing program.

Domain 2: The Environment (office/small-group environment)
- Creating an environment of respect and rapport.
- Establishing a culture for health and wellness.
- Following health protocols and procedures.
- Supervising health associates.
- Organizing physical space.

Domain 3: Delivery of Service
- Assessing student needs.
- Administering medications to students.
- Promoting wellness through classes or classroom presentations.
- Managing emergency situations.
- Demonstrating flexibility and responsiveness.
- Collaborating with teachers to develop specialized educational programs and services for students with diverse medical needs. This ensures that equitable learning opportunities are available for all students.

Domain 4: Professional Responsibilities
- Reflecting on practice.
- Maintaining health records in accordance with policy and submitting reports in a timely fashion.
- Communicating with families.

FIGURE 5.5

Domain 1 for Library/Media Specialists: Planning and Preparation

COMPONENT	LEVEL OF PERFORMANCE			
	UNSATISFACTORY	BASIC	PROFICIENT	DISTINGUISHED
1a: **Demonstrating knowledge of literature and current trends in library/media practice and information technology**	Library/media specialist demonstrates little or no knowledge of literature and of current trends in practice and information technology.	Library/media specialist demonstrates limited knowledge of literature and of current trends in practice and information technology.	Library/media specialist demonstrates thorough knowledge of literature and of current trends in practice and information technology.	Drawing on extensive professional resources, library/media specialist demonstrates rich understanding of literature and of current trends in information technology.
1b: **Demonstrating knowledge of the school's program and student information needs within that program**	Library/media specialist demonstrates little or no knowledge of the school's content standards and of students' needs for information skills within those standards.	Library/media specialist demonstrates basic knowledge of the school's content standards and of students' needs for information skills within those standards.	Library/media specialist demonstrates thorough knowledge of the school's content standards and of students' needs for information skills within those standards.	Library/media specialist takes a leadership role within the school and district to articulate the needs of students for information technology within the school's academic program.
1c: **Establishing goals for the library/media program appropriate to the setting and the students served**	Library/media specialist has no clear goals for the media program, or they are inappropriate to either the situation in the school or the age of the students.	Library/media specialist's goals for the media program are rudimentary and are partially suitable to the situation in the school and the age of the students.	Library/media specialist's goals for the media program are clear and appropriate to the situation in the school and to the age of the students.	Library/media specialist's goals for the media program are highly appropriate to the situation in the school and to the age of the students and have been developed following consultations with students and colleagues.

FIGURE 5.5

Domain 1 for Library/Media Specialists: Planning and Preparation (continued)

COMPONENT	LEVEL OF PERFORMANCE			
	UNSATISFACTORY	BASIC	PROFICIENT	DISTINGUISHED
1d: **Demonstrating knowledge of resources, both within and beyond the school and district, and access to such resources as interlibrary loan**	Library/media specialist demonstrates little or no knowledge of resources available for students and teachers in the school, in other schools in the district, and in the larger community to advance program goals.	Library/media specialist demonstrates basic knowledge of resources available for students and teachers in the school, in other schools in the district, and in the larger community to advance program goals.	Library/media specialist is fully aware of resources available for students and teachers in the school, in other schools in the district, and in the larger community to advance program goals.	Library/media specialist is fully aware of resources available for students and teachers and actively seeks out new resources from a wide range of sources to enrich the school's program.
1e: **Planning the library/media program integrated with the overall school program**	Library/media program consists of a random collection of unrelated activities, lacking coherence or an overall structure.	Library/media specialist's plan has a guiding principle and includes a number of worthwhile activities, but some of them don't fit with the broader goals.	Library/media specialist's plan is well designed to support both teachers and students in their information needs.	Library/media specialist's plan is highly coherent, taking into account the competing demands of scheduled time in the library, consultative work with teachers, and work in maintaining and extending the collection; the plan has been developed after consultation with teachers.
1f: **Developing a plan to evaluate the library/media program**	Library/media specialist has no plan to evaluate the program or resists suggestions that such an evaluation is important.	Library/media specialist has a rudimentary plan to evaluate the library/media program.	Library/media specialist's plan to evaluate the program is organized around clear goals and the collection of evidence to indicate the degree to which the goals have been met.	Library/media specialist's evaluation plan is highly sophisticated, with imaginative sources of evidence and a clear path toward improving the program on an ongoing basis.

FIGURE 5.6

Domain 2 for Library/Media Specialists: The Environment

COMPONENT	LEVEL OF PERFORMANCE			
	UNSATISFACTORY	BASIC	PROFICIENT	DISTINGUISHED
2a: **Creating an environment of respect and rapport**	Interactions, both between the library/media specialist and students and among students, are negative, inappropriate, or insensitive to students' cultural backgrounds and are characterized by sarcasm, put-downs, or conflict.	Interactions, both between the library/media specialist and students and among students, are generally appropriate and free from conflict but may be characterized by occasional displays of insensitivity or lack of responsiveness to cultural or developmental differences among students.	Interactions, both between the library/media specialist and students and among students, are polite and respectful, reflecting general warmth and caring, and are appropriate to the cultural and developmental differences among groups of students.	Interactions among the library/media specialist, individual students, and the classroom teachers are highly respectful, reflecting genuine warmth and caring and sensitivity to students' cultures and levels of development. Students themselves ensure high levels of civility among students in the library.
2b: **Establishing a culture for investigation and love of literature**	Library/media specialist conveys a sense that the work of seeking information and reading literature is not worth the time and energy required.	Library/media specialist goes through the motions of performing the work of the position, but without any real commitment to it.	Library/media specialist, in interactions with both students and colleagues, conveys a sense of the importance of seeking information and reading literature.	Library/media specialist, in interactions with both students and colleagues, conveys a sense of the essential nature of seeking information and reading literature. Students appear to have internalized these values.
2c: **Establishing and maintaining library procedures**	Media center routines and procedures (for example, for circulation of materials, working on computers, independent work) are either nonexistent or inefficient, resulting in general confusion. Library assistants are confused as to their role.	Media center routines and procedures (for example, for circulation of materials, working on computers, independent work) have been established but function sporadically. Efforts to establish guidelines for library assistants are partially successful.	Media center routines and procedures (for example, for circulation of materials, working on computers, independent work) have been established and function smoothly. Library assistants are clear as to their role.	Media center routines and procedures (for example, for circulation of materials, working on computers, independent work) are seamless in their operation, with students assuming considerable responsibility for their smooth operation. Library assistants work independently and contribute to the success of the media center.

FIGURE 5.6

Domain 2 for Library/Media Specialists: The Environment (continued)

COMPONENT	LEVEL OF PERFORMANCE			
	UNSATISFACTORY	BASIC	PROFICIENT	DISTINGUISHED
2d: **Managing student behavior**	There is no evidence that standards of conduct have been established, and there is little or no monitoring of student behavior. Response to student misbehavior is repressive or disrespectful of student dignity.	It appears that the library/media specialist has made an effort to establish standards of conduct for students and tries to monitor student behavior and respond to student misbehavior, but these efforts are not always successful.	Standards of conduct appear to be clear to students, and the library/media specialist monitors student behavior against those standards. Library/media specialist's response to student misbehavior is appropriate and respectful to students.	Standards of conduct are clear, with evidence of student participation in setting them. Library/media specialist's monitoring of student behavior is subtle and preventive, and response to student misbehavior is sensitive to individual student needs. Students take an active role in monitoring the standards of behavior.
2e: **Organizing physical space to enable smooth flow**	Library/media specialist makes poor use of the physical environment, resulting in poor traffic flow, confusing signage, inadequate space devoted to work areas and computer use, and general confusion.	Library/media specialist's efforts to make use of the physical environment are uneven, resulting in occasional confusion.	Library/media specialist makes effective use of the physical environment, resulting in good traffic flow, clear signage, and adequate space devoted to work areas and computer use.	Library/media specialist makes highly effective use of the physical environment, resulting in clear signage, excellent traffic flow, and adequate space devoted to work areas and computer use. In addition, book displays are attractive and inviting.

FIGURE 5.7

Domain 3 for Library/Media Specialists: Delivery of Service

COMPONENT	LEVEL OF PERFORMANCE			
	UNSATISFACTORY	BASIC	PROFICIENT	DISTINGUISHED
3a: **Maintaining and extending the library collection in accordance with the school's needs and within budget limitations**	Library/media specialist fails to adhere to district or professional guidelines in selecting materials for the collection and does not periodically purge the collection of outdated material. Collection is unbalanced among different areas.	Library/media specialist is partially successful in attempts to adhere to district or professional guidelines in selecting materials, to weed the collection, and to establish balance.	Library/media specialist adheres to district or professional guidelines in selecting materials for the collection and periodically purges the collection of outdated material. Collection is balanced among different areas.	Library/media specialist selects materials for the collection thoughtfully and in consultation with teaching colleagues, and periodically purges the collection of outdated material. Collection is balanced among different areas.
3b: **Collaborating with teachers in the design of instructional units and lessons**	Library/media specialist declines to collaborate with classroom teachers in the design of instructional lessons and units.	Library/media specialist collaborates with classroom teachers in the design of instructional lessons and units when specifically asked to do so.	Library/media specialist initiates collaboration with classroom teachers in the design of instructional lessons and units.	Library/media specialist initiates collaboration with classroom teachers in the design of instructional lessons and units, locating additional resources from sources outside the school.
3c: **Engaging students in enjoying literature and in learning information skills**	Students are not engaged in enjoying literature and in learning information skills because of poor design of activities, poor grouping strategies, or inappropriate materials.	Only some students are engaged in enjoying literature and in learning information skills due to uneven design of activities, grouping strategies, or partially appropriate materials.	Students are engaged in enjoying literature and in learning information skills because of effective design of activities, grouping strategies, and appropriate materials.	Students are highly engaged in enjoying literature and in learning information skills and take initiative in ensuring the engagement of their peers.

FIGURE 5.7

Domain 3 for Library/Media Specialists: Delivery of Service *(continued)*

COMPONENT	LEVEL OF PERFORMANCE			
	UNSATISFACTORY	BASIC	PROFICIENT	DISTINGUISHED
3d: **Assisting students and teachers in the use of technology in the library/media center**	Library/media specialist declines to assist students and teachers in the use of technology in the library/media center.	Library/media specialist assists students and teachers in the use of technology in the library/media center when specifically asked to do so.	Library/media specialist initiates sessions to assist students and teachers in the use of technology in the library/media center.	Library/media specialist is proactive in initiating sessions to assist students and teachers in the use of technology in the library/media center.
3e: **Demonstrating flexibility and responsiveness**	Library/media specialist adheres to the plan, in spite of evidence of its inadequacy.	Library/media specialist makes modest changes in the library/media program when confronted with evidence of the need for change.	Library/media specialist makes revisions to the library/media program when they are needed.	Library/media specialist is continually seeking ways to improve the library/media program and makes changes as needed in response to student, parent, or teacher input.

FIGURE 5.8

Domain 4 for Library/Media Specialists: Professional Responsibilities

COMPONENT	LEVEL OF PERFORMANCE			
	UNSATISFACTORY	BASIC	PROFICIENT	DISTINGUISHED
4a: **Reflecting on practice**	Library/media specialist does not reflect on practice, or the reflections are inaccurate or self-serving.	Library/media specialist's reflection on practice is moderately accurate and objective, without citing specific examples and with only global suggestions as to how it might be improved.	Library/media specialist's reflection provides an accurate and objective description of practice, citing specific positive and negative characteristics. Library/media specialist makes some specific suggestions as to how the media program might be improved.	Library/media specialist's reflection is highly accurate and perceptive, citing specific examples. Library/media specialist draws on an extensive repertoire to suggest alternative strategies and their likely success.
4b: **Preparing and submitting reports and budgets**	Library/media specialist ignores teacher requests when preparing requisitions and budgets or does not follow established procedures. Inventories and reports are routinely late.	Library/media specialist's efforts to prepare budgets are partially successful, responding sometimes to teacher requests and following procedures. Inventories and reports are sometimes submitted on time.	Library/media specialist honors teacher requests when preparing requisitions and budgets and follows established procedures. Inventories and reports are submitted on time.	Library/media specialist anticipates teacher needs when preparing requisitions and budgets, follows established procedures, and suggests improvements to those procedures. Inventories and reports are submitted on time.
4c: **Communicating with the larger community**	Library/media specialist makes no effort to engage in outreach efforts to parents or the larger community.	Library/media specialist makes sporadic efforts to engage in outreach efforts to parents or the larger community.	Library/media specialist engages in outreach efforts to parents and the larger community.	Library/media specialist is proactive in reaching out to parents and establishing contacts with outside libraries, coordinating efforts for mutual benefit.

FIGURE 5.8

Domain 4 for Library/Media Specialists: Professional Responsibilities *(continued)*

COMPONENT	LEVEL OF PERFORMANCE			
	UNSATISFACTORY	BASIC	PROFICIENT	DISTINGUISHED
4d: **Participating in a professional community**	Library/media specialist's relationships with colleagues are negative or self-serving, and the specialist avoids being involved in school and district events and projects.	Library/media specialist's relationships with colleagues are cordial, and the specialist participates in school and district events and projects when specifically requested.	Library/media specialist participates actively in school and district events and projects and maintains positive and productive relationships with colleagues.	Library/media specialist makes a substantial contribution to school and district events and projects and assumes leadership with colleagues.
4e: **Engaging in professional development**	Library/media specialist does not participate in professional development activities, even when such activities are clearly needed for the enhancement of skills.	Library/media specialist's participation in professional development activities is limited to those that are convenient or are required.	Library/media specialist seeks out opportunities for professional development based on an individual assessment of need.	Library/media specialist actively pursues professional development opportunities and makes a substantial contribution to the profession through such activities as offering workshops to colleagues.
4f: **Showing professionalism**	Library/media specialist displays dishonesty in interactions with colleagues, students, and the public; violates copyright laws.	Library/media specialist is honest in interactions with colleagues, students, and the public; respects copyright laws.	Library/media specialist displays high standards of honesty and integrity in interactions with colleagues, students, and the public; adheres carefully to copyright laws.	Library/media specialist can be counted on to hold the highest standards of honesty and integrity and takes a leadership role with colleagues in ensuring there is no plagiarism or violation of copyright laws.

- Participating in a professional community.
- Engaging in professional development.
- Showing professionalism. This includes integrity, advocacy, and maintaining confidentiality.

Figures 5.9 through 5.12 present the levels of performance for each component of the four domains.

SCHOOL COUNSELORS

School counselors work with other educators to ensure student success. They address students' emotional needs and design approaches to help students chart a course for their lives and careers beyond school. Counselors may work from a separate office or counseling center, or they may take their program into classrooms for sessions with entire classes. Most counselors combine the two settings, selecting the approach that is appropriate to the school's schedule and student needs. Counselors are advocates for the appropriate level of instruction for students, and they engage in interventions designed to support student growth and the achievement of goals. These interventions are accomplished with students individually as well as in small-group and whole-class settings, and consist of both proactive and responsive services.

Proactive guidance services are often referred to as development guidance, in which counselors offer a curriculum of classroom presentations based upon the known developmental needs of children of the particular age group. Responsive services, on the other hand, emerge from issues that appear either in individual students (such as a school phobia) or within the school culture as a whole (for example, when a member of a class dies suddenly).

The role of counselors at the secondary level is quite different from that at the elementary level. With young children, the emphasis is on ensuring appropriate instruction and helping all students acquire communication skills, healthy self-images, and appropriate relationships with their peers. At the secondary level, the counselor's responsibilities typically shift to more individual postsecondary planning, helping students determine their strengths and optimal courses of action.

School counselors work at several levels of responsibility, serving as a resource to individual students, teachers, parents and guardians, and the school as a whole. They counsel individual students regarding such matters as excessive tardiness or behavior problems and help them design an appropriate academic program. They may also collaborate with teachers to present curriculum-based guidance lessons or to offer advice on behavior management or study hall procedures. Guidance counselors regularly confer with parents about any number of issues that affect student learning, typically including issues related to behavior and emotions. In addition, the counselor might work at the school level, interpreting cognitive, aptitude, and achievement tests; interpreting student records; and assisting the school principal and school psychologist in identifying and resolving student needs, issues, and problems.

The domains and components of a school counselor's responsibilities are as follows:

Domain 1: Planning and Preparation
- Demonstrating knowledge of counseling theory and techniques.
- Demonstrating knowledge of child and adolescent development.

FIGURE 5.9

Domain 1 for School Nurses: Planning and Preparation

COMPONENT	LEVEL OF PERFORMANCE			
	UNSATISFACTORY	BASIC	PROFICIENT	DISTINGUISHED
1a: Demonstrating medical knowledge and skill in nursing techniques	Nurse demonstrates little understanding of medical knowledge and nursing techniques.	Nurse demonstrates basic understanding of medical knowledge and nursing techniques.	Nurse demonstrates understanding of medical knowledge and nursing techniques.	Nurse demonstrates deep and thorough understanding of medical knowledge and nursing techniques.
1b: Demonstrating knowledge of child and adolescent development	Nurse displays little or no knowledge of child and adolescent development.	Nurse displays partial knowledge of child and adolescent development.	Nurse displays accurate understanding of the typical developmental characteristics of the age group, as well as exceptions to the general patterns.	In addition to accurate knowledge of the typical developmental characteristics of the age group and exceptions to the general patterns, nurse displays knowledge of the extent to which individual students follow the general patterns.
1c: Establishing goals for the nursing program appropriate to the setting and the students served	Nurse has no clear goals for the nursing program, or they are inappropriate to either the situation or the age of the students.	Nurse's goals for the nursing program are rudimentary and are partially suitable to the situation and the age of the students.	Nurse's goals for the nursing program are clear and appropriate to the situation in the school and to the age of the students.	Nurse's goals for the nursing program are highly appropriate to the situation in the school and to the age of the students and have been developed following consultations with students, parents, and colleagues.

(figure continues)

FIGURE 5.9

Domain 1 for School Nurses: Planning and Preparation *(continued)*

COMPONENT	LEVEL OF PERFORMANCE			
	UNSATISFACTORY	BASIC	PROFICIENT	DISTINGUISHED
1d: **Demonstrating knowledge of government, community, and district regulations and resources**	Nurse demonstrates little or no knowledge of governmental regulations and resources for students available through the school or district.	Nurse displays awareness of governmental regulations and resources for students available through the school or district, but no knowledge of resources available more broadly.	Nurse displays awareness of governmental regulations and resources for students available through the school or district and some familiarity with resources external to the school.	Nurse's knowledge of governmental regulations and resources for students is extensive, including those available through the school or district and in the community.
1e: **Planning the nursing program for both individuals and groups of students, integrated with the regular school program**	Nursing program consists of a random collection of unrelated activities, lacking coherence or an overall structure.	Nurse's plan has a guiding principle and includes a number of worthwhile activities, but some of them don't fit with the broader goals.	Nurse has developed a plan that includes the important aspects of work in the setting.	Nurse's plan is highly coherent and serves to support not only the students individually and in groups, but also the broader educational program.
1f: **Developing a plan to evaluate the nursing program**	Nurse has no plan to evaluate the program or resists suggestions that such an evaluation is important.	Nurse has a rudimentary plan to evaluate the nursing program.	Nurse's plan to evaluate the program is organized around clear goals and the collection of evidence to indicate the degree to which the goals have been met.	Nurse's evaluation plan is highly sophisticated, with imaginative sources of evidence and a clear path toward improving the program on an ongoing basis.

FIGURE 5.10

Domain 2 for School Nurses: The Environment

COMPONENT	LEVEL OF PERFORMANCE			
	UNSATISFACTORY	BASIC	PROFICIENT	DISTINGUISHED
2a: **Creating an environment of respect and rapport**	Nurse's interactions with at least some students are negative or inappropriate.	Nurse's interactions with students are a mix of positive and negative.	Nurse's interactions with students are positive and respectful.	Students seek out the nurse, reflecting a high degree of comfort and trust in the relationship.
2b: **Establishing a culture for health and wellness**	Nurse makes no attempt to establish a culture for health and wellness in the school as a whole, or among students or among teachers.	Nurse's attempts to promote a culture throughout the school for health and wellness are partially successful.	Nurse promotes a culture throughout the school for health and wellness.	The culture in the school for health and wellness, while guided by the nurse, is maintained by both teachers and students.
2c: **Following health protocols and procedures**	Nurse's procedures for the nursing office are nonexistent or in disarray.	Nurse has rudimentary and partially successful procedures for the nursing office.	Nurse's procedures for the nursing office work effectively.	Nurse's procedures for the nursing office are seamless, anticipating unexpected situations.
2d: **Supervising health associates**	No guidelines for delegated duties have been established, or the guidelines are unclear. Nurse does not monitor associates' activities.	Nurse's efforts to establish guidelines for delegated duties are partially successful. Nurse monitors associates' activities sporadically.	Nurse has established guidelines for delegated duties and monitors associates' activities.	Associates work independently, indicating clear guidelines for their work. Nurse's supervision is subtle and professional.
2e: **Organizing physical space**	Nurse's office is in disarray or is inappropriate to the planned activities. Medications are not properly stored.	Nurse's attempts to create a well-organized physical environment are partially successful. Medications are stored properly but are difficult to find.	Nurse's office is well organized and is appropriate to the planned activities. Medications are properly stored and well organized.	Nurse's office is efficiently organized and is highly appropriate to the planned activities. Medications are properly stored and well organized.

FIGURE 5.11

Domain 3 for School Nurses: Delivery of Service

COMPONENT	LEVEL OF PERFORMANCE			
	UNSATISFACTORY	BASIC	PROFICIENT	DISTINGUISHED
3a: **Assessing student needs**	Nurse does not assess student needs, or the assessments result in inaccurate conclusions.	Nurse's assessments of student needs are perfunctory.	Nurse assesses student needs and knows the range of student needs in the school.	Nurse conducts detailed and individualized assessment of student needs to contribute to program planning.
3b: **Administering medications to students**	Medications are administered with no regard to state or district policies.	Medications are administered by designated individuals, but signed release forms are not conveniently stored.	Medications are administered by designated individuals, and signed release forms are conveniently stored and available when needed.	Medications are administered by designated individuals, and signed release forms are conveniently stored. Students take an active role in medication compliance.
3c: **Promoting wellness through classes or classroom presentations**	Nurse's work with students in classes fails to promote wellness.	Nurse's efforts to promote wellness through classroom presentations are partially effective.	Nurse's classroom presentations result in students acquiring the knowledge and attitudes that help them adopt a healthy lifestyle.	Nurse's classroom presentations for wellness are effective, and students assume an active role in the school in promoting a healthy lifestyle.

FIGURE 5.11

Domain 3 for School Nurses: Delivery of Service *(continued)*

COMPONENT	LEVEL OF PERFORMANCE			
	UNSATISFACTORY	BASIC	PROFICIENT	DISTINGUISHED
3d: **Managing emergency situations**	Nurse has no contingency plans for emergency situations.	Nurse's plans for emergency situations have been developed for the most frequently occurring situations but not others.	Nurse's plans for emergency situations have been developed for many situations.	Nurse's plans for emergency situations have been developed for many situations. Students and teachers have learned their responsibilities in case of emergencies.
3e: **Demonstrating flexibility and responsiveness**	Nurse adheres to the plan or program, in spite of evidence of its inadequacy.	Nurse makes modest changes in the nursing program when confronted with evidence of the need for change.	Nurse makes revisions in the nursing program when they are needed.	Nurse is continually seeking ways to improve the nursing program and makes changes as needed in response to student, parent, or teacher input.
3f: **Collaborating with teachers to develop specialized educational programs and services for students with diverse medical needs**	Nurse declines to collaborate with classroom teachers to develop specialized educational programs.	Nurse collaborates with classroom teachers in developing instructional lessons and units when specifically asked to do so.	Nurse initiates collaboration with classroom teachers in developing instructional lessons and units.	Nurse initiates collaboration with classroom teachers in developing instructional lessons and units, locating additional resources from outside the school.

FIGURE 5.12

Domain 4 for School Nurses: Professional Responsibilities

COMPONENT	LEVEL OF PERFORMANCE			
	UNSATISFACTORY	BASIC	PROFICIENT	DISTINGUISHED
4a: **Reflecting on practice**	Nurse does not reflect on practice, or the reflections are inaccurate or self-serving.	Nurse's reflection on practice is moderately accurate and objective without citing specific examples and with only global suggestions as to how it might be improved.	Nurse's reflection provides an accurate and objective description of practice, citing specific positive and negative characteristics. Nurse makes some specific suggestions as to how the nursing program might be improved.	Nurse's reflection is highly accurate and perceptive, citing specific examples. Nurse draws on an extensive repertoire to suggest alternative strategies.
4b: **Maintaining health records in accordance with policy and submitting reports in a timely fashion**	Nurse's reports, records, and documentation are missing, late, or inaccurate, resulting in confusion.	Nurse's reports, records, and documentation are generally accurate, but are occasionally late.	Nurse's reports, records, and documentation are accurate and are submitted in a timely manner.	Nurse's approach to record keeping is highly systematic and efficient and serves as a model for colleagues across the school.
4c: **Communicating with families**	Nurse provides no information to families, either about the nursing program as a whole or about individual students.	Nurse provides limited though accurate information to families about the nursing program as a whole and about individual students.	Nurse provides thorough and accurate information to families about the nursing program as a whole and about individual students.	Nurse is proactive in providing information to families about the nursing program and about individual students through a variety of means.

FIGURE 5.12

Domain 4 for School Nurses: Professional Responsibilities *(continued)*

COMPONENT	LEVEL OF PERFORMANCE			
	UNSATISFACTORY	BASIC	PROFICIENT	DISTINGUISHED
4d: **Participating in a professional community**	Nurse's relationships with colleagues are negative or self-serving, and nurse avoids being involved in school and district events and projects.	Nurse's relationships with colleagues are cordial, and nurse participates in school and district events and projects when specifically requested to do so.	Nurse participates actively in school and district events and projects and maintains positive and productive relationships with colleagues.	Nurse makes a substantial contribution to school and district events and projects and assumes leadership role with colleagues.
4e: **Engaging in professional development**	Nurse does not participate in professional development activities, even when such activities are clearly needed for the development of nursing skills.	Nurse's participation in professional development activities is limited to those that are convenient or are required.	Nurse seeks out opportunities for professional development based on an individual assessment of need.	Nurse actively pursues professional development opportunities and makes a substantial contribution to the profession through such activities as offering workshops to colleagues.
4f: **Showing professionalism**	Nurse displays dishonesty in interactions with colleagues, students, and the public; violates principles of confidentiality.	Nurse is honest in interactions with colleagues, students, and the public; does not violate confidentiality.	Nurse displays high standards of honesty, integrity, and confidentiality in interactions with colleagues, students, and the public; advocates for students when needed.	Nurse can be counted on to hold the highest standards of honesty, integrity, and confidentiality and to advocate for students, taking a leadership role with colleagues.

• Establishing goals for the counseling program appropriate to the setting and the students served.

• Demonstrating knowledge of state and federal regulations and of resources both within and beyond the school and district.

• Planning the counseling program, integrated with the regular school program, and including developmental guidance, intervention, and responsive services. This involves individual and small-group sessions, in-class activities, and includes crisis prevention, intervention, and response.

• Developing a plan to evaluate the counseling program.

Domain 2: The Environment (office/small-group environment)

• Creating an environment of respect and rapport.
• Establishing a culture for productive communication.
• Managing routines and procedures.
• Establishing standards of conduct and contributing to the culture for student behavior throughout the school.
• Organizing physical space.

Domain 3: Delivery of Service

• Assessing student needs.
• Assisting students and teachers in the formulation of academic, personal/social, and career plans, based on knowledge of student needs.
• Using counseling techniques in individual and classroom programs.
• Brokering resources to meet needs.
• Demonstrating flexibility and responsiveness.

Domain 4: Professional Responsibilities

• Reflecting on practice.
• Maintaining records and submitting them in a timely fashion.
• Communicating with families.
• Participating in a professional community.
• Engaging in professional development.
• Showing professionalism. This includes integrity, advocacy, and maintaining confidentiality.

Figures 5.13 through 5.16 present the levels of performance for each component of the four domains.

SCHOOL PSYCHOLOGISTS

School psychologists typically chair the child study team and respond to referrals from classroom teachers and administrators. They consult with teachers to better understand a situation, and they may observe a student in the classroom setting before a formal evaluation. When appropriate, they will contact a student's physician or community mental health provider to better understand the larger context of the child's treatment. In addition, they secure the parents' permission for administering any evaluations.

School psychologists work with students individually and in groups. They also serve as a resource to teachers and guidance counselors, assisting them in their challenges in working with students with disabilities or special talents or students who abuse drugs and other substances. And, most critically, they work with the entire faculty to prevent and manage crises when they occur.

FIGURE 5.13

Domain 1 for School Counselors: Planning and Preparation

COMPONENT	LEVEL OF PERFORMANCE			
	UNSATISFACTORY	BASIC	PROFICIENT	DISTINGUISHED
1a: **Demonstrating knowledge of counseling theory and techniques**	Counselor demonstrates little understanding of counseling theory and techniques.	Counselor demonstrates basic understanding of counseling theory and techniques.	Counselor demonstrates understanding of counseling theory and techniques.	Counselor demonstrates deep and thorough understanding of counseling theory and techniques.
1b: **Demonstrating knowledge of child and adolescent development**	Counselor displays little or no knowledge of child and adolescent development.	Counselor displays partial knowledge of child and adolescent development.	Counselor displays accurate understanding of the typical developmental characteristics of the age group, as well as exceptions to the general patterns.	In addition to accurate knowledge of the typical developmental characteristics of the age group and exceptions to the general patterns, counselor displays knowledge of the extent to which individual students follow the general patterns.
1c: **Establishing goals for the counseling program appropriate to the setting and the students served**	Counselor has no clear goals for the counseling program, or they are inappropriate to either the situation or the age of the students.	Counselor's goals for the counseling program are rudimentary and are partially suitable to the situation and the age of the students.	Counselor's goals for the counseling program are clear and appropriate to the situation in the school and to the age of the students.	Counselor's goals for the counseling program are highly appropriate to the situation in the school and to the age of the students and have been developed following consultations with students, parents, and colleagues.

(figure continues)

FIGURE 5.13

Domain 1 for School Counselors: Planning and Preparation *(continued)*

COMPONENT	LEVEL OF PERFORMANCE			
	UNSATISFACTORY	BASIC	PROFICIENT	DISTINGUISHED
1d: Demonstrating knowledge of state and federal regulations and of resources both within and beyond the school and district	Counselor demonstrates little or no knowledge of governmental regulations and of resources for students available through the school or district.	Counselor displays awareness of governmental regulations and of resources for students available through the school or district, but no knowledge of resources available more broadly.	Counselor displays awareness of governmental regulations and of resources for students available through the school or district, and some familiarity with resources external to the school.	Counselor's knowledge of governmental regulations and of resources for students is extensive, including those available through the school or district and in the community.
1e: Planning the counseling program, integrated with the regular school program	Counseling program consists of a random collection of unrelated activities, lacking coherence or an overall structure.	Counselor's plan has a guiding principle and includes a number of worthwhile activities, but some of them don't fit with the broader goals.	Counselor has developed a plan that includes the important aspects of counseling in the setting.	Counselor's plan is highly coherent and serves to support not only the students individually and in groups, but also the broader educational program.
1f: Developing a plan to evaluate the counseling program	Counselor has no plan to evaluate the program or resists suggestions that such an evaluation is important.	Counselor has a rudimentary plan to evaluate the counseling program.	Counselor's plan to evaluate the program is organized around clear goals and the collection of evidence to indicate the degree to which the goals have been met.	Counselor's evaluation plan is highly sophisticated, with imaginative sources of evidence and a clear path toward improving the program on an ongoing basis.

FIGURE 5.14

Domain 2 for School Counselors: The Environment

COMPONENT	LEVEL OF PERFORMANCE			
	UNSATISFACTORY	BASIC	PROFICIENT	DISTINGUISHED
2a: **Creating an environment of respect and rapport**	Counselor's interactions with students are negative or inappropriate, and the counselor does not promote positive interactions among students.	Counselor's interactions are a mix of positive and negative; the counselor's efforts at encouraging positive interactions among students are partially successful.	Counselor's interactions with students are positive and respectful, and the counselor actively promotes positive student-student interactions.	Students seek out the counselor, reflecting a high degree of comfort and trust in the relationship. Counselor teaches students how to engage in positive interactions.
2b: **Establishing a culture for productive communication**	Counselor makes no attempt to establish a culture for productive communication in the school as a whole, either among students or among teachers, or between students and teachers.	Counselor's attempts to promote a culture throughout the school for productive and respectful communication between and among students and teachers are partially successful.	Counselor promotes a culture throughout the school for productive and respectful communication between and among students and teachers.	The culture in the school for productive and respectful communication between and among students and teachers, while guided by the counselor, is maintained by both teachers and students.
2c: **Managing routines and procedures**	Counselor's routines for the counseling center or classroom work are nonexistent or in disarray.	Counselor has rudimentary and partially successful routines for the counseling center or classroom.	Counselor's routines for the counseling center or classroom work effectively.	Counselor's routines for the counseling center or classroom are seamless, and students assist in maintaining them.

(figure continues)

FIGURE 5.14

Domain 2 for School Counselors: The Environment *(continued)*

COMPONENT	LEVEL OF PERFORMANCE			
	UNSATISFACTORY	BASIC	PROFICIENT	DISTINGUISHED
2d: **Establishing standards of conduct and contributing to the culture for student behavior throughout the school**	Counselor has established no standards of conduct for students during counseling sessions and makes no contribution to maintaining an environment of civility in the school.	Counselor's efforts to establish standards of conduct for counseling sessions are partially successful. Counselor attempts, with limited success, to contribute to the level of civility in the school as a whole.	Counselor has established clear standards of conduct for counseling sessions and makes a significant contribution to the environment of civility in the school.	Counselor has established clear standards of conduct for counseling sessions, and students contribute to maintaining them. Counselor takes a leadership role in maintaining the environment of civility in the school.
2e: **Organizing physical space**	The physical environment is in disarray or is inappropriate to the planned activities.	Counselor's attempts to create an inviting and well-organized physical environment are partially successful.	Counseling center or classroom arrangements are inviting and conducive to the planned activities.	Counseling center or classroom arrangements are inviting and conducive to the planned activities. Students have contributed ideas to the physical arrangement.

FIGURE 5.15

Domain 3 for School Counselors: Delivery of Service

COMPONENT	LEVEL OF PERFORMANCE			
	UNSATISFACTORY	BASIC	PROFICIENT	DISTINGUISHED
3a: **Assessing student needs**	Counselor does not assess student needs, or the assessments result in inaccurate conclusions.	Counselor's assessments of student needs are perfunctory.	Counselor assesses student needs and knows the range of student needs in the school.	Counselor conducts detailed and individualized assessments of student needs to contribute to program planning.
3b: **Assisting students and teachers in the formulation of academic, personal/social, and career plans, based on knowledge of student needs**	Counselor's program is independent of identified student needs.	Counselor's attempts to help students and teachers formulate academic, personal/social, and career plans are partially successful.	Counselor helps students and teachers formulate academic, personal/social, and career plans for groups of students.	Counselor helps individual students and teachers formulate academic, personal/social, and career plans.
3c: **Using counseling techniques in individual and classroom programs**	Counselor has few counseling techniques to help students acquire skills in decision making and problem solving for both interactions with other students and future planning.	Counselor displays a narrow range of counseling techniques to help students acquire skills in decision making and problem solving for both interactions with other students and future planning.	Counselor uses a range of counseling techniques to help students acquire skills in decision making and problem solving for both interactions with other students and future planning.	Counselor uses an extensive range of counseling techniques to help students acquire skills in decision making and problem solving for both interactions with other students and future planning.

(figure continues)

FIGURE 5.15

Domain 3 for School Counselors: Delivery of Service *(continued)*

COMPONENT	LEVEL OF PERFORMANCE			
	UNSATISFACTORY	BASIC	PROFICIENT	DISTINGUISHED
3d: **Brokering resources to meet needs**	Counselor does not make connections with other programs in order to meet student needs.	Counselor's efforts to broker services with other programs in the school are partially successful.	Counselor brokers with other programs within the school or district to meet student needs.	Counselor brokers with other programs and agencies both within and beyond the school or district to meet individual student needs.
3e: **Demonstrating flexibility and responsiveness**	Counselor adheres to the plan or program, in spite of evidence of its inadequacy.	Counselor makes modest changes in the counseling program when confronted with evidence of the need for change.	Counselor makes revisions in the counseling program when they are needed.	Counselor is continually seeking ways to improve the counseling program and makes changes as needed in response to student, parent, or teacher input.

FIGURE 5.16

Domain 4 for School Counselors: Professional Responsibilities

COMPONENT	LEVEL OF PERFORMANCE			
	UNSATISFACTORY	BASIC	PROFICIENT	DISTINGUISHED
4a: **Reflecting on practice**	Counselor does not reflect on practice, or the reflections are inaccurate or self-serving.	Counselor's reflection on practice is moderately accurate and objective without citing specific examples and with only global suggestions as to how it might be improved.	Counselor's reflection provides an accurate and objective description of practice, citing specific positive and negative characteristics. Counselor makes some specific suggestions as to how the counseling program might be improved.	Counselor's reflection is highly accurate and perceptive, citing specific examples that were not fully successful for at least some students. Counselor draws on an extensive repertoire to suggest alternative strategies.
4b: **Maintaining records and submitting them in a timely fashion**	Counselor's reports, records, and documentation are missing, late, or inaccurate, resulting in confusion.	Counselor's reports, records, and documentation are generally accurate but are occasionally late.	Counselor's reports, records, and documentation are accurate and are submitted in a timely manner.	Counselor's approach to record keeping is highly systematic and efficient and serves as a model for colleagues in other schools.
4c: **Communicating with families**	Counselor provides no information to families, either about the counseling program as a whole or about individual students.	Counselor provides limited though accurate information to families about the counseling program as a whole and about individual students.	Counselor provides thorough and accurate information to families about the counseling program as a whole and about individual students.	Counselor is proactive in providing information to families about the counseling program and about individual students through a variety of means.

(figure continues)

FIGURE 5.16

Domain 4 for School Counselors: Professional Responsibilities *(continued)*

COMPONENT	LEVEL OF PERFORMANCE			
	UNSATISFACTORY	BASIC	PROFICIENT	DISTINGUISHED
4d: **Participating in a professional community**	Counselor's relationships with colleagues are negative or self-serving, and counselor avoids being involved in school and district events and projects.	Counselor's relationships with colleagues are cordial, and counselor participates in school and district events and projects when specifically requested.	Counselor participates actively in school and district events and projects and maintains positive and productive relationships with colleagues.	Counselor makes a substantial contribution to school and district events and projects and assumes leadership with colleagues.
4e: **Engaging in professional development**	Counselor does not participate in professional development activities even when such activities are clearly needed for the development of counseling skills.	Counselor's participation in professional development activities is limited to those that are convenient or are required.	Counselor seeks out opportunities for professional development based on an individual assessment of need.	Counselor actively pursues professional development opportunities and makes a substantial contribution to the profession through such activities as offering workshops to colleagues.
4f: **Showing professionalism**	Counselor displays dishonesty in interactions with colleagues, students, and the public; violates principles of confidentiality.	Counselor is honest in interactions with colleagues, students, and the public; does not violate confidentiality.	Counselor displays high standards of honesty, integrity, and confidentiality in interactions with colleagues, students, and the public; advocates for students when needed.	Counselor can be counted on to hold the highest standards of honesty, integrity, and confidentiality and to advocate for students, taking a leadership role with colleagues.

School psychologists consult with teachers, parents, and administrators to find the optimal approach in a situation. They evaluate students to determine eligibility for special services. They also work directly with students and their families to resolve interpersonal or family problems that interfere with progress in school. Psychologists also design prevention programs and promote tolerance and appreciation of diversity throughout the school. They may provide training in anger management and social skills and help students and their families deal with crises, such as death, illness, or community trauma.

In interactions with students and families, it is essential for a psychologist to establish rapport and trust. Psychologists must refrain from conveying the attitude that there is something "wrong" with the student; rather, it is important to learn the unique ways in which the student learns in order to tailor the learning environment to the student's needs. A battery of tests is designed to reveal important aspects of the student's approach to learning, enabling the psychologist to plan an intervention appropriate for that student.

Because of the sensitive nature of a psychologist's work, confidentiality is absolutely essential. Records must be scrupulously maintained and kept in a secure location. Professional guidelines must be carefully adhered to and state and federal regulations followed.

The domains and components of a school psychologist's responsibilities are as follows:

Domain 1: Planning and Preparation

• Demonstrating knowledge and skill in using psychological instruments to evaluate students.

• Demonstrating knowledge of child and adolescent development and psychopathology.

• Establishing goals for the psychology program appropriate to the setting and the students served.

• Demonstrating knowledge of state and federal regulations and of resources both within and beyond the school and district.

• Planning the psychology program, integrated with the regular school program, to meet the needs of individual students and including prevention.

• Developing a plan to evaluate the psychology program.

Domain 2: The Environment

• Establishing rapport with students. This includes using interpersonal skills such as empathy to establish trust and reduce anxiety.

• Establishing a culture for positive mental health throughout the school.

• Establishing and maintaining clear procedures for referrals.

• Establishing standards of conduct in the testing center.

• Organizing physical space for testing of students and storage of materials.

Domain 3: Delivery of Service

• Responding to referrals; consulting with teachers and administrators.

• Evaluating student needs in compliance with National Association of School Psychologists (NASP) guidelines.

• Chairing evaluation team.

• Planning interventions to maximize students' likelihood of success.

• Maintaining contact with physicians and community mental health service providers.
• Demonstrating flexibility and responsiveness.

Domain 4: Professional Responsibilities

• Reflecting on practice.
• Communicating with families. This is accomplished by, for example, establishing rapport and securing permissions.
• Maintaining accurate records.
• Participating in a professional community. This includes providing inservice training when appropriate.
• Engaging in professional development.
• Showing professionalism. This includes integrity, advocacy, and maintaining confidentiality.

Figures 5.17 through 5.20 present the levels of performance for each component of the four domains.

THERAPEUTIC SPECIALISTS

Professional specialists include the following:

• Speech/language pathologists, who provide services to students with speech and language challenges.
• Audiologists, who provide assistance to hearing-impaired learners.
• Physical therapists, who offer specialized services to physically challenged children.
• Occupational therapists, who offer life-skills training.
• Learning support specialists, who assist classroom teachers with students who have mental health diagnoses.

Therapists are an integral part of the school community, working as members of the entire team of educators. Their work is not "extra"; rather, it is central to ensuring that certain students have full access to the school's offerings. However, not every school staff includes each of the therapeutic specialists on a full-time basis. The consequence, as with other shared resources, is that communication between the specialist and both administrators and classroom teachers is a critical aspect of the role.

The domains and components of a therapeutic specialist's responsibilities are as follows:

Domain 1: Planning and Preparation

• Demonstrating knowledge and skill in the specialist therapy area; holding the relevant certificate or license.
• Establishing goals for the therapy program appropriate to the setting and the students served.
• Demonstrating knowledge of district, state, and federal regulations and guidelines.
• Demonstrating knowledge of resources, both within and beyond the school and district.
• Planning the therapy program, integrated with the regular school program, to meet the needs of individual students.
• Developing a plan to evaluate the therapy program.

Domain 2: The Environment

• Establishing rapport with students.
• Organizing time effectively.
• Establishing and maintaining clear procedures for referrals.

FIGURE 5.17

Domain 1 for School Psychologists: Planning and Preparation

COMPONENT	LEVEL OF PERFORMANCE			
	UNSATISFACTORY	BASIC	PROFICIENT	DISTINGUISHED
1a: **Demonstrating knowledge and skill in using psychological instruments to evaluate students**	Psychologist demonstrates little or no knowledge and skill in using psychological instruments to evaluate students.	Psychologist uses a limited number of psychological instruments to evaluate students.	Psychologist uses 5–8 psychological instruments to evaluate students and determine accurate diagnoses.	Psychologist uses a wide range of psychological instruments to evaluate students and knows the proper situations in which each should be used.
1b: **Demonstrating knowledge of child and adolescent development and psychopathology**	Psychologist demonstrates little or no knowledge of child and adolescent development and psychopathology.	Psychologist demonstrates basic knowledge of child and adolescent development and psychopathology.	Psychologist demonstrates thorough knowledge of child and adolescent development and psychopathology.	Psychologist demonstrates extensive knowledge of child and adolescent development and psychopathology and knows variations of the typical patterns.
1c: **Establishing goals for the psychology program appropriate to the setting and the students served**	Psychologist has no clear goals for the psychology program, or they are inappropriate to either the situation or the age of the students.	Psychologist's goals for the treatment program are rudimentary and are partially suitable to the situation and the age of the students.	Psychologist's goals for the treatment program are clear and appropriate to the situation in the school and to the age of the students.	Psychologist's goals for the treatment program are highly appropriate to the situation in the school and to the age of the students and have been developed following consultations with students, parents, and colleagues.

(figure continues)

FIGURE 5.17

Domain 1 for School Psychologists: Planning and Preparation (continued)

COMPONENT	LEVEL OF PERFORMANCE			
	UNSATISFACTORY	BASIC	PROFICIENT	DISTINGUISHED
1d: **Demonstrating knowledge of state and federal regulations and of resources both within and beyond the school and district**	Psychologist demonstrates little or no knowledge of governmental regulations or of resources for students available through the school or district.	Psychologist displays awareness of governmental regulations and of resources for students available through the school or district, but no knowledge of resources available more broadly.	Psychologist displays awareness of governmental regulations and of resources for students available through the school or district and some familiarity with resources external to the district.	Psychologist's knowledge of governmental regulations and of resources for students is extensive, including those available through the school or district and in the community.
1e: **Planning the psychology program, integrated with the regular school program, to meet the needs of individual students and including prevention**	Psychologist's plan consists of a random collection of unrelated activities, lacking coherence or an overall structure.	Psychologist's plan has a guiding principle and includes a number of worthwhile activities, but some of them don't fit with the broader goals.	Psychologist has developed a plan that includes the important aspects of work in the setting.	Psychologist's plan is highly coherent and preventive and serves to support students individually, within the broader educational program.
1f: **Developing a plan to evaluate the psychology program**	Psychologist has no plan to evaluate the program or resists suggestions that such an evaluation is important.	Psychologist has a rudimentary plan to evaluate the psychology program.	Psychologist's plan to evaluate the program is organized around clear goals and the collection of evidence to indicate the degree to which the goals have been met.	Psychologist's evaluation plan is highly sophisticated, with imaginative sources of evidence and a clear path toward improving the program on an ongoing basis.

FIGURE 5.18

Domain 2 for School Psychologists: The Environment

COMPONENT	LEVEL OF PERFORMANCE			
	UNSATISFACTORY	BASIC	PROFICIENT	DISTINGUISHED
2a: **Establishing rapport with students**	Psychologist's interactions with students are negative or inappropriate; students appear uncomfortable in the testing center.	Psychologist's interactions are a mix of positive and negative; the psychologist's efforts at developing rapport are partially successful.	Psychologist's interactions with students are positive and respectful; students appear comfortable in the testing center.	Students seek out the psychologist, reflecting a high degree of comfort and trust in the relationship.
2b: **Establishing a culture for positive mental health throughout the school**	Psychologist makes no attempt to establish a culture for positive mental health in the school as a whole, either among students or teachers, or between students and teachers.	Psychologist's attempts to promote a culture throughout the school for positive mental health in the school among students and teachers are partially successful.	Psychologist promotes a culture throughout the school for positive mental health in the school among students and teachers.	The culture in the school for positive mental health among students and teachers, while guided by the psychologist, is maintained by both teachers and students.
2c: **Establishing and maintaining clear procedures for referrals**	No procedures for referrals have been established; when teachers want to refer a student for special services, they are not sure how to go about it.	Psychologist has established procedures for referrals, but the details are not always clear.	Procedures for referrals and for meetings and consultations with parents and administrators are clear to everyone.	Procedures for all aspects of referral and testing protocols are clear to everyone and have been developed in consultation with teachers and administrators.

(figure continues)

FIGURE 5.18

Domain 2 for School Psychologists: The Environment *(continued)*

COMPONENT	LEVEL OF PERFORMANCE			
	UNSATISFACTORY	BASIC	PROFICIENT	DISTINGUISHED
2d: **Establishing standards of conduct in the testing center**	No standards of conduct have been established, and psychologist disregards or fails to address negative student behavior during an evaluation.	Standards of conduct appear to have been established in the testing center. Psychologist's attempts to monitor and correct negative student behavior during an evaluation are partially successful.	Standards of conduct have been established in the testing center. Psychologist monitors student behavior against those standards; response to students is appropriate and respectful.	Standards of conduct have been established in the testing center. Psychologist's monitoring of students is subtle and preventive, and students engage in self-monitoring of behavior.
2e: **Organizing physical space for testing of students and storage of materials**	The testing center is disorganized and poorly suited to student evaluations. Materials are not stored in a secure location and are difficult to find when needed.	Materials in the testing center are stored securely, but the center is not completely well organized, and materials are difficult to find when needed.	The testing center is well organized; materials are stored in a secure location and are available when needed.	The testing center is highly organized and is inviting to students. Materials are stored in a secure location and are convenient when needed.

FIGURE 5.19

Domain 3 for School Psychologists: Delivery of Service

COMPONENT	LEVEL OF PERFORMANCE			
	UNSATISFACTORY	BASIC	PROFICIENT	DISTINGUISHED
3a: **Responding to referrals; consulting with teachers and administrators**	Psychologist fails to consult with colleagues or to tailor evaluations to the questions raised in the referral.	Psychologist consults on a sporadic basis with colleagues, making partially successful attempts to tailor evaluations to the questions raised in the referral.	Psychologist consults frequently with colleagues, tailoring evaluations to the questions raised in the referral.	Psychologist consults frequently with colleagues, contributing own insights and tailoring evaluations to the questions raised in the referral.
3b: **Evaluating student needs in compliance with National Association of School Psychologists (NASP) guidelines**	Psychologist resists administering evaluations, selects instruments inappropriate to the situation, or does not follow established procedures and guidelines.	Psychologist attempts to administer appropriate evaluation instruments to students but does not always follow established time lines and safeguards.	Psychologist administers appropriate evaluation instruments to students and ensures that all procedures and safeguards are faithfully adhered to.	Psychologist selects, from a broad repertoire, those assessments that are most appropriate to the referral questions and conducts information sessions with colleagues to ensure that they fully understand and comply with procedural time lines and safeguards.
3c: **Chairing evaluation team**	Psychologist declines to assume leadership of the evaluation team.	Psychologist assumes leadership of the evaluation team when directed to do so, preparing adequate IEPs.	Psychologist assumes leadership of the evaluation team as a standard expectation; prepares detailed IEPs.	Psychologist assumes leadership of the evaluation team and takes initiative in assembling materials for meetings. IEPs are prepared in an exemplary manner.

(figure continues)

FIGURE 5.19

Domain 3 for School Psychologists: Delivery of Service *(continued)*

COMPONENT	LEVEL OF PERFORMANCE			
	UNSATISFACTORY	BASIC	PROFICIENT	DISTINGUISHED
3d: **Planning interventions to maximize students' likelihood of success**	Psychologist fails to plan interventions suitable to students, or interventions are mismatched with the findings of the assessments.	Psychologist's plans for students are partially suitable for them or are sporadically aligned with identified needs.	Psychologist's plans for students are suitable for them and are aligned with identified needs.	Psychologist develops comprehensive plans for students, finding ways to creatively meet student needs and incorporate many related elements.
3e: **Maintaining contact with physicians and community mental health service providers**	Psychologist declines to maintain contact with physicians and community mental health service providers.	Psychologist maintains occasional contact with physicians and community mental health service providers.	Psychologist maintains ongoing contact with physicians and community mental health service providers.	Psychologist maintains ongoing contact with physicians and community mental health service providers and initiates contacts when needed.
3f: **Demonstrating flexibility and responsiveness**	Psychologist adheres to the plan or program, in spite of evidence of its inadequacy.	Psychologist makes modest changes in the treatment program when confronted with evidence of the need for change.	Psychologist makes revisions in the treatment program when it is needed.	Psychologist is continually seeking ways to improve the treatment program and makes changes as needed in response to student, parent, or teacher input.

FIGURE 5.20

Domain 4 for School Psychologists: Professional Responsibilities

COMPONENT	LEVEL OF PERFORMANCE			
	UNSATISFACTORY	BASIC	PROFICIENT	DISTINGUISHED
4a: **Reflecting on practice**	Psychologist does not reflect on practice, or the reflections are inaccurate or self-serving.	Psychologist's reflection on practice is moderately accurate and objective without citing specific examples, and with only global suggestions as to how it might be improved.	Psychologist's reflection provides an accurate and objective description of practice, citing specific positive and negative characteristics. Psychologist makes some specific suggestions as to how the counseling program might be improved.	Psychologist's reflection is highly accurate and perceptive, citing specific examples that were not fully successful for at least some students. Psychologist draws on an extensive repertoire to suggest alternative strategies.
4b: **Communicating with families**	Psychologist fails to communicate with families and secure necessary permission for evaluations or communicates in an insensitive manner.	Psychologist's communication with families is partially successful; permissions are obtained, but there are occasional insensitivities to cultural and linguistic traditions.	Psychologist communicates with families and secures necessary permission for evaluations and does so in a manner sensitive to cultural and linguistic traditions.	Psychologist secures necessary permissions and communicates with families in a manner highly sensitive to cultural and linguistic traditions. Psychologist reaches out to families of students to enhance trust.
4c: **Maintaining accurate records**	Psychologist's records are in disarray; they may be missing, illegible, or stored in an insecure location.	Psychologist's records are accurate and legible and are stored in a secure location.	Psychologist's records are accurate and legible, well organized, and stored in a secure location.	Psychologist's records are accurate and legible, well organized, and stored in a secure location. They are written to be understandable to another qualified professional.

(figure continues)

FIGURE 5.20

Domain 4 for School Psychologists: Professional Responsibilities *(continued)*

COMPONENT	LEVEL OF PERFORMANCE			
	UNSATISFACTORY	BASIC	PROFICIENT	DISTINGUISHED
4d: **Participating in** **a professional** **community**	Psychologist's relationships with colleagues are negative or self-serving, and psychologist avoids being involved in school and district events and projects.	Psychologist's relationships with colleagues are cordial, and psychologist participates in school and district events and projects when specifically requested.	Psychologist participates actively in school and district events and projects and maintains positive and productive relationships with colleagues.	Psychologist makes a substantial contribution to school and district events and projects and assumes leadership with colleagues.
4e: **Engaging in** **professional** **development**	Psychologist does not participate in professional development activities, even when such activities are clearly needed for the ongoing development of skills.	Psychologist's participation in professional development activities is limited to those that are convenient or are required.	Psychologist seeks out opportunities for professional development based on an individual assessment of need.	Psychologist actively pursues professional development opportunities and makes a substantial contribution to the profession through such activities as offering workshops to colleagues.
4f: **Showing** **professionalism**	Psychologist displays dishonesty in interactions with colleagues, students, and the public and violates principles of confidentiality.	Psychologist is honest in interactions with colleagues, students, and the public, plays a moderate advocacy role for students, and does not violate confidentiality.	Psychologist displays high standards of honesty, integrity, and confidentiality in interactions with colleagues, students, and the public, and advocates for students when needed.	Psychologist can be counted on to hold the highest standards of honesty, integrity, and confidentiality and to advocate for students, taking a leadership role with colleagues.

• Establishing standards of conduct in the treatment center.

• Organizing physical space for testing of students and providing therapy.

Domain 3: Delivery of Service

• Responding to referrals and evaluating student needs.

• Developing and implementing treatment plans to maximize students' success.

• Communicating with families.

• Collecting information; writing reports.

• Demonstrating flexibility and responsiveness.

Domain 4: Professional Responsibilities

• Reflecting on practice.

• Collaborating with teachers and administrators.

• Maintaining an effective data-management system.

• Participating in a professional community. This includes providing inservice training when appropriate.

• Engaging in professional development.

• Showing professionalism, including integrity, advocacy, and maintaining confidentiality.

Figures 5.21 through 5.24 present the levels of performance for each component of the four domains.

FIGURE 5.21

Domain 1 for Therapeutic Specialists: Planning and Preparation

COMPONENT	LEVEL OF PERFORMANCE			
	UNSATISFACTORY	BASIC	PROFICIENT	DISTINGUISHED
1a: **Demonstrating knowledge and skill in the specialist therapy area; holding the relevant certificate or license**	Specialist demonstrates little or no knowledge and skill in the therapy area; does not hold the necessary certificate or license.	Specialist demonstrates basic knowledge and skill in the therapy area; holds the necessary certificate or license.	Specialist demonstrates thorough knowledge and skill in the therapy area; holds the necessary certificate or license.	Specialist demonstrates extensive knowledge and skill in the therapy area; holds an advanced certificate or license.
1b: **Establishing goals for the therapy program appropriate to the setting and the students served**	Specialist has no clear goals for the therapy program, or they are inappropriate to either the situation or the age of the students.	Specialist's goals for the therapy program are rudimentary and are partially suitable to the situation and to the age of the students.	Specialist's goals for the therapy program are clear and appropriate to the situation in the school and to the age of the students.	Specialist's goals for the therapy program are highly appropriate to the situation in the school and to the age of the students and have been developed following consultations with administrators and teachers.
1c: **Demonstrating knowledge of district, state, and federal regulations and guidelines**	Specialist demonstrates little or no knowledge of special education laws and procedures.	Specialist demonstrates basic knowledge of special education laws and procedures.	Specialist demonstrates thorough knowledge of special education laws and procedures.	Specialist's knowledge of special education laws and procedures is extensive; specialist takes a leadership role in reviewing and revising district policies.

FIGURE 5.21

Domain 1 for Therapeutic Specialists: Planning and Preparation *(continued)*

COMPONENT	LEVEL OF PERFORMANCE			
	UNSATISFACTORY	BASIC	PROFICIENT	DISTINGUISHED
1d: **Demonstrating knowledge of resources, both within and beyond the school and district**	Specialist demonstrates little or no knowledge of resources for students available through the school or district.	Specialist demonstrates basic knowledge of resources for students available through the school or district.	Specialist demonstrates thorough knowledge of resources for students available through the school or district and some familiarity with resources outside the district.	Specialist demonstrates extensive knowledge of resources for students available through the school or district and in the larger community.
1e: **Planning the therapy program, integrated with the regular school program, to meet the needs of individual students**	Therapy program consists of a random collection of unrelated activities, lacking coherence or an overall structure.	Specialist's plan has a guiding principle and includes a number of worthwhile activities, but some of them don't fit with the broader goals.	Specialist has developed a plan that includes the important aspects of work in the setting.	Specialist's plan is highly coherent and preventive and serves to support students individually, within the broader educational program.
1f: **Developing a plan to evaluate the therapy program**	Specialist has no plan to evaluate the program or resists suggestions that such an evaluation is important.	Specialist has a rudimentary plan to evaluate the therapy program.	Specialist's plan to evaluate the program is organized around clear goals and the collection of evidence to indicate the degree to which the goals have been met.	Specialist's evaluation plan is highly sophisticated, with imaginative sources of evidence and a clear path toward improving the program on an ongoing basis.

FIGURE 5.22

Domain 2 for Therapeutic Specialists: The Environment

COMPONENT	LEVEL OF PERFORMANCE			
	UNSATISFACTORY	BASIC	PROFICIENT	DISTINGUISHED
2a: **Establishing rapport with students**	Specialist's interactions with students are negative or inappropriate; students appear uncomfortable in the testing and treatment center.	Specialist's interactions are a mix of positive and negative; the specialist's efforts at developing rapport are partially successful.	Specialist's interactions with students are positive and respectful; students appear comfortable in the testing and treatment center.	Students seek out the specialist, reflecting a high degree of comfort and trust in the relationship.
2b: **Organizing time effectively**	Specialist exercises poor judgment in setting priorities, resulting in confusion, missed deadlines, and conflicting schedules.	Specialist's time-management skills are moderately well developed; essential activities are carried out, but not always in the most efficient manner.	Specialist exercises good judgment in setting priorities, resulting in clear schedules and important work being accomplished in an efficient manner.	Specialist demonstrates excellent time-management skills, accomplishing all tasks in a seamless manner; teachers and students understand their schedules.
2c: **Establishing and maintaining clear procedures for referrals**	No procedures for referrals have been established; when teachers want to refer a student for special services, they are not sure how to go about it.	Specialist has established procedures for referrals, but the details are not always clear.	Procedures for referrals and for meetings and consultations with parents and administrators are clear to everyone.	Procedures for all aspects of referral and testing protocols are clear to everyone and have been developed in consultation with teachers and administrators.

FIGURE 5.22

Domain 2 for Therapeutic Specialists: The Environment *(continued)*

COMPONENT	LEVEL OF PERFORMANCE			
	UNSATISFACTORY	BASIC	PROFICIENT	DISTINGUISHED
2d: **Establishing standards of conduct in the treatment center**	No standards of conduct have been established, and specialist disregards or fails to address negative student behavior during evaluation or treatment.	Standards of conduct appear to have been established for the testing and treatment center. Specialist's attempts to monitor and correct negative student behavior during evaluation and treatment are partially successful.	Standards of conduct have been established for the testing and treatment center. Specialist monitors student behavior against those standards; response to students is appropriate and respectful.	Standards of conduct have been established for the testing and treatment center. Specialist's monitoring of students is subtle and preventive, and students engage in self-monitoring of behavior.
2e: **Organizing physical space for testing of students and providing therapy**	The testing and treatment center is disorganized and poorly suited to working with students. Materials are usually available.	The testing and treatment center is moderately well organized and moderately well suited to working with students. Materials are difficult to find when needed.	The testing and treatment center is well organized; materials are available when needed.	The testing and treatment center is highly organized and is inviting to students. Materials are convenient when needed.

FIGURE 5.23

Domain 3 for Therapeutic Specialists: Delivery of Service

COMPONENT	LEVEL OF PERFORMANCE			
	UNSATISFACTORY	BASIC	PROFICIENT	DISTINGUISHED
3a: **Responding to referrals and evaluating student needs**	Specialist fails to respond to referrals or makes hasty assessments of student needs.	Specialist responds to referrals when pressed and makes adequate assessments of student needs.	Specialist responds to referrals and makes thorough assessments of student needs.	Specialist is proactive in responding to referrals and makes highly competent assessments of student needs.
3b: **Developing and implementing treatment plans to maximize students' success**	Specialist fails to develop treatment plans suitable for students, or plans are mismatched with the findings of assessments.	Specialist's plans for students are partially suitable for them or sporadically aligned with identified needs.	Specialist's plans for students are suitable for them and are aligned with identified needs.	Specialist develops comprehensive plans for students, finding ways to creatively meet student needs and incorporate many related elements.
3c: **Communicating with families**	Specialist fails to communicate with families and secure necessary permission for evaluations or communicates in an insensitive manner.	Specialist's communication with families is partially successful; permissions are obtained, but there are occasional insensitivities to cultural and linguistic traditions.	Specialist communicates with families and secures necessary permission for evaluations, doing so in a manner sensitive to cultural and linguistic traditions.	Specialist secures necessary permissions and communicates with families in a manner highly sensitive to cultural and linguistic traditions. Specialist reaches out to families of students to enhance trust.

FIGURE 5.23

Domain 3 for Therapeutic Specialists: Delivery of Service *(continued)*

COMPONENT	LEVEL OF PERFORMANCE			
	UNSATISFACTORY	BASIC	PROFICIENT	DISTINGUISHED
3d: **Collecting information;** **writing reports**	Specialist neglects to collect important information on which to base treatment plans; reports are inaccurate or not appropriate to the audience.	Specialist collects most of the important information on which to base treatment plans; reports are accurate but lacking in clarity and not always appropriate to the audience.	Specialist collects all the important information on which to base treatment plans; reports are accurate and appropriate to the audience.	Specialist is proactive in collecting important information, interviewing teachers and parents if necessary; reports are accurate and clearly written and are tailored for the audience.
3e: **Demonstrating** **flexibility and** **responsiveness**	Specialist adheres to the plan or program, in spite of evidence of its inadequacy.	Specialist makes modest changes in the treatment program when confronted with evidence of the need for change.	Specialist makes revisions in the treatment program when they are needed.	Specialist is continually seeking ways to improve the treatment program and makes changes as needed in response to student, parent, or teacher input.

FIGURE 5.24

Domain 4 for Therapeutic Specialists: Professional Responsibilities

COMPONENT	LEVEL OF PERFORMANCE			
	UNSATISFACTORY	BASIC	PROFICIENT	DISTINGUISHED
4a: **Reflecting on practice**	Specialist does not reflect on practice, or the reflections are inaccurate or self-serving.	Specialist's reflection on practice is moderately accurate and objective without citing specific examples, and with only global suggestions as to how it might be improved.	Specialist's reflection provides an accurate and objective description of practice, citing specific positive and negative characteristics. Specialist makes some specific suggestions as to how the therapy program might be improved.	Specialist's reflection is highly accurate and perceptive, citing specific examples that were not fully successful for at least some students. Specialist draws on an extensive repertoire to suggest alternative strategies.
4b: **Collaborating with teachers and administrators**	Specialist is not available to staff for questions and planning and declines to provide background material when requested.	Specialist is available to staff for questions and planning and provides background material when requested.	Specialist initiates contact with teachers and administrators to confer regarding individual cases.	Specialist seeks out teachers and administrators to confer regarding cases, soliciting their perspectives on individual students.
4c: **Maintaining an effective data-management system**	Specialist's data-management system is either nonexistent or in disarray; it cannot be used to monitor student progress or to adjust treatment when needed.	Specialist has developed a rudimentary data-management system for monitoring student progress and occasionally uses it to adjust treatment when needed.	Specialist has developed an effective data-management system for monitoring student progress and uses it to adjust treatment when needed.	Specialist has developed a highly effective data-management system for monitoring student progress and uses it to adjust treatment when needed. Specialist uses the system to communicate with teachers and parents.

FIGURE 5.24

Domain 4 for Therapeutic Specialists: Professional Responsibilities *(continued)*

COMPONENT	LEVEL OF PERFORMANCE			
	UNSATISFACTORY	BASIC	PROFICIENT	DISTINGUISHED
4d: **Participating in a professional community**	Specialist's relationships with colleagues are negative or self-serving, and specialist avoids being involved in school and district events and projects.	Specialist's relationships with colleagues are cordial, and specialist participates in school and district events and projects when specifically asked to do so.	Specialist participates actively in school and district events and projects and maintains positive and productive relationships with colleagues.	Specialist makes a substantial contribution to school and district events and projects and assumes a leadership role with colleagues.
4e: **Engaging in professional development**	Specialist does not participate in professional development activities, even when such activities are clearly needed for the development of skills.	Specialist's participation in professional development activities is limited to those that are convenient or are required.	Specialist seeks out opportunities for professional development based on an individual assessment of need.	Specialist actively pursues professional development opportunities and makes a substantial contribution to the profession through such activities as offering workshops to colleagues.
4f: **Showing professionalism, including integrity, advocacy, and maintaining confidentiality**	Specialist displays dishonesty in interactions with colleagues, students, and the public and violates principles of confidentiality.	Specialist is honest in interactions with colleagues, students, and the public, plays a moderate advocacy role for students, and does not violate norms of confidentiality.	Specialist displays high standards of honesty, integrity, and confidentiality in interactions with colleagues, students, and the public and advocates for students when needed.	Specialist can be counted on to hold the highest standards of honesty, integrity, and confidentiality and to advocate for students, taking a leadership role with colleagues.

6

USING THE FRAMEWORK

Since late 1996, hundreds of teacher preparation programs, schools and school districts, and government agencies (both in the United States and in other countries) have found the framework for teaching to be a useful tool in defining good teaching. Educators have discovered that by having clear standards of practice and descriptions of how those standards are manifested in various contexts, they are able to be increasingly thoughtful and reflective about their work. This chapter describes the different uses of the framework for teaching and offers some suggestions based on the experience of thousands of educators.

USING THE FRAMEWORK FOR REFLECTION AND SELF-ASSESSMENT

The most powerful use of the framework—and one that should accompany any other use—is for reflection and self-assessment. Research has clearly demonstrated that reflection on practice improves teaching. Using a framework to guide such reflection enhances the value of the activity and makes teaching more purposeful, thoughtful, and rewarding.

Reflection and self-assessment are, first of all, individual activities, conducted in the privacy of a teacher's own classroom or home. Although the results of reflection and self-assessment may play a part in other, shared activities—such as mentoring or peer coaching—reflection and self-assessment are typically conducted individually. But although thinking is, by definition, an individual activity, it is stimulated by conversation. Many users of the framework have reported having much deeper and more productive discussions about teaching since they have been using the framework; they attribute these deeper conversations to both the clarity of the language and the reflection that the discussion encourages.

Reflection is a natural and highly productive human activity. All of us tend to engage in reflection as we mull over the results of our activities and how we could have been more effective. In other words, as pointed out by John Dewey in the early days of the 20th century, we learn not from our experience but from our thinking *about* that experience. It is the *thinking* that matters.

However, those new to the profession tend to engage in somewhat superficial, global reflection. When asked about a lesson after its completion, a new teacher might report that it was "fine" or "terrible" or make some other general statement. (It is possible, of course, that in the culture of the school, teachers feel they must say "fine"—that it is not safe to admit deficiency—but even where the environment permits it, many new teachers honestly believe that the lesson was "fine" even in the face of evidence to the contrary.) Accurate reflection, in other words, is a *learned* skill, one that many teachers early in their careers have not yet acquired.

To be productive, reflection on practice must be systematic and analytic. When a lesson has not gone well, it is important for a teacher not only to recognize that it was not successful but also to be able to determine the reasons for that outcome. Only if those reasons are understood can a teacher improve the lesson (or others like it) the next time. Therefore, to improve skills in reflection, one must learn how to analyze all the decisions made in the course of designing the lesson and the on-the-spot adjustments made during the course of the lesson itself.

Cooperating teachers, mentors, supervisors of student teachers, and even evaluators have found that they can help inexperienced teachers improve their skills at reflection by structuring the conversations that take place after a lesson. Because of the power of reflection, it is essential that the discussion take place in a comfortable and safe environment; teachers should know, in other words, that the important point is not whether or not a lesson proceeds perfectly. What *is* important is that they are able to determine what about the lesson was not satisfactory (unsuitable activity or materials? poor pacing? not the right student groupings?) so it can be remedied the next time. Teaching involves such a complex set of skills that lessons are almost never perfect. The key to being an accomplished teacher is acquiring the skill to continually improve one's practice; an important vehicle for this is reflection and conversation.

Once inexperienced teachers have acquired skill in reflection, they can do it on their own. They will have acquired the habits of mind that enable them to mentally "run through" lessons after they teach them, considering the different aspects of the lesson, to determine what they might want to change before they teach the lesson again (either next period or a year from now) while it is fresh in their minds. They may write themselves a note, for example, that the directions for the activity were not clear and should be rewritten, or that the materials used did not work for some students.

The types of questions that might structure a reflection conversation or a teacher's independent reflection appear in Figure 6.1.

A natural result of reflection on practice is a teacher's sense of which areas of teaching would be the most important ones to strengthen. In that way, the reflection is inherent in self-assessment, which leads inevitably to a focus for professional learning and growth. And although the two activities—reflection and self-assessment—might be considered to be distinct conceptually, in practice they are intertwined; one cannot happen without the other. This application of the framework for teaching is its most powerful and is integral to every other use of it.

Some educators and policymakers have suggested that different frameworks for different stages of a teacher's career would be useful to promote learning. They argue that because the work of beginners is a specific stage of a teacher's career, a unique set of standards should describe that work. Indeed, several attempts have been made to promulgate beginning teaching standards, most notably those of INTASC, illustrated in Chapter 1. However, it is the position of this framework for teaching that the work of experienced teachers is essentially identical to that of beginning teachers; experienced teachers just do it *better.* That is, the work of teaching is the same, but as teachers acquire experience, and therefore expertise, they do the various tasks with greater skill and automaticity.

USING THE FRAMEWORK FOR TEACHER PREPARATION

Universities and teacher preparation programs in many countries around the world have found the framework for teaching to be useful in the design and implementation of their programs. In some settings, particularly outside the United States, slight adaptations of the framework have been necessary, but the essential organizational structure has remained intact. The framework has contributed to the preparation of teachers in several distinct, though related, areas: organizing program offerings, observing experienced teachers, and supervising student teachers.

Organizing Program Offerings

Because the framework for teaching describes the important work of teaching, courses can be analyzed according to whether students have the opportunity to acquire the concepts and skills presented in the framework. The courses themselves, of course, may be structured around the important ideas that underlie teaching—for example, child and adolescent development, the major ideas within each of the disciplines, designing engaging instruction, managing complex learning environments, specific instructional skills, and so on. But taken together, a teacher preparation program should include all the elements of the framework for teaching. And the course syllabi can be analyzed in light of the components of the framework. Therefore, a course on child and adolescent development

FIGURE 6.1

Interview Protocol for a Post-observation (Reflection) Conference

Name of Teacher _____ School _____

1. In general, how successful was the lesson? Did the students learn what you intended for them to learn? How do you know?

2. If you were able to bring samples of student work, what do those samples reveal about those students' levels of engagement and understanding?

3. Comment on your classroom procedures, student conduct, and your use of physical space. To what extent did these contribute to student learning?

4. Did you depart from your plan? If so, how, and why?

5. Comment on different aspects of your instructional delivery (e.g., activities, grouping of students, materials, and resources). To what extent were they effective?

6. If you had a chance to teach this lesson again to the same group of students, what would you do differently?

would help teachers-in-training acquire the knowledge and skills required for Component 1b (Demonstrating Knowledge of Students); one in classroom management would address both Components 2c (Managing Classroom Procedures) and 2d (Managing Student Behavior.) Moreover, some important course offerings in university programs address areas that, in the framework, are included in the common themes, such as cultural competence and the use of technology.

Observing Experienced Teachers

Most teacher preparation programs include an opportunity for students to observe in schools. However, many such observations are largely unstructured, with the benefits to students essentially random. With the framework for teaching as a guide, students can make a point of watching how experienced teachers establish, for example, classroom routines (Component 2c) or how the teachers structure a class discussion so all students participate (Component 3b). Furthermore, students can interview experienced teachers using an instrument common across the program to ensure that everyone is obtaining at least some common insights from the teachers they observe. Individuals could, of course, elaborate on the established questions, but they would at least share a core set. The post-observation questions included in Figure 6.1 could be used for this purpose.

Supervising Student Teachers

Many teacher preparation programs use the framework for teaching as the basis of an instrument to observe student teachers. Every teacher preparation program includes some type of

clinical practice, in which students assume increasingly greater responsibility for the class of a teacher to whom they are assigned. The students receive feedback from both their cooperating teacher and the program supervisor. Clearly, the more consistent this feedback is from the two sources, the more valuable it is for the student. In addition, however, when a teacher preparation program structures its observation instrument around the framework for teaching, students can be absolutely clear as to what the observers will be looking for; there are no secrets or mysteries.

When cooperating teachers and supervisors observe student teachers, it is not sufficient to simply watch; they must watch for *certain things* so the feedback can be meaningful. For example, when using the framework, it is clear to both parties what characterizes an environment of respect and rapport. An observer can watch a class, making notes about those things that provide evidence of such an environment. This requires purposeful observation and then consideration of the evidence in light of the rubrics in the framework.

It is not only during a lesson that student teachers demonstrate their teaching skill. They have also had to *plan* the lesson, revealing their proficiency in the components of Domain 1 (Planning and Preparation). Student teachers should be able to answer the questions listed in Figure 6.2 (either orally or in writing) to either a cooperating teacher or a university supervisor.

Of course, there are some aspects of teaching that student teachers do not do, or do not do to the same extent as do regular teachers. For example, they will communicate with families, if at all, on a much more limited basis than do regular teachers. Similarly, most student teachers don't participate as actively in a professional community by, for example, serving

---

FIGURE 6.2

Interview Protocol for a Pre-observation (Planning) Conference

---

Questions for discussion:

1. To which part of your curriculum does this lesson relate?

2. How does this learning "fit" in the sequence of learning for this class?

3. Briefly describe the students in this class, including those with special needs.

4. What are your learning outcomes for this lesson? What do you want the students to understand?

5. How will you engage the students in the learning? What will you do? What will the students do? Will the students work in groups, or individually, or as a large group? Provide any worksheets or other materials the students will be using.

6. How will you differentiate instruction for different individuals or groups of students in the class?

7. How and when will you know whether the students have learned what you intend?

8. Is there anything that you would like me to specifically observe during the lesson?

on a curriculum committee, as do teachers who are full members of the faculty. Such adaptations do not suggest that the framework for teaching does not describe the work of student teachers, only that they do not yet carry the full responsibility of teaching.

USING THE FRAMEWORK FOR RECRUITMENT AND HIRING

Many school districts using the framework for teaching have discovered that structuring their recruitment and hiring process around the domains and components can greatly enhance the likelihood that they will hire teachers who will be successful in the district. The framework can be woven into the hiring process in several related, though distinct, ways.

The first use of the framework in recruitment and hiring is as the basis for interview questions. Many school district officials have crafted questions based on the framework to use when they interview teacher candidates. For example, "How do you establish standards of conduct in your classroom?" These questions enable those conducting the interview to learn about a number of important aspects of a teacher's approach to teaching and to working with both colleagues and families.

When interviewing teaching candidates who are just completing their training and who therefore don't have much actual teaching experience, interview questions, naturally, must be modified to some degree. For example, student teachers may not have had the opportunity to work with a class to establish routines and procedures, but if they have interviewed experienced teachers on this matter and observed the results of routines being effectively (or perhaps ineffectively) established,

they will have worked out an approach in their own minds.

In addition, the framework can be used as the basis for analyzing videotapes and teacher portfolios. Some school districts require their teacher candidates to submit a videotape of their teaching and perhaps a professional portfolio. These can be analyzed as to the teacher's effectiveness in the different areas of skill described in the framework for teaching.

When a school district uses the framework for recruitment and hiring, that very fact can help teaching candidates decide that they do (or do not) want to join that professional staff. That is, the district is saying, in a clear manner, that this is how it defines good teaching, and it wants candidates to know that before they even apply for a position.

USING THE FRAMEWORK FOR MENTORING AND INDUCTION

The complexity of teaching can be daunting for those new to the profession. Teaching is one of the few professions in which novices must assume the same responsibilities as veterans in the field. In some teaching environments, rookies are presented with the most challenging students, the largest number of preparations, inadequate or limited materials, and the least attractive rooms. First-year teachers are far more likely than veterans not to have their own room, which results in working on an itinerant basis, moving their supplies from room to room on a cart.

All these conditions lead to stress for a novice teacher, which can lead to high rates of attrition. All schools and districts want to help new teachers be successful, but their first concern is to retain them in the profession. People who enter the field of education often have other career options. If teaching is too difficult, too stressful, too unrewarding, or too highly politicized, they may take their talents into another arena.

The task for an induction program and for mentors in such a program is not to make teaching easy; that is probably impossible, given the realities of classroom life. Teaching is not an easy job, period. But it is rewarding—or at least it can be. The challenge, then, is for a mentor teacher to help a novice experience sufficient rewards in daily life so that the novice wants to master the complex details needed to become truly accomplished. Once the thousands of small skills are mastered, the patterns established, the curriculum understood, and the procedures organized in a routine, teachers are free to exercise their creativity. But in the beginning, accomplishing these activities can seem hopeless; there is far too much to do, and the students and their parents do not tolerate many false starts.

One of the greatest gifts an experienced teacher can offer the profession is to serve as a mentor to a novice. By sharing acquired wisdom, the veteran can spare the beginner hours of time and countless occasions of self-doubt. By serving as a friendly critic or just a patient listener, the mentor can assist the novice in identifying those areas of teaching that will benefit most from focused attention. The mentor can help by analyzing the novice's plans and classroom interactions and by making specific and substantive suggestions for improvement. In addition, the mentor can serve as a demonstration teacher, modeling techniques of effective instruction.

The framework for teaching plays an important role in the mentor-novice relationship. If the novice has conducted a self-assessment using the framework, this analysis is most helpful in determining which areas of teaching need primary attention.

Alternatively, the mentor may observe the novice in action or review lesson and unit plans and make suggestions, using the framework to show areas needing attention. The components provide a road map to teaching; by using the road map, both the mentor and the beginning teacher can focus their energies on those areas of teaching where improvement will have the greatest overall effect.

With beginning teachers, the first area for teaching that usually needs to be mastered is the classroom environment (Domain 2). Components in Domain 2 relate to aspects of the classroom that are not directly instructional, such as creating an environment of respect and rapport, establishing a culture for learning, managing student behavior, and organizing physical space. Probably most important for the novice, Domain 2 also includes establishing and maintaining routines and procedures. Most educators find that they must have these procedural matters mastered before they can let their creative energies loose on the instructional aspects of teaching.

Another rich area for mentoring is content and, more specifically, content-related pedagogical expertise. A new teacher of high school history can learn much about the teaching of history from a mentor in the same department. A teacher with expertise in teaching elementary mathematics has much to offer a novice preparing a 3rd grade math lesson. Such expertise is valuable and should be made available whenever possible.

Novice teachers can also learn from a mentor whose expertise lies in a different content area or with students of a different level, particularly with respect to general pedagogical issues and the classroom environment (Domain 2). In general, a mentor doesn't need content expertise to notice that some students are dominating the discussion or that students are not engaged in the activities. A teacher's skill in questioning and discussion techniques is independent of the content being explored. Therefore, even though content expertise is valuable from a mentor, much assistance may be derived from a mentoring relationship with a teacher with a different specialty. In fact, such cross-fertilization can provide other benefits not available when the novice and the mentor share a similar background and teaching assignment.

Mentors who work with novice teachers must cultivate the skills of providing feedback and suggestions constructively. These consultative skills enable a mentor to offer support that may otherwise be perceived as criticism. One technique involves making positive comments about a lesson or a unit plan. Sometimes the tendency is to focus exclusively on the areas of performance that need improvement and omit references to the many strengths displayed. All teachers, particularly those new to the profession, need to hear their good points described and commented upon. They may not be sure that a particular approach is a good one, and hearing it praised by a respected teacher can go a long way toward building confidence. An effective mentor builds on the identified strengths of the novice and provides for training in areas needing refinement or growth.

When a mentor sees room for improvement, a wise approach is to focus on purposes and to ask questions before making suggestions. Most novices are eager to adopt better practices, but advice makes more sense when it is presented as a method to better achieve the novice teacher's purposes. Therefore, conversations about the teacher's intentions and ways to achieve the teacher's goals help a novice appreciate that all instructional decisions have consequences and that some accomplish the teacher's purposes better than others.

USING THE FRAMEWORK FOR PEER COACHING

Professional educators continually try to learn. They recognize that their education does not end when they receive their degrees, and they continue to incorporate research findings into their practice. They have internalized the idea that all good teaching can improve; they seek out other outstanding teachers and learn from, as well as teach, their colleagues. The peer coaching relationship is one of professional synergy, with each participant offering insights that result in the improvement of teaching. Teachers who engage in a peer coaching relationship acknowledge that even excellent teaching can improve and that in a profession as demanding and as subject to new research findings as teaching, everyone's professional responsibility involves enhancing one's skills.

The framework for teaching enhances the peer coaching relationship among educators. Time is well spent when peers conduct self-assessments and then discuss areas of perceived weakness and strength with each other. When teachers use the same framework for teaching, they improve communication because they're using the same set of concepts and terms to describe phenomena. In addition, by using the framework, they can be sure that the areas chosen for improvement are truly those most in need of work.

Colleagues can use the framework in many ways to enhance the peer coaching process. First, self-assessments show which areas need improvement. Then, in consultation with their colleagues, teachers can request assistance in those areas, asking their peers to review lesson and unit plans or to observe a lesson. The subsequent conversations are rich even if they are not based on the framework. When such dialogue is grounded in the language of the framework, however, it is enhanced by the shared understanding that derives from a common view of the teaching process.

Considerations that apply to the mentor-novice relationship also apply to the peer coaching partnership. For example, expertise in content and skills in providing substantive and supportive feedback benefit both individuals. But because the people involved in a peer coaching relationship are both experienced teachers, the dialogue reflects that parity. Experienced teachers recognize one another's strengths—how they offer and accept instructional suggestions is a mark of professionalism.

USING THE FRAMEWORK FOR SUPERVISION AND EVALUATION

Current supervision theory states that to be effective, supervisory practices must be regulated in large part by the teacher. The teacher decides what happens in a classroom, and instructional practice cannot improve without these decisions being the best possible. The framework for teaching can transform what is generally the rather meaningless ritual of supervisory evaluation into a powerful process for thinking about instructional excellence.

How to develop evaluation procedures that simultaneously ensure high-quality teaching and promote professional learning by teachers has been thoroughly described elsewhere (see Danielson & McGreal, 2000). The fundamental principles of such an approach are described here.

Ensuring High-Quality Teaching

Schools have an ethical and statutory requirement to ensure teaching of high quality for all their students. Schools accept funds, either from a government agency (in the case of publicly funded schools) or from parents (in the case of private and parochial schools); the parents have a right to expect teaching of high quality. The evaluation system is the one system designed specifically to provide that assurance.

The challenges confronting a school or a district in ensuring high-quality teaching include several essential features:

• The criteria used to define good teaching must both be grounded in research and reflect the professional wisdom of educators who will use the system. The conversations among educators to establish those criteria can make a substantial contribution to the professional culture of the school.

• The system must include the opportunity for teachers to provide evidence of all the different criteria, and the criteria must be known in advance.

• Everyone in the school or district must have access to sufficient training to ensure that administrators can make consistent judgments based on evidence of practice and that teachers understand the system well enough to demonstrate their skill.

To the extent that the framework for teaching is a research-based definition of good teaching used by a school or a district, then the obligation to ensure good teaching is a matter of ensuring that teachers can demonstrate the knowledge and skill described in the framework. Doing so requires conducting classroom observations, to be sure, because much of what is important about good teaching can be observed during classroom interactions. But classroom observations must be accompanied by conferences both before and after the lesson. The preconference (or, to use a more descriptive term, the planning conference) provides essential evidence of a teacher's skill in planning a lesson. The teacher's plan can be considered in light of various factors, such as the extent to which the instructional outcomes represent important learning aligned to content standards or the lesson is situated within a larger coherent sequence of lessons. In addition, when a preconference is integral to an observation, teachers become accustomed to considering such questions. Figure 6.2 offers a series of questions that teachers could be asked before an observed lesson.

Of course, although the conference before an observed lesson can provide evidence of a teacher's skill in planning for the lesson, it gives no indication of the teacher's skill in long-range planning. For that, a unit plan is needed, such as that outlined in Figure 6.3. By completing three-week unit plans, teachers demonstrate the thinking that has resulted in how they treat a topic with a group of students. The unit plan suggested here is brief, consisting of a single page. The boxes for each day are used to note the topic for the day and generally how students will engage with that topic. Obviously units vary in length. Teachers can adapt the form to accommodate longer units by using more than one form, or they can adapt it to accommodate shorter units by using only a portion of the form. The unit plan illustrates a teacher's skill in Component 1e, Designing Coherent Instruction.

Component 1f (Designing Student Assessments) is a critical aspect of instructional planning. In fact, along with determining what they want students to learn, teachers must decide how

FIGURE 6.3

Three-Week Unit Plan

Name _____ School _____

Grade Level _____ Subject _____ Dates of Unit _____

Daily Topic and Activities				
Monday	**Tuesday**	**Wednesday**	**Thursday**	**Friday**

they will know if the students have learned it. Assessment is important for both single lessons and longer units, although a teacher's plan for assessing student learning in a single lesson may be fairly informal. But there are times when systematic assessment is called for and must be planned. A unit plan, therefore, is not complete without the inclusion of assessment methodologies to be used, the criteria or standards by which student work will be assessed, and a scoring guide or rubric, if appropriate.

The postconference (or reflection conference) plays an important role in the observation process. The discussion enables the evaluator to gain access to the teacher's thinking about the lesson, how it might have been done differently, and how it could have been improved. Indeed, many experienced users of the framework for teaching find the postobservation conference to be the most valuable aspect of the entire observation process.

Many important aspects of teaching happen "behind the scenes" and are not captured in a classroom observation at all. For example, an evaluator will not obtain any evidence of the components of Domain 4 (except Component 4a—Reflecting on Teaching—which is revealed during a postobservation conference). Therefore, it may be necessary to ask teachers to assemble a collection, or portfolio, of evidence to demonstrate their skill in, for example, communicating with families, participating in a professional community, contributing to the profession, and engaging in professional growth. Sample log forms for teachers to use in documenting their activities for the components in Domain 4 are included as Figures 6.4 through 6.8.

Teachers can also supply other indications of their work in the classroom through analyzing an assignment and student work in response to the assignment. Assignments for students are not equal in their value in engaging students in learning or in their level of cognitive challenge. Analyzing student work provides another window into classroom practice that is not available from any other source. The questions in Figure 6.9 can provide a structure for that analysis.

Analyzing student work is an immensely powerful activity for teachers to undertake; it indicates the level of student engagement and the degree of understanding by individual students. By examining all the student work from an assignment, teachers can gain insight not only into their students' learning but also into their own teaching. As a result of this analysis, they may determine that a different approach to a topic would be more effective in the future. It is worth noting in this regard

FIGURE 6.4

Family Contact Log

Name _____

School _____ School Year _____

Date	Person Contacted	Type of Contact (person, phone)	Purpose	Outcome

FIGURE 6.5

School and District Contribution Log

Name _____

School _____ School Year _____

Date	Event (e.g., committee meeting, open house)	Contribution

FIGURE 6.6

Professional Contribution Log

Name _____

School _____ School Year _____

Date	Event or Service (e.g., conference presentation, mentoring)	Contribution

FIGURE 6.7

Professional Development Log

Name _____

School _____ School Year _____

Date	Event or Service (e.g., workshop, conference, course)	Benefits Derived

FIGURE 6.8

Research Log

Name _____ School _____

Grade Level _____ Subject _____ Dates of Unit _____

1. Write a question that you would like to answer about student learning or your teaching.

2. What information do you need to answer the question?

3. In the Action Plan, indicate how you plan to answer the question.

Action Plan		
Step	**Actions**	**Time Line**
1		
2		
3		
4		

4. Summary and Conclusions: If you are able to complete the research, answer the following questions on separate paper:

   - What have you learned from this project?
   - What additional questions do you have?
   - Do you plan to alter your practice as a result of this project? If so, how?

FIGURE 6.9

Questions for Analyzing an Activity or Assignment

Attach activity directions or an assignment that engages students in learning an important concept. This might be a homework assignment, a worksheet, project guidelines, or a problem to solve. After looking at student papers, select several examples of student work in response to the assignment. These should reflect the full range of student ability in the class and should include any feedback you offered to students on their work.

Consider the following questions, as appropriate:

1. What is the concept you intend for your students to learn or explore?

2. How does this assignment "fit" within the prior and future learning of students in this class?

3. Why did you decide to organize the assignment in this manner? That is, how does this approach advance student understanding?

4. Consider the student work, both of the class as a whole and of those for whom you have samples.

   • What does it tell you about their level of understanding?

   • What does it say about their perseverance?

5. If you had the opportunity to make this same assignment again, would you do it in the same way? If not, how might you alter it, and why?

6. Given the student work, what do you plan to do next with these students?

---

that of all the activities teachers undertake in preparing their portfolios to submit for certification by the National Board for Professional Teaching Standards, many report that they find the analysis of student work to be the most rewarding.

Promoting Professional Learning

A second (and some would say even more important) reason to implement good teacher evaluation procedures is to engage teachers in important professional learning. Although many teachers—and some administrators—are skeptical that this can occur, many educators who have used the framework for evaluation purposes attest to its results in encouraging professional growth. However, just basing an evaluation system on a good definition of teaching is not sufficient to promote learning; the procedures themselves must ensure it. Important characteristics of such an evaluation system are (1) teacher engagement with the process, (2) teacher reflection and conversation, and (3) trust.

Teacher engagement with the process. In many schools, evaluation is something *done to* teachers, with the teachers themselves playing an *essentially passive* role. A typical sequence of activities in a traditional observation/ supervision system proceeds as follows: the evaluator comes to watch the teacher, the evaluator takes notes, the evaluator returns to his office, the evaluator writes up notes, and the evaluator returns and tells the teacher about her teaching. It is evident that in this system the evaluator is doing all the work, while the teacher is essentially passive.

One of the things we absolutely know about learning is that it is done by the *learner,* whether this person is an adult or a child. Therefore, if an evaluation system is to engage teachers in learning, it must require that they play an active role.

Teacher reflection and conversation. An evaluation system that promotes teacher learning will be one in which teachers reflect on their practice. This can be encouraged through the reflection conference following an observed lesson; indeed, even if time must be saved and corners cut, the reflection conference is so important that it should never be skipped. But teacher reflection can also accompany a teacher's portfolio, particularly if teachers are asked to comment on items in the portfolio, such as samples of student work, or on what they have derived from professional development courses and workshops. Indeed, one of the principal findings of those who have participated in the certification process of the National Board for Professional Teaching Standards is that the process itself is highly rewarding; even when they don't obtain certification, teachers report that they have learned a lot about their teaching from the process alone.

Trust. It is well known that fear shuts people down. Therefore, an evaluation system that teachers will learn the most from is one in which they don't feel threatened. Many districts have achieved such a system, at least with their teachers working under a continuing contract, by organizing the system around three tracks.

In the three-track system, probationary teachers are assigned to Track 1, in which their performance is evaluated against the components of the framework for teaching. This is, of course, a high-stakes evaluation. (For this reason, it is essential that mentors not be placed in the position of evaluating their mentees; if they do, it undermines the trusting relationship they have, which is so critical to the probationary teacher's honesty.)

In the three-track system, tenured (or continuing contract) teachers are placed in Track 2, which is a highly professional system of evaluation. It is assumed that the teacher is, at the very least, competent, so the focus of the evaluation shifts away from establishing basic quality. Such evaluation, then, can emphasize a professional relationship between the teacher and the evaluator and can concern itself with improvement of practice. In some school districts, teachers, in some years, don't engage in a formal evaluation at all; instead, they conduct a self-assessment, establish growth goals, and work to improve their practice on their own or with others in a study group.

Track 3 is that phase of the evaluation process designed to assist tenured (or continuing contract) teachers whose performance has slipped and whose performance is below standard. This may be for reasons independent of their teaching (e.g., the serious illness of a family member), but it may result from a teacher simply becoming stale. Track 3 is intended to provide structured assistance and support, so a teacher's performance improves sufficiently to return to the activities of Track 2.

The framework for teaching has proved to be extremely valuable to educators across the United States and in other countries as they work to strengthen the profession. It contributes to the concept of teaching as a profession and is a resource to all those who aim to prepare teachers for their work, to hire teachers for their schools, to mentor beginning teachers, and to improve their own practice. Its principal contribution to all those efforts is to provide a common language and to enable educators to develop a shared understanding of important aspects of practice.

APPENDIX: THE RESEARCH FOUNDATION

*Author's note:
Ann T. DeRosa,
an educator in the
Readington Township
School District in
New Jersey, contributed
to the update of the
research foundation.*

The framework for teaching is based on the Praxis III criteria developed by the Educational Testing Service (ETS) after extensive surveys of the research literature, consultation with expert practitioners and researchers, wide-ranging job analyses, summaries of the demands of state licensing programs, and fieldwork. The components include those aspects of teaching that are expected of experienced as well as beginning teachers. The research foundation for the Praxis III criteria is summarized here because it is relevant to this framework for teaching. Many of the findings presented derive from a work by Carol Anne Dwyer (1994) called *Development of the Knowledge Base for the Praxis III: Classroom Performance Assessments Assessment Criteria*. This appendix presents in an abbreviated form some results of the extensive research that ETS conducted that is described in detail in that publication.

The knowledge base for the assessment criteria used in Praxis III: Classroom Performance Assessments was derived over an extended period (1987 to 1993) from three distinct sources: the "wisdom of practice" (Shulman, 1987) of experienced teachers, the theory and data developed by educational researchers, and the requirements developed by state teacher-licensing authorities. These sources of information are interrelated: both experienced teachers and state licensing bodies draw on the educational research literature for their understanding of good teaching.

The process of developing the assessment criteria for Praxis III was iterative, drawing on extensive research on the tasks of teaching. Such work involved conducting job analyses of elementary, middle, and high school beginning teachers, as well as administrators. ETS staff prepared the surveys, with assistance from the American Association of Colleges for Teacher Education, the American Federation of Teachers, the National Association of Elementary School Principals, the National Association of Secondary School Principals, the National Association of State Directors of Teacher Education and Certification, and the National Education Association. ETS researchers also conducted an extensive literature search to summarize and synthesize the most reliable findings on effective teaching. Drafts of assessment criteria were reviewed by expert panels and subjected to the rigors of pilot and field testing. And the requirements of state licensing agencies were analyzed for their statements of teaching criteria. From this process emerged the assessment criteria used in ETS's Praxis III: Classroom Performance Assessments.

Although the framework for teaching derives from the same research base as the criteria for Praxis III, the framework differs from Praxis III in two important ways. First, the framework is intended to apply to the work of all teachers, not only newly licensed ones; second, it is designed to be used in professional conversations that accompany mentoring or peer coaching. In contrast, the Praxis III criteria were developed solely for assessment.

Leading practitioners extensively reviewed the framework, which was subjected to the rigors of testing in school situations. However, it is ultimately the validation of individual users (teachers and supervisors) that matters. The framework must resonate with the professional vision that individuals bring to their craft. Only when the components are found to be consistent with the way in which individuals view their work will the components be of value.

The framework divides the complex act of teaching into four broad realms of activity, or domains. Each domain consists of five or six components. Using the four domains as a structure, the rest of the appendix provides the research supporting the components.

DOMAIN 1: PLANNING AND PREPARATION

The research on planning and preparation for teaching is abundant and clear. Skowron (2001) underscores the importance of careful planning:

> Good planning sets the stage for good teaching, which in turn fosters optimal learning. Teachers who know how to plan know precisely what they want to accomplish—or more exactly, what they want their students to accomplish. Poor planning results in no one, including the teacher, having a clear understanding of what is to be accomplished. Effective instruction starts with an organized instructional plan. (p. 2)

Shulman's (1987) earlier work supports Component 1a (Demonstrating Knowledge of Content and Pedagogy):

> We expect teachers to understand what they teach and, when possible, to understand it in several

ways. They should understand how a given idea relates to other ideas within the same subject area and to ideas in other subjects as well. (p. 14)

He also illuminates the other components of Domain 1:

The key to distinguishing the knowledge base of teaching lies at the intersection of content and pedagogy, in the capacity of a teacher to transform the content knowledge he or she possesses into forms that are pedagogically powerful and yet adaptive to the variations in ability and background presented by the students. (p. 15)

Many other studies emphasize the central role of content knowledge and pedagogical expertise. Most states require some evidence of this knowledge as a prerequisite for licensing. One of the five main principles, or core propositions, that is assessed as part of the certification process through the National Board for Professional Teaching Standards refers to teachers understanding the material that they teach. The core proposition states, "Teachers know the subjects they teach and how to teach those subjects to students."

The importance of becoming familiar with and building on students' knowledge and skills (Component 1b) is also the focus of much research and writing. There has been an explosion of research on students' prior knowledge. The work of Sykes and Bird (1992) strongly demonstrates that prior conceptions exert a powerful hold and are difficult to alter.

Therefore, teachers are best positioned to help students engage in meaningful learning or dispel misconceptions when they understand and recognize the value of their students'

knowledge and strive to add to it. Marzano (2004) addresses major factors that influence the development of academic background knowledge. He believes that the number of experiences that students encounter in school will directly add to their knowledge of content. Jackson and Davis (2000) give the following advice to teachers: "Meet students where they are, since people learn best by connecting new information to old" (p. 83).

Other authors support the constructivist view of teaching and learning that underlies the framework for professional practice. Many researchers, including Brooks and Brooks (1993), assert that when teachers recognize and honor the human impulse to construct new understandings, they create unlimited possibilities for students. Also consistent with these findings, an American Psychological Association publication (McCombs, 1992) defines learning as "an individual process of constructing meaning from information and experience, filtered through each individual's unique perceptions, thoughts, and feelings."

The importance of setting clear instructional outcomes (Component 1c) is well documented in the research literature. Jones (1992) cites many studies demonstrating the link between effective teaching and learning and the teacher's formulation of learning goals that are appropriate to the students. Schmoker (1999) studied the importance of goals relative to schools. He states, "School success depends upon how effectively we select, define, and measure progress and how well we adjust effort toward goals" (p. 25).

An important element of the appropriateness of a goal relates to intellectual rigor. Lowered expectations are often manifested in rote exercises and teaching that remains at a literal level. Rhem (1999) discusses teacher expectations and Robert Rosenthal's viewpoint. Rhem quotes Rosenthal as saying, "If you think your students can't achieve very much, are perhaps not too bright, you may be inclined to teach simple stuff, do a lot of drills, read from your lecture notes, give simple assignments calling for simplistic factual answers" (p. 3).

The need for designing coherent instruction (Component 1e) is also highly supported by research literature. For example, Jackson and Davis (2000) make recommendations for organizing instruction. They believe that content should be organized around concepts because the brain searches for meaningful patterns as it connects parts to wholes. Another suggestion that they offer centers on selecting pertinent experiences:

> Connect what happens in the classroom to the students, either directly or by helping them discover links to the world beyond the classroom, since people learn best when what they are learning has relevance to themselves or their society. (p. 84)

Designing coherent instruction includes knowing what instructional materials may be used (Component 1d). Jackson and Davis (2000) also address the need for teachers to use resources available through collaboration. They discuss how special education teachers and other colleagues can be excellent resources when planning instruction. Additionally, they highlight the link between instruction and assessment and assert that assessment should be directly connected to instruction and designed to provide ongoing, useful feedback, to both students and teachers, on what students have learned (Component 1f). They go on to state the following:

> To decide what assessments will reveal evidence of familiarity, mastery, and enduring understanding, teachers must consider a range of assessment methods that allow for ongoing and cumulative feedback, otherwise known as formative and summative assessment. (p. 55)

Wiggins (1998) also believes that assessment feedback should be used to improve teaching and learning progressively, not just to audit student performance. Wiggins and McTighe (1998) discuss the role that teachers serve:

> Teachers are designers. An essential act of our profession is the design of curriculum and learning experiences to meet specified purposes. We are also designers of assessments to diagnose student needs to guide our teaching and to enable us, our students, and others (parents and administrators) to determine whether our goals have been achieved; that is, did the students learn and understand the desired knowledge? (p. 7)

DOMAIN 2: THE CLASSROOM ENVIRONMENT

Research on the development of expertise shows that novice teachers must master at least the rudiments of classroom management before they can become skilled at instruction. That is, attention to routines and procedures, the physical environment, and the establishment of norms and expectations for student behavior are prerequisites to good instruction.

Of course, the relationship is not a simple one. Research supports the need for classroom management, and evidence from both research and informal experience indicates that high student engagement in learning is both a cause and an effect of successful classroom management. Effective teachers attend to various elements of the classroom environment, creating and maintaining an atmosphere of respect, caring, and commitment to important work.

Distinguished teachers demonstrate genuine caring and respect for individual students (Component 2a). Whitaker (2004) notes that one of the hallmarks of effective teachers is that they create a positive atmosphere in their classrooms and schools. He goes on to state, "Effective teachers treat everyone with respect, every day" (p. 45). Tomlinson (1999) addresses how teachers can create a healthy classroom environment. She believes that teachers must appreciate each child as an individual and recognize that all children have intellect, emotions, and changing physical needs. Jackson and Davis (2000) recommend that teachers provide students with rich learning environments, a recommendation that is consistent with Component 2b. They describe intelligence as fluid, not fixed, and maintain that it will increase, given access to a diversity of materials, opinions, and options.

Evertson and Harris (1992) emphasize the need to establish routines and procedures and to teach them along with expectations for appropriate performance. The need for establishing clear routines to optimize learning (Component 2c) is also documented by Jensen (1998). He believes that teachers should provide predictability through school and classroom rituals, which serve as a way to reduce environmental stress for students.

Whitaker (2004) describes how effective teachers manage student behavior (Component 2d):

Great teachers are very clear about their approach to student behavior. They establish clear expectations at the start of the year and follow them consistently as the year progresses. (pp. 17–18)

He goes on to explain that although consequences for misbehavior are established, they are secondary to the expectations.

Research indicates that physical factors (Component 2e) have an impact on student learning and can serve to minimize student misbehavior. An online *Scholastic* article, referencing excerpts from Linda Shalaway's publication *Learning to Teach . . . Not Just for Beginners* (2005), examines the physical environments of successful classrooms. Shalaway claims that warm, well-run classrooms begin with the room's physical layout—the arrangement of desks and working space, the attractiveness and appeal of bulletin boards, the storage of materials and supplies. She also explains that easily accessible materials and supplies can eliminate delays, disruptions, and confusion as students prepare for activities. Finally, she addresses what she calls "other important environmental features," such as temperature, lighting, and noise level.

DOMAIN 3: INSTRUCTION

Recent educational research has emphasized constructivist learning (and therefore teaching) and a renewed interest in "teaching for understanding" and "conceptual learning." Much of the earlier research on effective teaching, however, is still relevant and useful to practitioners. One approach is not superior to the others. Rather, as explained earlier, effective practices are designed to achieve desired results. As educators expand their expectations for student learning to focus more on conceptual understandings and problem-solving skills, the instructional strategies used must correspondingly change.

Effective teachers communicate clearly about learning expectations, goals, and specific instructions for meeting these goals (Component 3a). The work of Skowron (2001) and Tomlinson (1999) strongly supports these tenets, as well as those associated with teacher flexibility and responsiveness to student needs (Component 3e).

The research base for questioning and discussion techniques (Component 3b) and student engagement with learning (Component 3c) is fairly consistent. Brooks and Brooks (1993) suggest that effective teachers encourage student inquiry by asking thoughtful, open-ended questions and encouraging students to ask questions of each other. They assert that complex, thoughtful questions challenge students to look beyond the apparent, to delve into issues deeply and broadly, and to form their own understandings of events and phenomena. Ellett's (1990) work states that student involvement is needed:

> In teaching students to think, the teacher deliberately structures and uses teaching methods and learning tasks that actively involve *students* [italics in original] in ample opportunities to develop concepts and skills in generating, structuring, transferring, and restructuring knowledge. (p. 47)

Skowron (2001) reviews the literature in this area and comes to a similar conclusion:

> The purpose of engagement is to involve students in developing important concepts, skills, and

processes. Engagement provides the condition in which concepts are made meaningful. (p. 15)

Using assessment in instruction (Component 3d) is also integral to providing superior educational opportunities. Skowron (2001) states:

> Monitoring students as they engage in a learning task is a crucial part of teaching. It is important for students to receive feedback on their progress throughout the learning activity. At times encouragement or positive affirmation is all that is needed. At other times clarification or instructional guidance is necessary to prevent misunderstandings. When confused, some students willingly ask for help. Other students do not. And still others do not even know they are confused. Monitoring all students is important to obtain diagnostic feedback and determine when intervention through reteaching or additional practice is necessary. (p. 24)

The National Board for Professional Teaching Standards (2004) recognizes the importance of teachers demonstrating flexibility and responsiveness (Component 3e). The concepts of lesson adjustment, response to students, and persistence are reflected in one of the five assessment principles used for national board certification. This core proposition reads as follows: "Teachers are responsible for managing and monitoring student learning."

Moore (2004) discusses the relationship between classroom research and teaching. She suggests that teachers who incorporate research into their daily teaching are eventually able to pinpoint patterns of learner response they may have never before realized. She continues,

> Reflecting on the patterns and making instructional changes based on authentic evidence (assignments, performance, observations of student work) is a natural part of this process for teachers who are experienced teacher researchers. (p. 1)

Research and the "wisdom of practice" (Shulman, 1987) have highlighted and continue to illuminate the limitations of using standardized tests as the sole measures of achievement. Educators are looking to other research methodologies, focusing less on single lessons and more on case studies of entire units of study and other success criteria (such as more performance assessments and other constructed-response formats). Research has also discovered (and in some cases rediscovered) the potential for problem- and project-based learning, with students asking their own questions and conducting their own investigations, and the teacher's role being one of facilitator and resource manager (Brandt, 1992, 1994; Cohen, McLaughlin, & Talbert, 1993; Gardner & Boix-Mansilla, 1994; Heckman, 1994; Nias, Southworth, & Campbell, 1992; Perkins & Blythe, 1994; Perrone, 1994; Wiske, 1994; Wolf, 1987; Woods, 1994).

As noted earlier, students benefit the most when permitted to "construct" rich new understandings based on prior knowledge. The focus on constructivist learning builds, of course, on earlier work by Dewey and educators committed to implementing the implications of Piaget's work in the classroom. For example, Wolk (1994) cites studies from the early part of the 20th century—Hennes (1921) and Kilpatrick (1918, 1925)—as a foundation for his work in project-based learning. Professional literature has cited and continues to cite examples of the benefits associated with students functioning as researchers engaged in authentic work. Even many years ago, the November 1994 issue of *Educational Leadership* was devoted to such strategies for success. Such emphasis differs greatly from the focus on skill-based instruction, administered in small steps and assessed using a norm-referenced, standardized, multiple-choice test. Ideally, students participate in the process and take ownership for their own growth, as the teacher structures experiences that promote complex, high-level learning. Torp and Sage (1998) provide details on how to effectively construct problem-based learning experiences for students at all grade levels. They stress the importance of helping students make strong connections in an authentic context using a standards-based approach in which students are accountable for their own learning, demonstrating proficiency when assessed.

DOMAIN 4: PROFESSIONAL RESPONSIBILITIES

Educators and researchers have gradually expanded the definition of teaching to include not only classroom interaction between teachers and students, but also the full range of responsibilities that constitute teaching. Three of the five key principles that the National Board for Professional Teaching Standards (2004) cites as the foundation for the assessment of accomplished teachers and the awarding of advanced certificates are aligned with Domain 4:

• Teachers are committed to students and their learning [included in Component 4f].

• Teachers think systematically about their practice and learn from experience [included in Components 4a and 4e].

• Teachers are members of learning communities [included in Components 4d and 4f].

Teacher professionalism (Domain 4) is still an evolving field. Much of the research is theoretical and grounded in logical and ethical rather than empirical studies. Some examples include studies on topics such as the teacher as researcher; dimensions of professional development; the benefits of contributing to the school, the district, and the profession; and the nature of professional decision making.

A number of studies do guide practitioners, however, particularly in the areas of teacher reflection, advocacy, collaboration with colleagues, and communication with families. Many studies document the value of teacher reflection, conducted alone or in collaboration with colleagues, by investigating the reflection on practice by either student teachers or more experienced professionals. Examples include Colton and Sparks-Langer (1992, 1993); Ellwein, Graue, and Comfort (1990); Ross and Regan (1993); and Tabachnick and Zeichner (1991).

Effective teachers are lifelong learners who take ownership for student learning and continually reflect on their efforts to ensure that they are providing focused, quality instruction (Component 4a). Such teachers engage in corrective problem-solving approaches with failing students rather than punishing them for their shortcomings. The positive effects of this sense of efficacy are demonstrated in such studies as Jones (1992), Pajares (1992), and Schunk (1991).

Many educators, as well as researchers, believe that the ability to reflect on teaching is the mark of a true professional.

Skowron (2001) supports this assertion as she claims that becoming an exceptional teacher is a learning process that some believe never ends. The teacher is in a continual state of learning, building, and refining teaching practices. Reeves (2004) notes that the reflective process is at the very heart of accountability. He goes on to state that through the process of reflection, educators are able to distinguish between the popularity of teaching techniques and their effectiveness.

Superior teachers contribute to and participate in a professional community by cultivating strong, supportive relationships with their colleagues and by assuming leadership roles among the faculty, as well as for events and projects (Component 4d). Tucker and Stronge (2005) studied successful teaching and found that qualities of effective teachers include collegiality, collaboration, a strong belief in efficacy, and contributions to the school and community. Gabriel (2005) promotes the nurturing of teacher leadership and efficacy in today's schools:

> For nearly a century, schools have functioned in the autocratic style of the line-staff model: principals are managers and teachers are their employees, often voiceless and powerless to influence their superiors' quest to improve student achievement. But with the growing emphasis on high-stakes testing and the advent of *No Child Left Behind,* many school leaders are seeking more effective organizational behavior by drawing on the leadership potential of all stakeholders, especially teachers. (p. 1)

Teachers who are committed to growing and developing professionally concern themselves with enhancing their content knowledge and pedagogical skills, as well as productively contributing to the profession (Component 4e). Although Fullan (2001) places value on the growth efforts of individual teachers and describes the importance of program coherence as a means to combat fragmentation of multiple innovations, his research on progress also emphasizes the role of the entire group in a school:

> Thus, professional development or training of individuals is not sufficient. For this reason schools must focus on creating schoolwide professional learning communities. (p. 64)

DuFour and Eaker (1998) succinctly summarize the same point:

> The most promising strategy for sustained, substantive school improvement is developing the ability of school personnel to function as professional learning communities. (p. xi)

MacIntyre, Flores, and Noddings, as cited in Sergiovanni (1994), identify "a commitment to not only one's own practice, but to the practice itself" as one of the four dimensions of "professional ideal" toward which all should strive (p. 142).

Action research is a process that also promotes professional development, collaboration, reflection, and efficacy in teachers. As Sagor (2000) describes it:

> Practitioners who engage in action research inevitably find it to be an empowering experience. Action research has this positive effect for many reasons. Obviously, the most important is that action research is always relevant to the participants. Relevance is guaranteed because the focus of

each research project is determined by the researchers, who are also the primary consumers of the findings.

> Perhaps even more important is the fact that action research helps educators be more effective at what they care most about—their teaching and the development of their students. Seeing students grow is probably the greatest joy educators can experience. When teachers have convincing evidence that their work has made a real difference in their students' lives, the countless hours and endless efforts of teaching seem worthwhile. (p. 3)

Calhoun (1994) simplifies the concept of action research by describing it as another way of saying, "Let's study what's happening at our school, decide if we can make it a better place by changing what and how we teach and how we relate to students and the community; study the effects; and then begin again" (p. 1).

Teachers who are most effective implement efficient systems to maintain accurate records, while empowering students to participate in monitoring and maintaining such records (Component 4b). Wormeli (2003) discusses the importance of keeping accurate classroom records, including those documenting grades, missed assignments, work habits, incidents of tardiness, and absences. He suggests that teachers give students the responsibility for some of the record keeping in the classroom.

Exceptional teachers also display professionalism by serving as advocates for children (Component 4f). Jackson and Davis (2000) underscore the importance of students having an advocate and claim that when students make a lasting connection with at least one caring adult in school, academic and personal outcomes improve. They also cite earlier research from the 1989 report *Turning Points: Preparing American Youth for the 21st Century* when they state that students should have adults to "act on their behalf to marshal every school and community resource needed for students to succeed, and help to fashion a promising vision for the future" (pp. 142–143).

The link between parent involvement in schools and student learning is well established (Component 4c). Jones (1992) and Cruickshank (1990) compiled research suggesting that, in general, student learning is enhanced when teachers work at parent involvement. Powell, Casanova, and Berliner (1991) provide a review of research on parent involvement and its effect on student learning. In this set of readings, they establish that parent involvement is intimately associated with academic achievement and that there are a variety of ways for teachers to establish and enhance such involvement. In 1997, the U.S. Department of Education produced a publication titled *Family Involvement in Children's Education: Successful Local Approaches,* which contends that when educators, families, and communities work together, schools get better. The document suggests that parent involvement can be an important contributor to student achievement because when parents are fully involved, they are typically willing to assume equal responsibility for the success of their children:

> Successful partnerships are those that involve the sustained mutual collaboration, support, and participation of school staffs and families at home and at school in activities and efforts that can directly and positively affect the success of children's learning and progress in school. (p. 2)

Jackson and Davis (2000) have compiled the results of extensive research on parent involvement to improve student learning. They also emphatically conclude that parents' participation in the life of the school and in their children's schoolwork has a positive impact on student outcomes. Bucknam, as cited in Marzano (2003), states that schools that involve parents and community in their day-to-day operations have lower absenteeism, truancy, and dropout rates.

Research in favor of maintaining parental connections with the school is so overwhelming that the national Parent Teacher Association (PTA) developed standards for parent/family involvement programs (Chadwick, 2004). Therefore, it is essential for teachers to regularly communicate with parents and engage them in the total school experience.

REFERENCES

Berliner, D. C. (2001). Learning about teaching from expert teachers. *International Journal of Educational Research, 35,* 463–482.

Berliner, D. C. (2004). Describing the behavior and documenting the accomplishments of expert teachers. *Bulletin of Science, Technology, & Society, 21*(3), 200–212.

Brandt, R. (1992). On research on teaching: A conversation with Lee Shulman. *Educational Leadership, 49*(7), 14–19.

Brandt, R. (1994). On making sense: A conversation with Magdalene Lampert. *Educational Leadership, 51*(5), 26–30.

Brooks, J. G., & Brooks, M. G. (1993). *In search of understanding: The case for constructivist classrooms.* Alexandria, VA: Association for Supervision and Curriculum Development.

Calhoun, E. F. (1994). *How to use action research in the self-renewing school.* Alexandria, VA: Association for Supervision and Curriculum Development.

Carnegie Forum on Education and the Economy's Task Force on Teaching as a Profession (1986, May). *A nation prepared: Teachers for the 21st century.* Hyattsville, MD: Author.

Chadwick, K. G. (2004). *Improving schools through community engagement: A practical guide for educators.* Thousand Oaks, CA: Corwin Press.

Cohen, D. K., McLaughlin, M. W., & Talbert, J. E. (Eds.). (1993). *Teaching for understanding: Challenges for policy and practice.* San Francisco: Jossey-Bass.

Colton, A. B., & Sparks-Langer, G. M. (1992). Restructuring student teaching experiences. In C. D. Glickman (Ed.), *Supervision in transition* (pp. 155–168). Alexandria, VA: Association for Supervision and Curriculum Development.

Colton, A. B., & Sparks-Langer, G. M. (1993). A conceptual framework to guide the development of teacher reflection and decision making. *Journal of Teacher Education, 44*(1), 45–54.

Cruickshank, D. R. (1990). *Research that informs teachers and teacher educators.* Bloomington, IN: Phi Delta Kappa Educational Foundation.

Danielson, C., & McGreal, T. (2000). *Evaluation to enhance professional practice.* Alexandria, VA: Association for Supervision and Curriculum Development.

DuFour, R., & Eaker, R. (1998). *Professional learning communities at work: Best practices for enhancing student achievement.* Bloomington, IN: National Educational Service.

Dwyer, C. A., & Villegas, A. M. (1993). *Guiding conceptions and assessment principles for the Praxis series: Professional assessments for beginning teachers.* (Research Report No. 93-17). Princeton, NJ: Educational Testing Service.

Dwyer, C. A. (1994). *Development of the knowledge base for the Praxis III: Classroom performance assessments assessment criteria.* Princeton, NJ: Educational Testing Service.

Ellett, C. (1990). *A new generation of classroom-based assessments of teaching and learning: Concepts, issues and controversies from pilots of the Louisiana STAR.* Baton Rouge: College of Education, Louisiana State University.

Ellwein, M. C., Graue, M. E., & Comfort, R. E. (1990). Talking about instruction: Student teachers' reflections on success and failure in the classroom. *Journal of Teacher Education, 41*(4), 3–14.

Evertson, C. M., & Harris, A. H. (1992). What we know about managing classrooms. *Educational Leadership, 49*(7), 74–78.

Fullan, M. (2001). *Leading in a culture of change.* New York: Jossey-Bass.

Fullan, M. (2005, February). Resiliency and sustainability. *School Administrator, 62*(2), 16–18.

Gabriel, J. G. (2005). *How to thrive as a teacher leader.* Alexandria, VA: Association for Supervision and Curriculum Development.

Gage, N. L. (1977). *The scientific basis of the art of teaching.* New York: Teachers College Press.

Gardner, H., & Boix-Mansilla, V. (1994). Teaching for understanding—within and across the disciplines. *Educational Leadership, 51*(5), 14–18.

Guskey, T. R. (2005, April). *Formative classroom assessment and Benjamin S. Bloom: Theory, research, and implications.* Paper presented at the annual meeting of the American Educational Research Association, Montreal, Canada.

Heckman, P. E. (1994). Planting seeds: Understanding through investigation. *Educational Leadership, 51*(5), 36–39.

Hennes, M. (1921). Project teaching in an advanced fifth grade. *Teachers College Record, 19*(2), 137–148.

Irvine, J. J. (1990, May). *Beyond role models: The influence of black teachers on black students.* Paper presented at Educational Testing Service, Princeton, NJ.

Jackson, A. W., & Davis, G. A. (2000). *Turning points 2000: Educating adolescents in the 21st century.* New York: Teachers College Press.

Jensen, E. (1998). *Teaching with the brain in mind.* Alexandria, VA: Association for Supervision and Curriculum Development.

Jones, J. (1992). *Praxis III teacher assessment criteria research base.* Princeton, NJ: Educational Testing Service.

Kilpatrick, W. H. (1918). The project method. *Teachers College Record, 19*(4), 319–335.

Kilpatrick, W. H. (1925). *Foundations of method: Informal talks on teaching.* New York: Macmillan.

Marzano, R. J. (2003). *What works in schools: Translating research into action.* Alexandria, VA: Association for Supervision and Curriculum Development.

Marzano, R. J. (2004). *Building background knowledge for academic achievement.* Alexandria, VA: Association for Supervision and Curriculum Development.

McCombs, B. L. (1992). *Learner-centered psychological principles: Guidelines for school redesign and reform.* Washington, DC: American Psychological Association.

Moore, R. A. (2004). *Classroom research for teachers: A practical guide.* Norwood, MA: Christopher-Gordon Publishers.

National Board for Professional Teaching Standards. (1991). *Toward high and rigorous standards for the teaching profession* (3rd ed.). Detroit, MI: Author.

National Board for Professional Teaching Standards. (2004). *The five core propositions.* Available: www.nbpts.org/the_standards/the_five_core_propositio

Newmann, F. M., Secada, W. G., & Wehlage, G. G. (1995). *A guide to authentic instruction and assessment: Vision, standards, and scoring.* Madison, WI: Wisconsin Center for Education Research.

Nias, J., Southworth, G., & Campbell, P. (1992). *Whole school curriculum development in the primary school.* London: Falmer Press.

Pajares, M. F. (1992). Teachers' beliefs and educational research: Cleaning up a messy act. *Review of Educational Research, 62*(3), 307–332.

Perkins, D., & Blythe, T. (1994). Putting understanding up front. *Educational Leadership, 51*(5), 4–7.

Perrone, V. (1994). How to engage students in learning. *Educational Leadership, 51*(5), 11–13.

Powell, J. H., Casanova, U., & Berliner, D. C. (1991). *Parental involvement: Readings in educational research, a program for professional development.* Washington, DC: National Education Association.

Reeves, D. B. (2004). *Accountability for learning: How teachers and school leaders can take charge.* Alexandria, VA: Association for Supervision and Curriculum Development.

Reynolds, A. (1992). What is competent beginning teaching? A review of the literature. *Review of Educational Research, 62*(1), 1–35.

Rhem, J. (1999). Pygmalion in the classroom. *The National Teaching and Learning Forum, 8*(2). Available: www.ntlf.com/html/pi/9902/pygm_1.htm

Richardson, J. (2004, February/March). Lesson study. *Tools for Schools.* Available: www.nsdc.org/library/publications/tools/tools2-04rich.cfm

Ross, J. A., & Regan, E. M. (1993). Sharing professional experience: Its impact on professional development. *Teaching and Teacher Education, 9*(1), 91–106.

Sagor, R. (2000). *Guiding school improvement with action research.* Alexandria, VA: Association for Supervision and Curriculum Development.

Schmoker, M. (1999). *Results: The key to continuous school improvement* (2nd ed.). Alexandria, VA: Association for Supervision and Curriculum Development.

Schunk, D. H. (1991). Self-efficacy and academic motivation. *Educational Psychologist, 26,* 207–231.

Sergiovanni, T. J. (1994). *Building community in schools.* San Francisco: Jossey-Bass.

Shalaway, L. (2005). *Learning to teach . . . not just for beginners: The essential guide for all teachers.* New York: Scholastic.

Shulman, L. S. (1987). Knowledge and teaching: Foundations of the new reform. *Harvard Educational Review, 57*(1), 1–22.

Skowron, J. (2001). *Powerful lesson planning models: The art of 1,000 decisions.* Arlington Heights, IL: SkyLight Training and Publishing.

Strategies for success. (1994, November). *Educational Leadership, 52*(3) [entire issue].

Sykes, G., & Bird, T. (1992, August). Teacher education and the case idea. *Review of Research in Education, 18,* 457–521.

Tabachnick, B. R., & Zeichner, K. (1991). Reflections on reflective teaching. In B. Tabachnick & K. Zeichner (Eds.), *Issues and practices in inquiry-oriented teacher education*. Philadelphia: Falmer Press.

Tomlinson, C. A. (1999). *The differentiated classroom: Responding to the needs of all learners*. Alexandria, VA: Association for Supervision and Curriculum Development.

Torp, L., & Sage, S. (1998). *Problems as possibilities: Problem-based learning for K–16 education* (2nd ed.). Alexandria, VA: Association for Supervision and Curriculum Development.

Tucker, P. D., & Stronge, J. H. (2005). *Linking teacher evaluation and student learning*. Alexandria, VA: Association for Supervision and Curriculum Development.

U.S. Department of Education. (1997). *Family involvement in children's education: Successful local approaches*. Washington, DC: Author.

Villegas, A. M. (1991). *Culturally responsive pedagogy for the 1990s and beyond*. Unpublished manuscript. Princeton, NJ: Educational Testing Service.

Whitaker, T. (2004). *What great teachers do differently: Fourteen things that matter most*. Larchmont, NY: Eye on Education.

Wiggins, G. (1998). *Educative assessment: Designing assessments to inform and improve performance*. San Francisco: Jossey-Bass.

Wiggins, G., & McTighe, J. (1998). *Understanding by design*. Alexandria, VA: Association for Supervision and Curriculum Development.

Wiliam, D. (2004, June). *Keeping learning on track: Integrating assessment with instruction*. Invited address to the 30th annual conference of the International Association for Educational Assessment (IAEA), Philadelphia.

Wiske, M. S. (1994). How teaching for understanding changes the rules in the classroom. *Educational Leadership, 51*(5), 19–21.

Wittrock, M. C. (Ed.). (1986). *Handbook of research on teaching* (3rd ed.). New York: Macmillan.

Wolf, D. P. (1987, Winter). The art of questioning. *Academic Connections,* 1–7.

Wolk, S. (1994). Project-based learning: Pursuits with a purpose. *Educational Leadership, 52*(3), 42–45.

Woods, R. K. (1994). A close-up look at how children learn science. *Educational Leadership, 51*(5), 33–35.

Wormeli, R. (2003). *Day one & beyond: Practical matters for new middle-level teachers*. Portland, ME: Stenhouse Publishers, and Westerville, OH: National Middle School Association.

INDEX

Page numbers followed by *f* indicate reference to a figure.

About the Author

Charlotte Danielson is an educational consultant based in Princeton, New Jersey. She has taught at all levels, from kindergarten through college, and has worked as an administrator, a curriculum director, and a staff developer in school districts in several regions of the United States. In addition, she has served as a consultant to hundreds of school districts, universities, intermediate agencies, and state departments of education in virtually every state and in many other countries. In her consulting work, Danielson has specialized in aspects of teacher quality and evaluation, curriculum planning, performance assessment, and professional development. Her work has ranged from the training of practitioners in aspects of instruction and assessment, to the design of instruments and procedures for teacher evaluation, to keynote presentations at major conferences. For several years she served on the staff of Educational Testing Service (ETS) and was involved with many significant projects, including designing the assessor training program for Praxis III: Classroom Performance Assessments.

Danielson is the author of several books for teachers and administrators. These include *Enhancing Professional Practice: A Framework for Teaching* (1996), the Professional Inquiry Kit *Teaching for Understanding* (1996), *Teacher Evaluation to Enhance Professional Practice* (in collaboration with Tom McGreal, 2000), *Enhancing Student Achievement: A Framework for School Improvement* (2002), and *Teacher Leadership That Strengthens Professional Practice* (2006), all published by ASCD. In addition, she has written several *Collections of Performance Tasks and Rubrics,* published by Eye on Education.

Charlotte Danielson can be reached at charlotte_danielson@hotmail.com.